A MATTER OF BREEDING

A MATTER OF BREEDING

A Biting History of Pedigree Dogs and How the Quest for Status Has Harmed Man's Best Friend

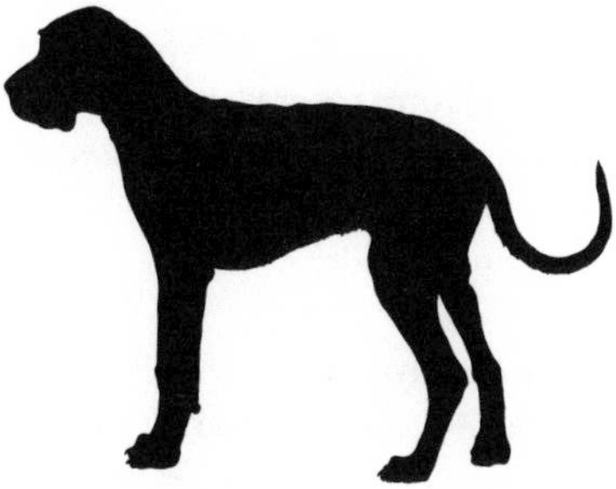

Michael Brandow

Beacon Press
Boston

Beacon Press
Boston, Massachusetts
www.beacon.org

Beacon Press books
are published under the auspices of
the Unitarian Universalist Association of Congregations.

Printed in the United States of America

18 17 16 15 8 7 6 5 4 3 2 1

This book is printed on acid-free paper that meets the uncoated paper ANSI/NISO specifications for permanence as revised in 1992.

Text design and composition by Kim Arney

Many names and other identifying characteristics of people mentioned in this work have been changed to protect their identities. The communal voice is not intended to presume upon the memories and experiences of others but to reflect the shared nature of the event itself, as the author remembers it.

Library of Congress Cataloging-in-Publication Data
Brandow, Michael.
A matter of breeding : a biting history of pedigree dogs and how the quest for status has harmed man's best friend / Michael Brandow.
pages cm
Includes bibliographical references and index.
ISBN 978-0-8070-3343-2 (pbk. : alk. paper)
ISBN 978-0-8070-3344-9 (ebook)
1. Dogs—Breeding. 2. Dogs—Pedigrees. I. Title.
SF427.2.B73 2014
636.7'0887—dc23

2014022861

For Samantha and Josie

CONTENTS

Foreword by Dr. Marc Bekoff ix
Introduction 1

CHAPTER ONE The English Vice 10
CHAPTER TWO Perfectionists Gone Wild 31
CHAPTER THREE Royal Precedents and Ruff Drafts 53
CHAPTER FOUR Eugenics, You, and Fido Too 74
CHAPTER FIVE A Frickin' Menagerie 103
CHAPTER SIX The Midas Touch 125
CHAPTER SEVEN Aristocracy for Sale 151
CHAPTER EIGHT Some Hunting Dogs 173
CHAPTER NINE Coming Home 200
CONCLUSION Frankenstein's Lab 214

Acknowledgments 236
Notes 237
Index 262

FOREWORD

For many years I've researched human-animal interactions, writing several books, including *The Emotional Lives of Animals* and, with Jane Goodall, *The Ten Trusts*, and cofounding the organization Ethologists for the Ethical Treatment of Animals. I am profoundly committed to the notion that we are our companions' trusted guardians, not their owners. Additionally, I feel strongly that dogs (and other animals) are not commodities and that causing intentional pain to them is unethical, inhumane, and unnecessary.

From this standpoint, I believe it's time—indeed, it's long overdue—to have reasoned discussions and debates about dog breeding. Many major studies document a rising number of breed-specific health problems and suggest we're in the midst of an alarming health crisis. A two-month-old bulldog should not need routine eye surgery nor should a four-year-old Labrador show signs of hip dysplasia. Clearly there's something wrong in the world of pedigree dogs. I've argued that we don't need any more "purebred" dogs, and as Michael Brandow asks in this most important book, "Why do we go on hurting the ones we love?"

With a background in journalism, dog care, and community activism, Michael Brandow is a close observer of canine culture. His eye-opening book, *A Matter of Breeding*, is what I regard as an ethically urgent and essential read. Brandow addresses head on the issues of snobbery and consumerism inherent to "purebreds," with remarks on "designer dogs," the second-largest but fastest-growing segment of the dog industry. Rich in history, the book traces the commercial origins of the Boston terrier, English bulldog, and other types that were marketed as highfalutin' status symbols beginning in the nineteenth century.

Upper classes, the author reminds us, have long set the benchmark for valuing dogs according to the social status they confer. From ancient court dogs and royalty's highly formalized hunting rites to the creation of kennel clubs by Gilded Age elites and the strict but often arbitrary standards used in competitions to judge on style, not substance, Brandow demonstrates that a major motivation for owning identifiable types has been their aristocratic appeal. And, while we satisfy our self-centered desires, millions upon millions of dogs unnecessarily suffer and die way before their time.

While the modern cult of pedigree and the very concept of officially recognized breeds are inventions of Victorian England, these ideas have taken root in our culture with profound consequences for dogs and people alike. Then, as now, much of the impetus for having fancy pets has revolved around what they're supposed to say about the owner's position, spending power, connoisseurship, and taste—in other words, how they reflect upon their owner's breeding. In showing how far we humans have gone in refashioning dogs to freakish extremes that go against common sense, even exaggerating their behaviors in ways to denote rarity and lavish expenditure, the author urges us to think critically about our breed prejudices and ask ourselves whether preserving them is worth all the damage done to dogs in the process. By examining a person's preference for a purebred to a nonbreed, we can see how these consumer choices are anything but neutral. We must also ask ourselves how we—as dog lovers—can justify bringing more animals into this world when millions are already dumped in shelters, often because they've failed to live up to expectations that are unrealistic and, according to Brandow, somewhat hypocritical.

Brandow's provocative analysis makes it clear that our everyday assumptions about dogs have implications for the social biases we have against each other, sources of much injustice. As he points out, if we're going to impose human beliefs on other animals, we could at least use those we claim to have. This contradiction, he suggests, could explain why so little effort has been made to purge dog breeding of misplaced priorities and pseudoscience of the past. In fact, those entrusted with the welfare and improvement of man's best friend—kennel clubs and the scientists they fund, breed clubs, puppy mills, and "reputable" breeders alike, and local veterinarians who clean up the mess without comment—constitute a colossal dog industry that all too often privileges a recognized brand with class connotations (papillon, golden, Portuguese) over an individual animal's health. As I've said before, we shouldn't breed for qualities that appeal to humans but do little for the dogs. There's nothing noble about encouraging anatomical, physiological, or genetic maladies that guarantee compromised lives, pain, suffering, and early deaths. When I hear a dog with a squashed face pant as if he or she is going to pass out it sickens me. The best way to stop the breeding of purebreds is to stop buying them.

Brandow's unflinching social history, viewed with humor and sarcasm, remains a very serious, significant, and timely message and is a very important first step toward reforming our cultural prejudices against mongrels due to their uncertain origins and substandard appearance. He unmasks the sordid past of dog shows, the impromptu creation of the oddities we've come to accept as normal, and the alarming conservatism of some experts who still insist, against all evidence to the contrary, that purebred dogs are likely to be healthier, smarter, or more loyal and trainable than common mutts. My hope is that after reading *A Matter of Breeding*, people eager to adopt a canine companion will first look to their local shelters and not a breed directory. Adopting a dog in need is the compassionate and, it turns out, often the more rational consumer choice. It's a win-win situation for the dogs and the people. What could be better? Breeding—meaning both the disturbing legacy of bias and inequality celebrated each year at the Westminster Kennel Club dog show, and the ongoing production of surplus pets while millions await rescue or death—needs to be reconsidered in a major way. This landmark book will surely motivate people to begin to ask the hard questions and to answer them, so that dogs benefit from these discussions. I'm sure the dogs who are chosen will be forever thankful for people who make this decision. It's a malicious double-cross to betray their deep feelings of trust in our having their best interests in mind.

Once again, to quote the author, "Breeding for blood 'purity' and formal perfection is pure madness and always has been." Amen.

—Dr. Marc Bekoff

INTRODUCTION

I found my inspiration for this impolite volume while trying to dodge something else. Wandering the sidewalks of Manhattan in the midst of an unsavory study on poop-scoop laws with my new-found mutt from a local shelter, I started wondering: what was so appealing about "purebred" dogs? I know many of us grew up with them. These were, after all, what good middle-class families had in those days, and preferably the latest model. But what gave birth to the widespread belief that being seen with a fancy breed makes you fancier than someone with a good old-fashioned mutt?

Pounding the pavement as a dog walker for ten years, I had as wide a catalog selection as my powers of observation could handle, a continual pooch panorama with all the standard shapes, sizes, and colors competing for attention. In a sense, I didn't need this rainbow coalition to tell me anything new. Having spent my life with breeds and nonbreeds alike, sat for hundreds in the homes of New York's elite, apprenticed with a dog trainer, performed with my own on national television, and passed thousands of hours volunteering at a dog park chatting with every imaginable breed of owner, I'd learned to love all dogs *despite* their pigmentation and social ties. I knew before starting this study that, unless they had specific skills for tasks like jumping through hoops, working on my grandmother's farm, hunting with my dad, or helping the blind lady who lived down the block, their dazzling diversity was mostly superficial. Bird dogs were out of their element in the rarified atmosphere of upper-class Manhattan. Portuguese water dogs were fish out of water. Take Weimaraners out of their Wegman coats and they were still half-crazed lapdogs. Dobies and rotties could be better guardians than some, but owners wanted signature stances and ears that stood right. Bassets were once used for tracking, and with a little more brains or less skin, the show versions might find a trail if you rubbed their noses in it. Black Labs and golden retrievers summoned ancient memories of Scottish moors and aristocratic estates, but at the end of the day, they were couch potatoes like the rest.

The actual subject of my study became not hounds but the humans hooked on their looks—and what fascinating creatures these were. In all those years spent walking privileged pets for one of the most visible and affluent communities in the world, the most challenging part of my job wasn't picking up the poop but sidestepping people who wanted dogs to be so much more. My sworn duty to my charges was to give them a good leg-stretching, including pit stops on the way, but also to get them to the nearest dog run safe and sound for an hour of off-leash freedom from those attempting to reward their unconditional love with a long list of preconditions. What my crew of pups needed was a chance to be themselves, and the clock was ticking for each and every individual regardless of breed, creed, or color. Cool shade and fresh grass called out universally to noses of all shades, and not even squirrels discriminated based on pedigree when taunting from the nearest branch.

Wrist burns as my witness, the last thing my dogs wanted or needed was to stop on hot concrete to be admired by total strangers looking for the latest Westminster champ. Normal boundaries, the rules designed to help people coexist in crowded places, came down in one tsunami of unbridled puppy love as I navigated my team through some of the hairiest social situations known to man or beast. Purebreds brought out the child in people, and grown adults from all walks of life brought ours to a screeching halt by pointing from a distance, rushing up to pet without permission, then blocking our path to ask questions.

If a new breed was in the White House and I was walking an inbred cousin, the *puparazzi* demanded in no uncertain terms to know: "Is that a Portuguese water dog?" or "Is it perchance a Petit Basset Griffon Vendéen?" When Charlotte got a Cavalier King Charles on *Sex and the City*, I had no choice but to answer, countless times, the query of the season: "Is that a Cavalier?" Nine weeks after *Best in Show* hit the theaters, a wave of Norwich terriers hit the sidewalks, followed by "Is that a Norwich or a Nor*folk?*" Border collies became burdensome when shown at Westminster. I stopped accepting Saint Bernards after *Beethoven's 2nd*, *3rd*, *4th*, and *5th*. When Disney released another sequel-to-a-remake, pavements were blighted with black spots and all of New York resounded with: "Isn't that a Dalmatian?"

Meanwhile, any mutts in my care were invisible to the purists, completely off their social radar. Like bird watchers in Central Park, the hobbyists were looking for particular *types*, specimens they could call out and label, then store upstairs for obscure and arcane purposes. Canine cataloging seems to bring some strange sense of pride and accomplishment, and the more esoteric the question, the better it reflects upon the inquirer who, in the vast majority of cases, already knows the answer. The real goal in the breed guessing game is to make known, to the dog's owner, walker, and anyone within earshot, that the contestant is up on all the four-legged facts as revealed on *Animal Planet* or Hollywood's latest Chihuahua extravaganza.

How many dog lovers are aware that, despite the praise and admiration we shower upon our best friends, not everything we do for them is in their own best interests? Sure, the coats are pretty, but

Labs and shepherds need hydrotherapy for hip dysplasia if they're to continue sidewalk entertaining. Shar-peis and boxers look distinctive with those folds on the face, but owners book return visits to animal hospitals for interminable allergies and epilepsy, while goldens and Scottish deerhounds take pet taxis to oncology wards and ICUs. We're so busy dragging Boomer and Bailey around town that we don't stop to think that much of their special care is only necessary because of problems their biggest fans have helped inflict upon them.

There can no longer be any doubt. As was long suspected, ample studies confirm that requiring breeds to be distinctive has led to dramatically higher levels of cancer, structural deformities, skin conditions, eye and ear infections, and a host of afflictions that are multiplying. Many purebreds are officially in peril and dog lovers must confront this sad reality. Forcing Labs to go on looking Labby and pugs pugnacious—expecting them to "conform," as they say in the show ring, to arbitrary beauty-pageant ideals—has resulted in creatures esthetically pleasing to behold, depending on your personal tastes, but physically and often mentally inferior to the average mutt. Compromising health and temperament with a concern for surface appearance has given dogs a host of defects including "extreme anatomies," say concerned vets, cartoon features that consumers find cute but are in fact deformities causing discomfort, pain, and shorter lives—and the agony owners feel when having to make that final decision sooner than they thought.

Why do we go on hurting the ones we love? Why must German shepherds limp through life and French bulldogs barely breathe? Enthusiasts attached to the breeds they had growing up surely don't wish to see their beloved favorites suffer, but they might want to be more aware that congenital illness and certain signature looks, even in the so-called hypoallergenic models, have become serious problems in recent years. I argue that the root of the problem lies in the past. Rigid tastes, latent class consciousness, a belief in blood "purity," naive notions on authenticity—and a tendency to sometimes love dogs for the wrong reasons—override a wealth of information available on the dangers of inbreeding, the downsides to extreme anatomies, and the evils of the pet industry today. Well-intentioned animal lovers with minds open to this broader historical perspective might wake up one morning to a revelation: dogs don't need to be neatly standardized, packaged, and sealed to be our friends. How much easier it would make people's lives to learn that for every prepaid, photogenic purebred ordered months in advance of birth with promises of "predictability" from "reputable" breeders, perfectly wonderful specimens of dog are available minutes away at the local shelter, with at least as much happiness to offer and often with no breeding at all.

Maybe dogs never lie about love, but some people still see what they want to see. No self-styled dog expert of the old school, in all my time pooch perambulating, has ever stopped me on a Manhattan sidewalk to ask, "Is it true that over 60 percent of all golden retrievers in this country are dying of cancer?" If by chance they did, I'd point them to an article in the *Wall Street Journal* (published over a decade after the study was released) or an eye-opening BBC documentary called "Pedigree Dogs Exposed" showing many breeds to be in serious trouble.[1] I might mention, if they had a moment to chat, that the BBC dropped its coverage of Crufts, the world's premier dog show and role model for our own Westminster, until cyno-social clubs reexamined their values and reset their priorities. Not a single hound hide enthusiast, respectful of tradition and awed by "good" breeding and "good" families, deigned to grab my arm and confirm that Queen Elizabeth herself withdrew royal patronage from England's famed Kennel Club, the forerunner of our American Kennel Club (AKC), to force its hand at reform.

The cult of pedigree and formal perfection comes to us via the British, and the many downsides are being seen on both sides of the pond. Little is it known that progress toward simply acknowledging a canine health crisis actually began in the United States, if only at an English bulldog's pace. Eighteen years before highly publicized calls to action were heard in the UK, Mark Derr's bold landmark essay, "The Politics of Dogs," appeared in the *Atlantic Monthly*[2] at a time when most national media feared lawsuits from the great and powerful AKC. Since then, books, magazines, and major studies have sounded alarms about problems with pedigree dogs,[3] and Americans have gradually withdrawn support from old authorities whose judgment appears unsound.[4] "Pedigree Dogs Exposed" surpassed an English tradition of whipping pretentious pet owners with social commentary and wit, taking the Kennel Club to court with charges more serious than snobbery. The *Economist* described many modern breeds not as the epitome of British know-how but as "a grotesque distortion of the underlying wolf."[5]

Reconsidering the dog, this isn't to say that the fancy—those who own, breed, show, and judge "purebreds"—consists entirely of dastardly villains bent on profiting from animal cruelty. Whether they're affiliated with the AKC or the more health- and performance-oriented United Kennel Club, breed buffs certainly don't wish to see their customized types discontinued. Breed clubs and kennel clubs, it's true, raise large sums to combat the diseases that have come to characterize individual breeds as unmistakably as their coat colors or ear shapes. That said, it has been argued that many of these efforts will have a limited effect within the present system. Adhering to the same strict and narrow practices to create breeds, and then to keep them "pure" in blood and "correct" in appearance, can make DNA-testing schemes to breed out illnesses self-defeating endeavors.[6] A rising number of veterinary scientists are calling for some of the most troubled types, ranging from pugs to

Cavaliers, to be banned despite their large followings, if only out of mercy for the dogs themselves.[7]

Progress has been slow, to say the least, but animal lovers on either side of the Atlantic shouldn't need to get their news from scientists, and certainly not from their dog walker. Simple farmers and nomadic hunters reached the same conclusions tens of thousands of years ago and with no help from evolutionary biology or population genetics, or the steady stream of coverage on *Nightline*, the *Today Show*, and local stations across the country. Breeding for blood "purity" and formal perfection is pure madness and always has been. So why do purists cling to this idea that "traditional" breeds they can't imagine in other shapes, sizes, or colors are anything more than commercial inventions of Victorian England? What keeps socially aware, politically correct, otherwise educated consumers from seeing that investing in a golden retriever is like buying derivatives from Goldman Sachs, and that saving the brand is like saving the Mars bar?

The answer is often as simple as snobbery, a motivation as old as the hills and an impulse that archaic institutions are vested in preserving. *A Matter of Breeding* is a critical social history of the dog fancy in England and America, an odyssey of wonder and disbelief. This does not pretend to be a scientific study, but plenty of those are waiting just keystrokes away from anyone who *really* wants to know. Combined herein are years of observation of people and pets in places public and private with as many years of research in archives underground. I'm eager to share my mystification over (1) how dogs came to occupy their wide array of shapes, sizes, and coat colors; (2) who decided how they had to look and for what elaborate reasons; (3) what possesses people to continue respecting their questionable judgment today; and finally (4) the price dogs have had to pay for living up to misplaced priorities. Breeds as we know them on sidewalks and green carpets didn't fall from the sky. They were deliberately designed and packaged for appeal, like any other luxury products. Applying the same baseless biases to humans would invite charges of shallowness, callousness, racism, or insanity. Imposing stringent but unnecessary standards on dogs is what dog lovers think they're doing in their best friends' best interests.

The history is here, some old and some recent, for readers to decide how much has changed. "It is very pleasing to have a new suit, a new car, a new wife, and it loses much unless you are able to exhibit it," as English historian Edward Ash explained in 1934 the timeless appeal of "fancy" pets—the reason they were invented in the first place.[8] Another noted English authority cut closer to the heart of the matter when he wrote: "I somehow never feel the same respect for a man who allows himself to be accompanied by a badly-bred cur, for dog and master are so often of one type."[9] His fashion advice in the 1890s: "Nobody who is anybody can afford to be followed by a mongrel dog."[10] Director Christopher Guest confirms this observation while explaining his inspiration for *Best in Show*: "I noticed a real dynamic that existed between owners and their pets. The pure-breds looked down on our mutts in the same way their owners looked down on us."[11]

Dogs are not science experiments, artworks, or historical artifacts with traditions to uphold. They live very much in the here and now, which is where our hearts and minds ought to be. Our dear friends have faced avoidable health problems for some time, and while these have grown to extremes, none of this is news. What's changed is how we value our companion species, after taking a wrong turn about a hundred fifty years ago, and how far we feel we can fairly bend them to please us. If only it were possible to step back and recall falling in love with our first puppy, before the fussbudgets told us *why*.

I leave you with a final word from a leading British authority on matters canine, his expert advice to Americans back in 1875 when we were still acquiring our taste for show rings, rosettes, and aping English royalty. That same fine gentleman who advised against wearing the wrong dog in public warned in no uncertain terms: "The market-price of a mongrel is the price of his hide, *minus* the value of the rope you buy to hang him."[12]

Now, how do you suppose we should respond—knowing what we do?

CHAPTER ONE

THE ENGLISH VICE

Inserting the key, I could already hear the sound of whimpering from somewhere deep inside the apartment. Two strained yaps barely penetrated the darkness as I stood in the entry feeling the wall for a light switch. I'd been working as a dog walker for years and there was something not quite right about this. Normal puppies were energetic and unstoppable when I arrived to give them their midday walks. They barked and clawed and I couldn't open the cages and attach their leashes fast enough to rush them outside before an accident happened on the nearest rug. The dog I was about to liberate didn't sound average at all. He was too reserved, or maybe something was holding him back. Pathetic yelps were muffled and punctuated by unsettling silences. This pup knew very well that I was in the apartment and tried to react but seemed to be struggling for breath. His snorting, coughing, and wheezing accelerated as I slid my hand along the wall, stepping carefully into the living room where indirect light paved my way, then moving down a dark hall into the kitchen. Still no light switch, though I could make out the grey outline of a cage. The creature gave all his strength to the next cry before this tapered off into a strange gurgling sound. Then silence.

Bob the baby bulldog had his own personal way of expressing happiness, and the cartoon noises resumed in full force as I approached the oblong box at the back of the room. I couldn't see the dog yet but knew him from our first meeting a few nights before. A five-month-old English bull, one of the more popular breeds these days, Bob looked just like any other of the dozens of his kind I passed each day along tree-lined streets with brownstone stoops. He had that same distinctive look, centuries of selective breeding having led him far astray of his ancestor the wolf. Wide, bulging eyes frightened other dogs on the street. Expressive folds of skin draped his opulent forehead. Ears drooped as they never would dare in nature. The snout was collapsed like a child's nose pressed against a pet shop window. This brute looked all muscle, but he didn't seem to be a survivor. The massive frame, sumo-wrestler shoulders, and truck driver's neck brought to mind his two gay dads who had obviously spent a good portion of their lives pumping up at the local gym. This dog was pear-shaped, only upside down like his man-parents. He had that "waspish waist" said to be distinctive to the breed over a century ago. Also like his dads, Bob had muscles that were purely cosmetic. In fact, he barely had the strength to walk. Even more extravagant than his frame, his super-sized skull was larger than life, completely out of proportion to his body.

Preposterous heads are one of the most prized features on this breed and are encouraged despite all the health complications created by such an extreme anatomy. Long before Bob was born, the standard skull for bulldogs had expanded to such proportions that Cesarean birth was the only way out for them, and mating had also become an unnatural act. Manly hips, on males and females alike, were made extremely narrow by inbreeding to accentuate the larger upper half of the body, making artificial insemination a normal practice. The imposing physique, like the muscle-magazine bodies on his two gay dads—together measuring no more than eleven feet high, and deflating like hot-air balloons the moment these guys opened their mouths—somehow didn't seem threatening. The short and stumpy legs would make this little fellow "bear meat" in any woodland setting, and the sudden, slapstick motions that people find so entertaining distracted from the fact that he had trouble moving at all.

Still, you had to love this dog, and his two dads, perfectly nice people who spent endless hours at the gym but lacked the self-discipline to resist going with the crowd. They clearly worshipped their new designer-label puppy with all their hearts, and with genuine love. A few nights before, when I came for the interview, they were sitting on opposite ends of a high-end, state-of-the-art living room praising precious, disabled Bob for hobbling back and forth between his two jacked dads as they took turns calling out his name. I, too, took some sort of perverse pleasure in watching the challenged pup struggle more than a five-month-old should to move only a few feet. All three of us laughed and cheered as he huffed and puffed like the Little Engine That Could. I knew that his long list of handicaps could have been prevented—Bob could not have been born—and yet the familiar story of ambition in the face of adversity always sells. I'd try laughing again, a few days later, as the small, tightly packed pooch popped out of his cage with a cannonball thrust, then slowed to a waddle halfway across the kitchen floor and labored to raise his concrete head high enough to look at me with those startling bloodshot eyes. In his cage were three piles of half-digested food he couldn't hold down from breakfast. I would clean up the mess when we got back. For the moment, we had a schedule to keep. I'd been instructed to give the dog water before our walk because he was often dehydrated from all the vomiting. But even the liquid might come up in the elevator, and so I'd been told to carry paper towels.

There's nothing quite like the sound of a bulldog drinking. The sickening sound effect made by the pitiful mutant golden retriever in *The Fly II* as he sucks up gruel is the closest anything comes. After Bob's long, slurpy inhalation from the porcelain bowl bearing his name, I reached down to slip an impressive black-leather studded harness over his beefcake frame. Then came the mad rush to the sidewalk, twelve floors and a slow elevator ride below. Bob was getting better at "holding it," but he didn't always make it to the curb on 23rd Street. Trying to hurry, I passed the kitchen counter and couldn't help marveling at an extensive collection of bottles, jars, and cans in all shapes and sizes. Here was the power center of this home. Protein powders, steroids, energy elixirs, all sorts of muscle-building concoctions for his dads, and about a dozen other products I couldn't make out, were mixed indiscriminately among the dog's hundreds of pills and potions. Prescriptions for Bob's endless list of ailments had the familiar brown label of a local animal hospital. My morbid curiosity satisfied, I guided Bob toward the hall, remembering the warning about possible seizures. His owners had assured me that, like his inability to hold down food and water, or to walk more than a few feet at a time without resting, fainting was normal and I shouldn't be alarmed and go dragging this dog to the vet for every little thing.

Turning the corner out of the kitchen with my charge tagging faithfully far behind, I caught a last ray of morning light that streamed through a back window. A blade of fire cut across the length of the room only to land mundanely in the sink. In the deepest recesses, at the bottom near the drain, a bowl was tilted to one side where it had been left unwashed after a hurried meal. Floating in a puddle of milk, as though positioned at center stage by the sun's golden spotlight, was a huge, waterlogged wheat flake, the remains of a breakfast of champions, hideously bloated and freakishly deformed.

Any writer not gay himself would never get away with poking fun at the fads and fashions that come out of homo heavens like the few square blocks in Manhattan known as Chelsea. I live only a few blocks away, and share the sexual preference, but the comparison stops there. The whole place seems alien to me. As in so many trendsetting gay neighborhoods, the outward forms of things are forever changing at a dizzying pace. It's hard to keep up with the mutating facades of buildings, the restocked shop windows and refurbished front lobbies, the new clothes on the street. If I weren't a dog walker carrying keys to a large number of apartments in this neighborhood, I might have been stuck in the 1980s as my nearby Greenwich Village apartment still is. Being constantly on the move gave me an educated eye. Every few years, I learned, any self-respecting Chelsean is required to redecorate, to change his wardrobe—and his mind. Food that wasn't edible yesterday is suddenly a staple. This year's designer drugs will soon share the fate of last year's variation on a boxer brief. And it's not just the appendages that mutate. Entire bodies come and go. After decades of allowing the slender, androgynous type, everyone was expected to beef up and look like a Marine. Smooth, hairless chests reigned supremely for a time, then body hair was back and "treasure trails" were carefully sculpted with razors by men who didn't have them naturally. Heads were buzzed clean for the "Dachau look"—a style that soon caught on across corporate America—only to grow into plush seventies shags with blond highlights before anyone had noticed. Silly and arbitrary as all this rapid change might seem to naive outsiders, it would be a mistake to underestimate this gay ghetto's influence. Oddly enough, a minority of people considered far from normal ultimately determine what is au courant in the outside world. So many outward aspects of being average are decided in this place, and by the time something has reached Boise, it's already socially unacceptable in Chelsea.

The same rule applies to tastes in dogs, which are in a constant state of flux. That's how Bob got here, and only recently. Not long ago, the cute and feisty Jack Russell terrier was the breed of choice for trendsetters. The *Frasier* show featured one of these misleadingly sweet, tightly wound time bombs that managed to resemble puppies their entire lives. Being forever young and toylike was their gay appeal, but even Peter Pan pets were short-lived. Soon these dogs du jour grew old and tired, and along came the foxy Shiba Inu, which was sleek, chic, and Japanese—only to be displaced by the lean, mean, athletic basenji, billed as the wild dog of Africa. The whole tundra story was a sham. The breed was a calculated cross between several domesticated dogs, but a mix that the gay boys found compelling and the nation soon learned to love. Little do people know that the feral ruggedness of the breed, like the manly silence of a dog that didn't bark, expanded in our eyes only after my straight model friend, Richard, and his basenji named Gunner, were plastered to the sides of city buses in an ad for Canali suits in the year 2000. After that campaign, all of Chelsea decided that if it couldn't have Richard, then it would have to settle for his dog.

The exotic basenji sat for a few years in the limelight, and then along came the French bulldog, a kind of transition to Bob. The more continental version of a bulldog was less blunt and bullish, more delicate and refined, like a young English gentleman returning from his grand tour with breeding and a fake accent. Only recently had the inelegant English bull, created before the French-ified model, returned to the cutting edge when I arrived in Bob's apartment that afternoon. Who knew how long this dog would be in style? Thick and top-heavy with wads of folded skin, and faces that only a mother—or Bob's dads—could love, these creatures began emerging from fashionable homes at about the same time as the release of a popular gay coffee table book, the one in the living room as we passed, conspicuously displayed and stuffed with torrid photos depicting Spanish matadors and their bulging crotches.

The English bulldog has always been a sort of freak-show oddity, even though it's been the national dog of that island nation for centuries. Across the pond where Anglophiles were eager to imitate, the breed became the official mascot for Yale's football team in the 1880s, possibly due to its resemblance to the players.[1] The bull remains a breed apart, not only owing to its tough, hulky appearance, but because of the original use still preserved in the name. Other dogs were bred to herd sheep, hunt birds, haul carts, or guard children. Not Bob's ancestor. Believed to have been born of a mastiff and a terrier of some sort in the sixteenth century, this stubborn, allegedly fearless hybrid was conceived, like some "creature of a diseased imagination,"[2] as one critic put it, for one reason and one reason alone: to entertain. This performer's role was to fight a tethered bull, to lock his powerful jaws on its screaming face, ideally on the snout, and to hold on tightly, legend says, sometimes for hours until the poor beast suffocated in its own blood.

Tall tales aside, bulldogs really did fight bulls and were, indeed, bred to approach a restrained animal face-to-face, unlike wolves that attack running prey from behind—that is, if they weren't kicked in the head first. Most surprising is not the fact that bull baiting was allowed to go on for several centuries and was avidly pursued by Englishmen of all classes, but that it is socially acceptable even today for anyone to harbor a latent nostalgia for the ghastly game. For reasons not quite explained, people who are normally opposed to violence and to animal cruelty find the breed charming. Even vegans, who won't drink cow milk and shy away from leather Hush

Puppies, are allowed to retain a soft spot for a dog designed to be nothing less than a celebration of bullish bloodlust. Dog breeding as a whole, as we'll see in chapters to come, is a favorite hiding place for values and beliefs we're no longer supposed to have.

Despite all high-minded ideals to the contrary, this ugly appetite for pitting dogs against bulls was indulged without reservation or apology since medieval times in England. Before bull baiting was outlawed by an act of Parliament in 1835, it was the national sport among a people said to have rivaled all others in its love for brutal animal hobbies. In retrospect, Spanish bullfights look like puppy mixers compared to the elaborate shows once staged for the elevation of the national character, as Lord Canning and anti-abolitionist William Windham defended the heinous practice about to be banned amidst fierce resistance.[3] Dog fanciers, people who are today considered lovers and protectors of animals, were in those days the very opposite. These were the spectators who gambled on the outcome of events and who cheered as flesh was torn, bones were crushed, and agonized cries filled the air. Right up until the nineteenth century when dog shows as we know them first appeared, "fancier" meant "bettor."

Before the breed learned to sit prettily for judges and resist the impulse to grab onto a leg, it was actually expected to *do* something for a living, if only "to bayte and take the bull by the eare, when occasion so requireth," as England's original hound historian, John Caius, prescribed.[4] This dog took his job very seriously. As in "pit bull" (not an official breed but perceived as one) fighting today, high wagers were staked on a dog's brute force and blind courage that bordered on stupidity. Bulldogs were encouraged to be mad fighting machines that would stop at nothing to subdue and kill their opponent. They were believed to be unthinking, which was considered a virtue in their line of work. Was this the hallmark of British national character that had to be preserved at any cost?

As one enthusiast remarked, it was "the diminution of the brain" that was the breed's most desirable quality. The skull or brain box was overly large, but the organ inside was believed to be somehow diminutive. "The cerebral capacity of the Bulldog is sensibly smaller than in any other race, and it is doubtless to the decrease in the encephalon that we must attribute its inferiority to all others in everything related to intelligence. The Bulldog is scarcely capable of any education and is fitted for nothing but for combat and ferocity."[5] This manmade monstrosity was presented as a sort of canine Sylvester Stallone with a Cockney accent. Bets were taken on how many of these thoughtless soldiers would have their backs broken when angry bulls flung them into the hysterical crowd surrounding Westminster pit. One of many forums where animals of all species were turned against each other and forced into mortal combat, this most famous theater of cruelty, coincidentally, had the same name as a prestigious dog show that takes place each year in New York City, and to a crowd of cheering millions around the world.

The English aren't entirely to blame for such reprehensible behavior toward other animals. They no more invented blood sport than they can rightly take credit for having conceived of dog breeding, though they did expand upon both traditions through creative innovation. Animal fighting was widely enjoyed by the Romans long before they acquired the taste. The "sport" went back beyond the Greeks and Egyptians. Ancients enjoyed a good goring, and not just bulls and dogs were featured in their public arenas. Like the gladiators who shared these same stages, bears, wildcats, buffaloes, elephants, and animals of all kinds died badly, to the delight of the mob. Like human slaves, it was believed, they were born for the sole purpose of suffering to entertain. In just one day at the Colosseum, over five thousand animals perished in fights with their own kind, or perhaps with other species, as in matches between man and beast. Jews and Muslims were baited in Europe during the Middle Ages, though at a distinct disadvantage. There was never a dull moment at any of these events because their variety gave spice to life.

The English apparently took this very old idea of animal fighting from the Romans, who arrived to occupy them in the first century AD. But the novelty dog they fashioned was their own exciting variation on a canine theme, and since that time the English have become famous for their ability to concoct so many different breeds. Mastiffs had been the preferred prize fighters before bulldogs appeared on the scene. These were the original stars in medieval animal fights, where they were pitted against each other or against bulls, bears, and sometimes lions for the royal games. Victims were often handicapped by having their eyes burned out to give the dogs a slight edge. The legs of bulls were sometimes cut at the hooves, forcing them to stand and defend themselves on bloody stumps. Mastiffs had foreboding faces thought to resemble that of the lion, another national symbol that goes back further than the bulldog. These kingly giants were highly valued but expensive to keep, and replacing them after savaged was problematic for all but the very wealthy. They were decorated with rosettes made of colored fabric before entering the ring, an unsettling prediction of blue ribbons in centuries to come.[6]

That's where the bulldog made his entrance. Said to have been born of a mastiff and something else, this was a smaller dog but equally courageous. The upkeep was cheaper, as these dogs were more easily replaced if they fell in the ring or got tossed into the crowd. A more democratic version of the mastiff, the animal was lower to the ground, where he stood a better chance than his noble ancestor of approaching an angry bull. He, too, had a leonine look but was never considered aristocratic. The bulldog was an Everyman's dog. He wasn't so much a king's pride as a butcher's, which gave him plenty of opportunities for practicing at what he did best and living off merits alone. His master always had on hand a supply of fresh animals waiting to be slaughtered. Poor brutes were tethered in private so the dogs could have a few rounds at them before they were finished off by the butcher's knife. Seasoned bullfighters went on to win large sums for their owners in the gaming pits. But forcing the dog to work for the honor of victory was not frowned upon, and making these events more interesting attracted higher wagers. To make approaching an angry bull more of a challenge, one match believed to have been fought in the early nineteenth century is said to have tested the dog's devotion to duty and his singularity of purpose. During the legendary baiting, a gentleman supposedly chopped off one of his dog's paws to show how tough the animal was. Apparently, the dog kept on going at the bull, and at regular intervals the other three paws were methodically removed, proving this breed would not shy away from a fight no matter what. Here was a natural-born killer. "These dogs were carefully bred by selection," wrote a historian of the breed. "Beauty and symmetry of form were in no way desirable, the appearance of the dog counted for nothing—courage, power and ferocity for everything."[7]

Though mastiffs and, much later, bull terriers were also used for gladiatorial events, the bulldog came to represent bull baiting, a favorite form of entertainment for kings and commoners, an almost sacred ritual that was celebrated for centuries in towns and villages across the land. Evil as the practice would be considered by today's standards, it once represented quite the opposite. How did this particular breed, before all others, come to be a national symbol? And what kind of Frankenstein would want to manufacture, much less admire, such a ghoulish creation? Perhaps it was believed that witnessing savage performances instilled in Englishmen from all walks of life the virtue of unquestioning self-sacrifice, a tendency that could come in handy when proclaiming wars. Burning, raping, and plundering might be made more palatable to someone who'd attended these mindless displays of carnage. Calculatedly cruel as blood sports were, they could be linked to a sense of national purpose, even imbued with the scent of Christian charity.

One of the most famous annual matches started in a town called Staines near London around 1660. George Staverton, a man of wealth, is said to have seen a butcher's dogs pursuing a bull in the street, which gave him an idea. In his will, he left the town enough money to buy a fresh bull each year and stage a formal baiting six days before Christmas. Spectators would be charged admittance and the proceeds used to buy shoes and stockings for poor children. Bull baiting, like a more famous public sacrifice once arranged by the Romans, was transformed from a cruel and senseless act of violence into a hallowed annual custom that only a heathen would dare to condemn. Something ugly was made beautiful. Base pleasures were ennobled. Cruelty became kind.[8]

How on earth did anyone ever get the idea that there was anything *cute* about these dogs? Probably from the certainty, as soon as they were standardized for dog shows in the nineteenth century, that they were no longer a threat. Crossed with Chinese pugs for the show ring, today's bulldog has been so thoroughly deformed that it wouldn't stand a chance against a bull, or anything else for that matter. A curious blend of Victorian sensibility and gothic horror, this is among the most expensive dogs for veterinary care today,[9] a fact that hasn't decreased its popularity.[10] On the contrary, like an antique figurine left to collect dust in a tchotchke shop for nearly a century, the bulldog has been shined up and restored to its former glory. The breed made the American Kennel Club's top-ten list in 2007 for the first time since the 1930s. Little Bobs are more sought after all the time, and they're being churned out like sausage links (with the help of a surgeon's cleaver, since virtually all births, again, are of the Cesarean kind). Proud owners can be heard on Manhattan street corners singing the praises of these fashionable retro-dogs, announcing like town criers their legendary past to curious passersby. "Yeah, they took this big, mean bull, you know, and tied it to a stake," I've heard said many times. "The dog would latch onto its snout and suck the life outta the thing." Bulldogs are celebrations of a bloody past that apparently hasn't lost its appeal.

For better or worse, Americans have an old, unshakable habit of imitating the English. "Those who once take to the breed," remarked dog man James Watson, "seem to imbibe something of the holding-on power of the dogs themselves, and it is noticeable in America, perhaps more so than in England, that our staunchest bulldog men have good square jaws and a look displaying character and resolution."[11] Baiting wasn't banned in New York City slaughterhouses until as late as 1867, although it had been officially frowned upon in England for decades. It was still widely believed that setting dogs loose on animals made the meat tender. Once the legal pursuit of this "sport" was thwarted on both sides of the Atlantic, admirers wanted to keep the dogs that had come to symbolize so much to so many people. Salvaging something civilized from a savage creature became the lifetime goal of many a devoted fan during the second half of the nineteenth century. In time, the English would find a way to keep their national mascot, and unwavering Anglophiles the world over could have as a pet an animal that had outlived its original purpose. When bullfighting was banned in England for humane reasons almost two hundred years ago, the national hero didn't have a forum. He couldn't perform the task for which he'd been designed. Short of stuffing the breed with sawdust and exhibiting him at the Crystal Palace, there seemed to be no more practical "utility," as is said of working animals before they're made into pets. Fans couldn't imagine a world without their old hero. "They no longer wanted a ferocious brute, whose one idea in life was to attack," another authority on the breed reminisced in the early twentieth century, "but they wished to retain all the splendid qualities of the dog without its ferocity."[12]

The being refashioned during these years has been called "a transition dog."[13] Innovations were needed to keep the crowd's attention, but repackaging the breed for a more squeamish audience was not as difficult as predicted. What better way to hold back an unwieldy beast, to reform a natural-born killer, than to cripple the monster so that it could barely do anything at all? To preserve bulldogs for posterity, their movement was slowed to a snail's pace. To suggest strength and vitality where there were none, bulldogs were emasculated, refashioned into caricatures of their former selves.

"It is a case resembling an attempt to convey to someone who has never seen lower Broadway," wrote Watson, "what that wonderful architectural canyon looks like merely by written description and without an accompanying photograph."[14] Bulldogs became enormous frames without substance, cartoon replicas unable to move very far but quite impressive to look at. As in popular stage melodramas of the nineteenth century, striking faces were essential. "Expression" in the show ring, not performance in the fighting ring, would be the new draw. Specimens born "very plain," wrote another expert, were devalued and "seldom saw the showbench." Folds on the forehead were singled out and retrospectively assigned an implausible purpose they most likely never had. Supposed to have served as channels for irrigating the pinned bull's blood around the dog's eyes while he held on for dear life, they were further deepened for emphasis. Dog show judges began using expressions like "good wrinkle" and "grand wrinkle"[15] to describe the marks of a new kind of champion. Eyes that had once stared into a dying bull's were made buggier, swelling and reddening to recall the gory scenes of old. The signature under-bite was heightened in vaudevillian style. Among other changes made to suggest what this breed *used* to do, this apparatus for holding on became the ultimate measure of dramatic effect. "The dog with lack of underjaw loses the proper expression," it was said of the more perfect specimens, "and in consequence does not show up the other portions of head to advantage—such as the eyes, ears, and skull."[16] The under-bite was further exaggerated, and the more skull, the more exciting. Soon breeders were skull-happy, horrifying some of the older devotees. Had fanciers perhaps gone too far in preserving this stalwart symbol of stoical English resolve? "The skull should be very large—the larger the better—and in circumference should measure (round the front of the ears) at least the height of the dog at the shoulders. . . . No point should be so much in excess of the others as to destroy the general symmetry, make the dog appear deformed, or interfere with its powers of motion."[17]

Deformity was in the eye of the beholder. Creating an illusion of mass in the lower jaw meant distracting from other parts of the head. "The craze for dished faces," recalled Edward Ash, "caused owners to use an appliance to get a shorter upper jaw. They set about it in this manner. When the puppies were quite young and the muscles and bones of the face yet tender, the cords on the middle and two sides of the lips were cut. A small wooden block, hollowed out to fit the face, was then attached, and struck a sharp blow with a mallet. This drove back the cartilage and bone of the nose. Jacks were then attached to hold the face in its new position until the bones and muscles had set."[18] Once the jaw was in place and the face sufficiently flattened, a wooly-coated version of the dog was promptly eliminated in the 1850s, as aficionados began to fight bitterly over what, exactly, the dog must look like and how it should be rated in competitions. Standardization was in order, and a system of points was needed if owners were to vie with each other for prizes. In 1875 the breed was "nearly approaching perfection," and the Bulldog Club, the oldest of all breed specialty clubs, was founded in England. The object of all this affection was soon recognized by the British Kennel Club and the American Kennel Club. Reformed dog fanciers—which by now meant lovers of a warlike past, but not fighters themselves—would in time subscribe to a set of formal breeding standards to produce animals that were more or less identical with their "broken-looking noses" and "'broken-back' appearance, which is very characteristic," as stern anti-mongrelist Gordon Stables noted approvingly.[19]

Not everyone agreed on the bulldog's new construction. "In your next article," canine chronicler Freeman Lloyd was once advised, "you ask the people if they ever saw an animal made by God with his lower canine teeth protruding outside or beyond the upper teeth."[20] Pushing the limits of common sense and redefining common cruelty, however, it might be said that focusing on exaggerated appearance rather than aggressive performance was a step in the direction of a more humane approach to dogs. Unfortunately, while it was true that the bulldog was no longer allowed to risk his life momentarily for the crowd's enjoyment, none of this repackaging was innocent or without long-term consequences for the dog himself. In the interest of earning points in the ring, standards for the breeding of animals that were tried and proven for thousands of years had to be lowered. The unnatural compression of the face soon led to breathing problems. The wrinkles in the skin caused infections and made a person wonder how many extra folds a dog really needed to have. The eyes grew so large that they were subject to a number of serious conditions. The chest was expanded to give a greater impression of strength—much like the puffed-up peacock breasts on Bob's two gay daddies—pushing the front legs so far apart that they became unstable. Thus the "malformation of the legs"[21] described nearly a century ago and seen in Bob as he hobbled so endearingly.

"To give it an appearance of great width of chest which it did not possess," wrote one expert, "various instruments of torture were used." Puppies were fitted with harnesses "so contrived that two large stuffed leather pads were secured between the fore legs of the dog, spreading them out and causing the unfortunate animal to waddle miserably about the kennel yard instead of enjoying his puppyhood as every puppy has a right to." Other breeders "placed heavy weights and secured them on the shoulders of the young and growing animal." The most barbaric method was "to confine the growing puppy in a hutch-like place of which the roof or top was so low that it was never possible for the wretched animal to stand upright."[22] In time, advances in inbreeding would make these instruments of torture obsolete. Mutant characteristics could be brought about more "naturally," that is, without the aid of hammers, vices, or iron maidens.

"Improvement," like beauty or deformity, was in the eye of the beholder. As early as 1904, Watson, who served on the AKC's Stud Book Committee, noted that female bulldogs did not typically like to mate and had to be restrained in the interest of fulfilling a growing demand for the breed. Thus the employment of gruesome "rape racks" that are still in use today. It was also observed, and by that same dependable source, that in the unlikely event that both bitch and pups survived the miracle of birth (aided by surgical means today, once again, due to the narrow hips on the former and the wide skulls on the latter), mothers very often did not want to care for their young.[23] Perhaps they knew that the pups were not fit for survival? Or maybe as two dog breeders who left the fancy and wrote *SOS Dog: The Purebred Dog Hobby Re-examined* suggest, "improved" breeding practices, often in isolation, have deprived many pedigree dogs of the sort of socialization needed for caregiving, and for mating without resorting to rape. Generations of selection for extreme aggression—the kind that would have driven wolves extinct before they had the chance to become dogs—may have left many modern bulldogs incapable of normal behavior, including mating, nurturing, and interacting socially. This has been suggested of their close cousins, bull terriers, which as pups can't typically even play ball with siblings without attacking each other and must be constantly monitored. Females must be muzzled to prevent them from biting or killing their young when they try to suckle. Such are the monstrous results of human meddling.[24]

Despite the many obstacles to the breed's continued success, and the countless casualties that mass production of these poor brutes must have entailed, bulldogs remained immensely popular for many years and the market was flooded with them. The new and improved bulldog had one small problem, though, among all the others: he wasn't agile enough to run. A dog that couldn't *run*? And this was considered the mark of a champion! As the practical abilities of the breed were sacrificed for dramatic effect, a walking contest was held in 1893 to determine which specimen most typified the "race" (as a breed was called in English until quite recently and still is in other languages).

Two top bulldogs were matched in the hope of silencing critics upset over how freakishly deformed the breed had become. The first champion, Orry, looked like a bulldog of the old school, being lighter boned and athletic. His opponent, Dockleaf, heavier set and smaller, came closer to the ideal for the modern theatrical version. Orry was the more agile of the two and won at walking—hardly a measure of athleticism—while Dockleaf showed fatigue and was withdrawn.[25] This didn't prevent breeders from reproducing a half-crippled Dockleaf for years to come. In the show ring, prizes would be showered upon dogs unfit for walking, much less running, but conforming to their official standard for appearance. Understandably, critics were concerned that "while these exaggerations of form were being produced, it was at the cost of the dog's stamina and health."[26]

In the 1970s, the breed was "improved" yet again, this time by an Anglophile American who created yet another fake replica breed altogether. Historical accuracy and improved health were the goals, though even this latest nostalgia-trip bulldog was remade for form first and had a questionable function as a house pet. According to dog designer David Leavitt, the traditional English bulldog—created a mere century before—no longer *looked* quite English enough. As is often done in "rescuing" rare dogs of the past, the breeder looked to old paintings, engravings, and statues when attempting to prop up this relic from a bygone era. After nearly two centuries of human fidgeting, the bulldog was repackaged once again, this time to be more convincing to an American audience that still had a taste for England's bloody past. "Extreme cruelty to animals was inherent in baiting sports," wrote Leavitt. "This cruelty was abhorrent to me, but I was fascinated by the great tenacity and courage of the over-matched underdog.[27] I was also drawn to the Bulldog because of his fierce appearance."[28] This authentic "Olde English Bulldogge" came complete with antique spelling as the name might appear in gold gothic letters above the bar in a quaint English pub—charming to some, pure nonsense to others. As added reminders of the dog's bellicose, breast-pounding past, a new brand of gin called "Bulldog" now wears a spiked collar around its neck, and "JOCKO," a line of manly jockstraps designed for gays bears the face of a tough and determined bulldog over the elastic waistband.

The odd-looking creature I was hired to walk that day was the 1890s theatrical version, not the 1970s remake of a remake. In fact, Bob's trip downstairs to the street was wrought with drama. As his dads had foretold, he threw up his water in the elevator. We moved as fast as the guy could limp across the polished marble floor of his front lobby until a sudden tug came to the leash. I looked down to learn that Bob had lost more of his breakfast even before I could prepare lunch with all of his prescriptions. The doorman knew from experience exactly what to do. He said not to worry because a mop and pail were nearby at all times. A grin came to the face of this keeper of the gates who'd grown attached to the tragicomical little figure, like everyone else who'd witnessed his daily ordeal. He opened the door so Bob could make it to the pavement without further delay.

"Good boy!" I said as the puppy squatted over the curb and released a small river of urine into the gutter. He waddled a few feet, did his other business, threw up some more, then snorted while looking up at me with eyes full of puss. I reminded myself not to be alarmed by this compact medicine ball oozing from every orifice. Bob coughed and rested before trying to walk again, only to stumble and swerve as though he was about to faint. We'd only been out a few minutes and already it was time to go home. I decided to carry Bob back into the building, but this was difficult to do without making breathing more difficult for him. Locking my arms around four deformed legs so as not to put pressure on the chest, I lifted with a grunt and ran through the doors, already opened by the doorman who'd been awaiting our return.

"It's almost like clockwork," he said, patting Bob on the head as we passed. "Let's hope he gets strong enough to take a *real* walk like other dogs some day."

Keeping this thought in mind, I turned the key again, Bob's signal to drag himself into the apartment and grab the nearest toy in sight. His dads had paid for a half-hour walk and he still had some time left. After I'd cleaned the puppy's cage, then fed and medicated him, we sat on a rug playing with his favorite toy of all, an old sock nearly chewed to bits. Tug-of-war made him growl happily, distracting for a time from his suffering, though he did throw up most of his lunch. I would have given him longer to play, but about a dozen other bulldogs were waiting, in their own respective dark apartments, to be walked. When the time came, Bob compliantly followed me into the kitchen with a snort, then waddled into his cage without a fuss. I don't know why I talk to dogs. Maybe to make myself feel less guilty for leaving, I said, "Don't worry, pal. I'll be back the same time tomorrow. And your dads will be home in a few hours." Bob seemed to understand and lay down on a powder-blue blanket with a kind of resolve I would've expected from a much older dog. He looked up with those bloodshot eyes that told a past he knew nothing about.

On the way out of this grand apartment decorated like an imperial palace and before hitting the switch, I took time to notice two large jade statues that flanked the main entrance leading to the outside hallway. These were animal figures and sort of looked like Bob in a sketchy way. Seated on two pedestals were translucent green dogs—or were they lions?—with tongues hanging out like serpents or maybe dragons. They had a demonic look to them with fiery eyes, catlike teeth, and bird claws. These were mythical creatures, or so I hoped. I darkened the room but turning to close the door behind me caught a glimpse of the coffee table again. In the spotlight of the opened door, next to the volume of well-hung matadors, was another glossy cover of a book called *Kennedy Style*. I'd never understood this obsession with old families and good breeding among a group of people who had no plans to do any themselves. There was the answer to my question.[29]

CHAPTER TWO

PERFECTIONISTS GONE WILD

Entering the grand old house on West Twelfth for an interview with a potential client, I was ushered in by a determined doggy who was flanked on both sides by two decorative felines. The cats paused cautiously while their pal, a funny French bulldog whose personality far exceeded her size, came rushing toward the door snorting and barking with a rough, whiskey voice. "This is Winnie," was my introduction to the being I befriended with a simple scratch behind one of her outlandish satellite-dish ears out of proportion to her head, which was itself supersized for the small, compact frame to which it looked bolted. "She's seven and loves cats," Winnie's mom continued, sensing my delight with the peaceable kingdom I'd just discovered in a narrow foyer. The dog approved, her owner was instantly set on giving me the job, and the rest was mere formality.

My new client gestured me down the hall and my new best friend followed, as though by instinct without being told, in a precise heel position by my side on round, feline feet. The cats scattered to right and left, disappearing into different rooms. "In fact she has two of her own. I like to call them the Three Musketeers. But you have to watch her on the sidewalk because she only loves *her* cats." A conversation followed in the front parlor where I sat on a sofa petting a quirky contraption that looked more like a cat than a dog. Attached to Winnie's dwarfed body was a domed lion's head with the punched-in face of a Persian. Puss-in-Boots ears were raised alertly, and her back was permanently arched like a frightened kitty's. Wide leonine eyes, a flat button nose, and a Cheshire grin carved into a globular skull resembling a Halloween pumpkin—a long tail was all that was missing to complete the comparison. Winnie's was reduced to a stub.

I smiled at the abbreviated cat-dog vying with her owner for attention while I was handed instructions on her idiosyncrasies. Endearing details were revealed, like what sorts of dogs frightened her on the street, which parks she preferred to promenade in, and favorite treats kept on the second shelf to the left. The top priority was a small cylindrical object made of rubber called a Kong toy, an alien shape I was told to impregnate with peanut butter and place precisely at the center of Winnie's red velvet bed in the library—*not* the pink satin bed in kitchen—after her daily walk. Winnie's intricate daily routine had to be respected strictly and punctually, I was warned in no uncertain terms, observed like rituals in a monk's book of hours, or else she might get confused and poop in the bedroom. Such are the intimate facts, some based on trial and error, others spawned of a dog owner's own private anthropomorphisms, that only a devoted parent would understand and care to impart to someone entering a circle of trust. Over the years, hit-or-miss habits become rules, and eventually these morph into sacred traditions. "I leave the TV on all day because she just loves *Animal Planet*," the woman continued with one of those wild claims that seemed at first to be "more about the people than the dogs," as they say, until I saw Winnie sitting mesmerized by shadows of tigers, zebras, and giraffes passing highly defined across an enormous flat screen. "She's very good on the leash. But keep an eye open for pizza crusts and chicken wings when you're walking her, because she's a real Hoover!"

Just as I was thinking that dogs would be dogs and there was nothing not to love about this one, some unseen presence entered the room and turned our conversation in a new direction. Winnie's mom and I sat civilized around a coffee table discussing doggy do's and don'ts, but as though guided by forces beyond her control, my host felt compelled to make an unsolicited confession. "The breeder told us she's not show quality," she confessed, apologizing for the perfectly sweet and innocent creature before us. "Her ears are too droopy, they said."

I'd heard it all before. No matter what the breed or how wonderful and unique the individual dog, there's always something wrong: a Frenchie's ears don't stand quite right, beagle's muzzle is too long, basenji's tail doesn't lean slightly to one side at a precise angle, cocker's eye rims lack that distinct "almond" shape . . . A person can adore a pet in or out of the show ring, but there's always that other presence looming, scrutinizing, and handing down judgments. It taxes the understanding of amateur dog lovers to discover that industry professionals, grown adults and many of them educated, devote their entire lives to maintaining the proper distance between a pair of nostrils and preserving the sanctity of a curly tail. Exacting rules for the canine form assume a complexity that pushes the limits of common sense and drags us back into a dark and primitive world of secret incantations and weird geometrical formulas.

Each of three sections on a dachshund, for example—head, torso, and hindquarters—should ideally make up, respectively, no more than one-third of the entire length. Otherwise, the pup might win no prize, and the price of its offspring, like the owner's esteem, will suffer. Likewise, a borzoi's height, platonically speaking, is equal to its length—in other words, the dog must form a perfect square.[1] This insistence on balance and mathematical precision can sometimes border on madness. If a Pembroke Welsh corgi wants to be fit for a queen or a kennel club, then it must be constructed as follows: "Distance from the occiput [or back of the head] to center of stop [where the muzzle begins] to be greater than the distance from stop to nose tip, the proportion being five parts of total distance for the skull and three parts for the foreface."[2] A line drawn from the nose tip through the eyes and then across the ear tips should form "an approximate equilateral triangle."[3] Professional show judges and average pet owners bow before rigid but arbitrary standards that have changed surprisingly little in years.

Coat color is also strictly governed on dogs wishing to be worthy of places in our hearts and homes. How quickly we've forgotten that throughout much of the nineteenth century, early attempts at Labrador retrievers were killed at birth if they were yellow, because no shade other than solid black was "desirable," as they say in the fancy. "There is no record of what happened to yellow dogs through this period," writes Richard Wolters in *The Labrador Retriever: The History—the People.* "The records of the restocking of the Buccleuch kennels from the Malmesbury line mentioned only blacks. It has to be assumed that if off-color puppies arrived they were not appreciated and consequently done away with."[4] To the present day at Westminster or Crufts, perfectionists can be very demanding, and a tiny wisp or "flash" of contrast on the chest or muzzle of an otherwise unblemished yellow, chocolate, or black Lab might handicap that dog in a judge's eyes. "A small white spot on the chest is permissible, but not desirable," reads the AKC standard out of sheer charity.[5] Any highlights such as graying on the face that can't be explained by age—though one of the Lab's possible ancestors, the Saint John's water dog, had these distinctions at birth—are grounds for disqualification. Heaven help the puppy born brindled.

Matching accessories are no less carefully thought out in advance. "Eye color should be brown in black and yellow Labradors, and brown or hazel in chocolates," reads the standard. "Black, or yellow eyes give a harsh expression and are undesirable. Small eyes, set close together or round prominent eyes are not typical of the breed. Eye rims are black in black and yellow Labradors; and brown in chocolates. Eye rims without pigmentation is a disqualification." It doesn't stop there. Black and yellow Labs must have black noses. Chocolate Labs must have brown. And the pink snout often seen on today's very popular yellow Lab is simply "unacceptable."[6] Skin, like fur, must be laid out as per instructions, especially on breeds with too much of it. English bulldogs and Dogues de Bordeaux, for example, cannot be champions if those distinctive folds aren't mapped symmetrically across the faces. A breeder of Rhodesian ridgebacks admitted to the BBC in 2008 that puppies born without that distinctive mark along the back—even though it's linked to a defect of the spine—are killed out of some (misguided) sense of mercy.[7]

Arbitrary but idealistic as this enormous body of rules might seem to outsiders, standards didn't fall from the sky. Winnie the French bulldog didn't inhabit her cartoon shape by accident. Before the AKC had the final word on her look, early pioneers fought long and hard to get this dog on a path to some preconception of perfection. Authorities back in the late nineteenth century bickered over whether the tail should be straight or curly, and the breed itself almost didn't happen. Three different runners-up vied for recognition from the kennel clubs and a lasting place in our hearts. The miniature bulldog, the toy bulldog, and the French bulldog all looked quite similar, and only one would live on to be ranked among the most popular breeds in the world. After some prolonged cat-fighting between ladies partial to each of these types, speculators on two variations stepped aside. The Frenchie was the social survivor.[8]

But with victory comes responsibility. The struggle wasn't over, because sponsors hadn't agreed on what it took to be a champion in the show ring, that celestial ideal to which any dog worthy of its name should aspire. The French bulldog had a good following, but the finer points were not yet etched in stone, and with no formal criteria for handing out trophies and rosettes—and nothing for the society column of the *New York Times* to write about the owners—the breed was "unstable," as fanciers call a type that has not achieved "breediness," or "reproductive uniformity."

Those funny, substandard ears on dear Winnie would have been no laughing matter to the elite corps of ladies who formed the French Bull Dog Club of America, the first of its kind devoted to this somewhat recent arrival on the purebred scene of 1897. Frenchies had come a long way in a short while. Originally English bulldogs whose size had been allowed to "deteriorate" in England, they are believed to have been transferred to the Continent by lace makers who migrated to Normandy.[9] While in France, the diminutive bulls grew smaller still by mating with local dogs. Isolated from their land of birth, they flourished and evolved in different ways, but until some grande dame from Paris snatched one up as a fashion accessory and made it a darling of urban elites, breeding was not controlled and pedigrees weren't recorded. In the early years, owners were typically working folk who made clothing for the rich but had no social use for pets that matched their wares. This dog wasn't even a breed yet because it lacked that couture perfection demanded by the big-city kennel clubs. Proto-Frenchies were kept for companionship and not for show. They were free to mix their blood indiscriminately with other dogs, a thought that strikes terror into the hearts of pooch purists.

Returning to this pressing question of head ornaments, a topic that occupied fine ladies for many an afternoon tea and the inspiration for forming the Frenchie club in the first place: "To what type of dog the toy bulldog was bred in France to create this particular ear formation," one writer recalled, "will, perhaps, always remain a mystery."[10] This was precisely the sort of ambiguity that fanciers could not abide. The ears had no known origin. A gap in the dog's family tree suggested something suspicious in its character. A minor detail drove a major wedge in the canine community, festering unfriendly feelings for years to come. When this rough draft of a recognized breed was thrust onto the social scene, it had the lack of distinction to be born with *two* types of ears. The first took a semi-erect, roselike shape. This was the ear on Winnie, and the style worn by her rightful ancestor, the hearty old snorting pride of England. But somewhere along the line, a mutation had occurred. A problematic protuberance struck a bold new stance, a posture as prickish and arrogant as one of those newfangled American skyscrapers. No one had taken the time or trouble yet to draw up an official standard for the dog, though this "bat" ear was considered a distinct disadvantage in some circles, while it was admired in others. Europeans frowned upon the pushy parvenu, and both English and French authorities agreed that only the "rose" variety should be considered in good taste. As far as they were concerned, the bat ear was a radical intrusion, and many American competitors at Westminster hedged their bets by importing rose specimens directly from purveyors in Paris. Owners of these pricy dogs expected their loyalty to pay off in cash prizes and silver cups, and more importantly, in social distinction and praise.

Little did authorities know that a small clique of New Yorkers with ideals of their own were preparing to step outside the circle and exploit a loophole. Worlds turned on minor details, and one can only imagine the bitter controversy ignited by a few wealthy women who violated an unwritten code and began a rebellion. Bat ears were being worn in some of the most prominent mansions along Fifth Avenue, and imposing matrons with names like

Cooper-Hewitt, Neilson, Haddon, Ronalds, Watrous, and Kernochan happened to have dogs that wore them. These influential figures wanted *their* pets to win at Westminster, and they were firmly committed to social change. This was surprising behavior. It wasn't like Americans to go against foreign tastes when it came to dogs, or anything else. The English had created most of the breeds that brought cachet upon their owners. Dog shows and official standards were also importations that civilized folk had learned to respect and revere as models of propriety. In a rare event for the fledgling fancy, the typically insecure, unquestioning, tail-between-the-legs attitude of newly monied Americans toward British role models was turning into something like national character. These women had the impudence to challenge the opinion of no less than an *English* show ring judge who had declared their dogs' ears to be unorthodox. The venerable judge George Raper must have been taken off guard. English authorities, like the dogs they were paid to visually dissect, were often shipped over and treated like royalty. High-born British dog owners were wasting no less time themselves rushing to American shows, where hefty prizes awaited. Their presence lent an air of class to these events, which, admittedly, they'd invented in the first place. Now a group of ambitious wives-of-so-and-so were suddenly taking it upon themselves to go against their better judgment, to question an English judge's authority and throw the final verdict back in his face. In the opinion of these contrarians, the only acceptable ear should bring to mind a winged nocturnal bloodsucker, not a fading flower.

Bitter infighting was not uncommon, as the pedigree dog cult struggled to define itself in the final hours of the Gilded Age. Breed clubs fought with kennel clubs and with each other, and just about everyone locked horns at one time or another with judges in the ring. Disgruntled players left in a huff and pulled their dogs out of events in shows of disdain. Until the American Kennel Club incorporated in 1909 and then consolidated its authority in 1929 by assuming control over all breed standards, competitions were more spirited than they are today. Dogdom wasn't centralized, and it was still possible to break with the powers that were, then return a few years later once everyone had cooled off. The events of 1897 were extreme. When the prize was awarded to a rose-eared Frenchie at Madison Square Garden, the tightly corseted gang of sharp-toothed biddies snapped their Chinese fans shut like dragon jaws and arose from their plush velvet seats. They threw luxuriant animal skins on their backs and stormed out of the exhibition hall, the plumage on their headdresses bristling with rage. Followed sheepishly by mogul husbands who'd come along for the ride and probably preferred a more sporting breed, they set about the difficult task of promoting their version of the Frenchie, the one born with the mutation they planned to perpetuate. A meeting was held later that day in the same hall. Angry voices demanded not only that any animal with rose ears be disqualified from all future competitions, but that the judge's decision be reversed and the silver cup returned. The howls were not heeded, so these women had their husbands create a club for them—that was how it was done in those days—and using their combined weight, they got in on the ground floor of the breed.

The French Bull Dog Club of America was formed one evening at Delmonico's restaurant, and a standard was hastily published in the *New York Times*, as if there had been no real news on April 7, 1897. "The ear shall hereafter be known as the 'bat' ear," read the ruling in defiance of international opinion, bringing fierce attacks from the foreign press, which was no less attuned to trivia, and inviting jabs from British loyalists at home.[11] How dare those upstart Americans take a dog that wasn't even their idea and butcher it beyond recognition? This was seen as a wanton act of barbarism, an affront to tradition, and perhaps an early warning that cultural dominance was beginning to flow in a new direction. The Yanks had pirated a status symbol. Then they had the audacity to hold an opulent victory bash at the Waldorf Astoria where only dogs with the wrong ears were displayed! Against a backdrop of marble columns, palm trees, and chandeliers that rivaled any European palace, New York aristocracy and its version of the perfect pet had emerged as a force with which to reckon. Pictured in an engraving in the *New York Herald* were rows of caged Frenchies wearing bat ears without shame.[12] They had fur collars and frilly names like Richelieu, Gamin, Babot, Ninette, Petite Fée, and Ange Pitou. The *New York Times* coverage of the event explained the central importance of the ears: "In order that the public may have a perfect idea of this distinctive quality special attention is called to the reproduction of the head of Schutto, to whom was awarded a magnificent cup as special prize for 'dog or bitch having the best ears, both in point of shape and carriage,' and he possesses this attribute in a most remarkable degree."[13]

As the new ear slowly gained social acceptance, resentment lingered. The usual donations for trophies were withheld when contests featured unsympathetic judges, and there were petty squabbles over details and tiffs about wording. Watson recalled in 1906 that "after a great deal of trouble the supporters of the bat-eared dog have received recognition and a classification has been made for the *Boule-Dogue Français*. This we think is a better title for the dog than that what we know it by, the propriety of translating it into English and thus making a bulldog of it being questionable."[14] Such were the preoccupations of society's elite of which kennel clubs like the AKC were very much a creation. Style was everything in the Land of Fancy, and the experts were determined to get this canine calibrated. Rules were set and every feature covered, from the length of its tail to the tip of its nose. The bat ear became the universal standard and the breed's most distinguishing characteristic.

Rose ears like Winnie's became instant grounds for disqualification. The new, Americanized Frenchies went on to attract idle matrons of the charity circuit with majestic names like Whitney, Belmont, Roosevelt, Vanderbilt, and Bennett, "for if there is anything the feminine heart dearly loves it is the one thing which no one else has, or, at best, that which but very few have," the *Times* explained. "Their grotesque appearance makes them also very striking either at walk or in the reception room."[15] As a result of the frivolous example set by a clique of socialites, these strange, half-crippled critters with monstrous skulls and bulging eyes were soon considered perfectly normal. For better or worse, peace was restored to dogdom. Never again would the war of the rose and bat ears rear its ugly head.

"We all love Winnie just the same," said her mom, praising her pooch's unique personality and many good qualities *despite* some terrible flaw. Substandard ears were the cross this dog's owners would have to bear with heads held high. Winnie's own head was a heavier burden still, not because it broke any of the rules, but because it fit the breed standard too well for her own wellness. Her breed club had decided on a proper cranium size back in the 1890s, leaving dogs like Winnie with special needs. This dog was so top-heavy that if her walker didn't hold the leash securely and guide her down the stairs, she'd go tumbling and could be seriously injured. No more aerodynamic was the precariously planar design of a Frenchie's face, doomed to further leveling over the years as judges interpreted a standard to further extremes, as it is their tendency to do. Freakish flatness became such an unhealthy preoccupation that fanciers forgot another "essential" called breathing. To this day, Frenchies, bulldogs, pugs, griffons, and many other dish-faced breeds have mouths so shallow that they can't cool themselves and have frequent heart attacks. Soft palate reduction is a surgery commonly performed on dogs with the misfortune of being born too perfect. Joint disease is another problem for Frenchies, thanks to the odd posture prescribed in their standard, and chronic eye infections due to those excess skin folds on the face. The whole mess of a cut-and-pasted cannibalized head is connected to an esophagus so malformed that frequent vomiting leads to pneumonia and death. Many "correct" specimens need spinal surgery due to the unnaturally arched back that's also a must. More incisions are on the horizon if dogs like Winnie are to survive as a breed. As with English bulls and many similar types with those skinny hips and hulky heads, Cesarean birth is the only way out. The French Bull Dog Club of America was founded, first and foremost, for a suitable ear style and was "the first organization in the world formed to promote the interests of French bulldogs."[16] But whose interests, exactly, were being promoted?

Breed standards are really no more than this: old recipes for the perfect dog that have little or nothing to do with health or sound construction, and everything to do with personal whim and a competitive spirit. How these curious criteria came about is a familiar story for many breeds. People in need of a hobby decided they liked a particular shape, size, and color of canine, something new and different from other dogs, something that would get them noticed and win them prizes. They formed their own breed club to promote themselves and their dogs, sometimes even before they had an exact breed whose interests they could further. Mixing and matching by trial and error—and sacrificing many puppies for not making the grade—they found a look to tickle their collective fancy. Generating animals that could be relied upon to breed "true," that is, with the limited set of arbitrary features they wanted to exaggerate—and allowing many unhealthy side effects to hitch a ride in the process—they mass-produced their genetically compromised ideal of perfection for consumers to buy. Sponsors waved their magic wand and voilà! A breed was born.

There's no mystery to any of this, nor should there be. Each time fans spot a particular breed on the street, rather than praise a thing of beauty, they might think back on the untold numbers destroyed to get this type. They might also consider the many mortalities to come when pups aren't born with idealized features, not to mention the price these dogs often pay in poor health if they're "correct." Once a dog of a pleasing aspect has been "stabilized," sponsors have their list of specifications enshrined among the other sacred texts guarded by an organization like the AKC or England's Kennel Club. Show ring judges, whose opinions are no less erratic than the breed's creators, refer to these documents when explaining random responses and justifying personal tastes in prestigious canine beauty pageants. Judges are the interpreters of the standards, the high priests of the fancy who ultimately decide which dogs approach their unseen ideals, which ones don't, and how each breed needs to be "improved" in the future, a self-sustaining process ensuring puppy sales will go on forever.

As the French bulldog's path to perfection illustrates, and contrary to popular knowledge, breed standards weren't passed down by the ancients from times immemorial. They're not steeped in tradition but were written very recently, often not more than a century ago.[17] Breeds as we know them are also new inventions, because you can't have a breed without a standard. Nor can you put on a dog show without both. Contrary to the huge backlog of misinformation passed down in history books and the sales pitches of commercial breeders, breed clubs, and registries, we now know from DNA that the vast majority of recognized breeds have only been walking sidewalks and show rings for a short while.[18] The sad truth is that scientific findings weren't really needed as proof. All anyone had to do was go back and look at the dates on breed standards to cast doubt on the fancy's claims to tradition. All it ever took was the daring to see beyond social and psychological barriers that made myth look like fact. The main appeal behind breeds has been the reassuring thought of delving into the distant past and digging up some authentic artifact. By safeguarding a relic, people feel they're part of something greater than themselves, as though they're preserving some rare species from extinction, rather than a simple commodity from failure. Judges are respected for upholding strange habits and protecting prototypes, and dog owners feel special for helping out by buying only animals resembling the latest champion, which was decided just yesterday.

In fact, the closest this whole process actually comes to anything antique is yet another myth. According to the Greeks, a meticulous fellow named Procrustes, aka "the stretcher," tied mortal humans to a rectangular iron frame to make them meet his own private standards. Procrustes sawed his victims' heads and legs until their torsos fit, or pulled them on a rack for falling short of expectations. This detail-oriented perfectionist was bent on improvement and would have gone on improving forever but for Theseus, slayer of the Minotaur, who cut off his head and ended this unhealthy obsession with the equiangular quadrilateral.

A breed standard might be seen as a "Procrustean bed," the expression used to describe an arbitrary and often archaic model to which a flawless fit is forced in some ruthless fashion. Throwing dogs into a ring and expecting them to conform to half-cocked calculations and color codes, imposing exaggerated styles severe enough to be identified on sight—forcing living, breathing, sentient creatures to fill molds cast for reasons nobody can remember but which everyone just assumes were good—is how pooches are kept "pure." No one needs to tell Winnie the French bulldog that Procrustean doggy beds aren't lined with satin or velvet.

Another inelegant fact from a no-frills history of dog breeds: no matter how you slice them, or how many blue ribbons and official papers you pile upon them, they're all mutts at the end of the day. In their misguided mission to preserve "perfect" types or keep working until they get one, fanciers conveniently forget that their cherished favorites were made by mating various dogs, often mongrels, that happened to have certain features someone wanted to enhance. Brief periods of rapid hybridization are what gave us the confusing catalog selection of types we've come to consider natural today. Many breeds were assembled by crossing already existent breeds. Either way, they're all mixed results because there was no pure dog in the first place. "It is a habit, if we can use the word," wrote Edward Ash in the 1930s, "for dog breeders to cover up the tracks which would show how a breed is made. Today it is a matter of self-protection. If breeders said that their high prices breed of dog were merely an Alsatian-Sealyham-Spaniel cross, who would give high prices?"[19] Purists cringe at the thought that prior to what they deemed purification by closing stud books and restricting gene pools—after an ideal type was produced more or less uniformly—their brands of choice were forged from impure unions. Pet owners who've invested in today's costly new "designer dogs," official breeds combined into blends like marriages arranged between royal families, are also due for a letdown. The "purebred" parents used to produce these hybrids have ancestors that were themselves the products of crossbreeding. This latest novelty is nothing new, except for the fact that designer dogs might stand a better chance of being healthy, and manufacturers haven't had the time to make up elaborate stories about previous owners who lived in castles.

An even less romantic, cut-rate version of many a breed's genesis reads as follows: some city people visiting the country one day spotted a farm dog that looked striking. They bought the nameless mongrel and returned to town where the dog and its progeny underwent the same grueling process as those mutilated Frenchies. Uniformity was the goal, and any dogs surviving the ordeal were designated purebreds by the local kennel club—when all along the founding father's social background was obscure, at best, and hardly worth writing home about. Breeds are no more than makeovers. At the risk of offending millions who've invested so much of their identities in purebred dogs, and spoiling fairy tales about princes and palaces, let it be finally said: *Never has there been such a thing as pure blood.* No such liquid exists, not in dogs or their owners—not unless, of course, royalty is for real, a belief still popular among those very same English who gave us the breeds, standards, and show rings we know and love today, and among Anglophiles the world over.

Not only is there no such liquid as pure blood, and though today's dogs are sufficiently inbred to account for vast numbers of health defects, the pedigrees that add to their market value are often worthless, even for purely snobbish purposes. An investigator for the Humane Society, Robert Baker, conducted an experiment in 1980 by successfully registering and receiving official AKC papers for several nonexistent Labrador retriever puppies to show just how easy it would be.[20] Likewise, no questions were asked in 2000 when NBC's *Dateline* registered eight golden retriever puppies—after mating a deceased male with a spayed female.[21] Considering the tens of thousands of puppy-mill dogs whose registration fees represent as much as 40 percent of the AKC's annual income, the potential numbers of fraudulent pedigrees (for either new dogs or their ancestors, whose origins were no more carefully scrutinized) should be sufficient to shatter any lingering illusions of pure blood and unbroken lineage in dogs.[22]

Yet pedigree prejudice is as old as history because people believe what they want to believe. John Caius, the unchallenged voice of dogdom for centuries—owing in no small part to his position as personal physician to two queens and a king—had no more use for "curres of the mungrell and rascal sort" than did his highnesses.

"Of such dogges as keep not their kinde," he wrote in 1570, "of such as are mingled out of sundry sortes not imitating the conditions of some one certaine spice, because they resemble no notable shape, nor exercise any worthy property of the true perfect and gentle kind, it is not necessarye that I write any more of them, but to banishe them as unprofitable implements, out of the boundes of my Booke."[23]

Wishful thinking has had such an influence that it took sticklers for DNA years to accept that dogs came from wolves, if only to stop short of reexamining their ideas on blood purity. *Canis familiaris*, Mark Derr suggests, is itself the result of both "inbreeding and admixture, or mongrelization" of dog wolves and their wolf ancestors, and backcrossing with wolves is an ongoing process that continues to blur the imaginary line between "pure" and "impure" blood, and between dogs and wolves as well.[24] Only in 1993 was definitive evidence found to prove a common origin for all dogs,[25] and until that time, the purists could deny ties to the shifty creature of the night and invent whatever aristocratic fairy tales they fancied. How, they asked, could a noble animal like the dog be descended from a wolf?

Some cultures have considered the wolf an aristocrat. Ours, for the most part, has not. Quite the contrary, many have tried to prune it from the family tree and cut pedigree dogs out of their rightful inheritance. A "cur" was long believed to be, unlike upper-class dogs, descended from the wolf. Canine blue bloods were seen as separate from mutts, which, like wolves, lacked nobility, and the current definition of a cur, "a mongrel or inferior dog," remains clear enough. One of the most frequent sales pitches from breeders, and an oath of fealty among fans partial to a breed, is that their brand of choice is as "loyal" toward them as they are for favoring it. This need to see character traits such as loyalty, intelligence, and courage in the animals we let live under our roofs—qualities that noble races surely must possess, or else why would they be so popular?—runs as deep as any other human concern. Wolves, on the other hand, have traditionally been viewed as killers of children and stealers of sheep, unholy beasts with satanic ties that are best avoided. These unwanted intruders were systematically extinguished on the British Isles long before the first dog shows were staged, leaving us with poofed-up pets that wear ribbons and can't breathe. But if nobility is what consumers crave, dogs aren't always as noble as they seem. Counter to ongoing claims that breeds are more civilized than mixes, or that golden retrievers are incapable of violence, there's still a lot more wolf in dogs than people want to admit, and even some disagreement over whether they should be considered separate species.[26]

"Do not demean him by clothing him in the shapeless shaggy coat of his remote and long forgotten ancestor," a Pekingese expert declared about a creature that might be many things but never a descendant of the lowly wolf. "Would *you* like to don the hairy robes of your pre-human existence?"[27] Canine consumers aren't entirely to blame for biases supported by quite a backlog of myth. Prior to modern classification of animals based on the principle of evolution, practically anything seemed possible. For centuries it was widely assumed that dogs took different shapes and sizes by mating with other species. Small terriers were thought to be the progeny of foxes, and larger dogs were said to be descended from bears. Theories like these sound ludicrous and laughable today, but they're no more unfounded than the notion that a breed is more pure than a mutt, or that a house pet who comes in a golden package with a "hallmark" from the AKC is somehow more regal than one that doesn't.[28] Dogs are an emotional topic, and people haven't had much time to absorb new evidence and bring their beliefs up to date. Until just yesterday, when modern genetics left less room for creative genealogy—or until someone took the time to read the dates on those breed standards at the kennel clubs—it was acceptable to say that purebred dogs and the ill-born sort were products of very distinct lines. “That all the different breeds of dogs of the present day were descended from the same primitive race, I should deem it preposterous to advance,” wrote Gordon Stables, the same sensitive soul who said that mongrels were only worth the rope required to hang them.[29] The pet dog business, the show-ring culture—and a vast veterinary industry built on the genetic havoc that both have wrought like Procrustes with his saws and stretchers—are founded on this crackpot notion that officially recognized dogs are racially superior to dogs that are not.

What goes for *Canis nobilis* goes manifold for all the minor details supposed to make up a dog’s character. Ever since a lone wolf stood beyond the warm glow of a campfire considering his options in the shadows, our best friends have been shape-shifting. Before they could win blue ribbons, dogs had to win our trust. Dangerous predators were not only expected to act harmless, they had to *look* the part. That meant being selectively bred to be more like playful puppies than predators, and remaining in a state of arrested development their entire lives because this was how to reassure us. Wolves seemed to adapt by some inner drive. Their foreheads were hammered out to take less severe and angular forms. Piercing eyes, set into great domed skulls, grew wide and “cute.”[30] Sharp, sneaky snouts were bashed in and long, conniving teeth were forced together to appear less threatening. The arrogant, prick ears on some dogs dropped into a humble posture never seen in animals prior to human contact (the elephant being the sole exception), exposing their wearers to chronic infections. Tails were raised as no slithering wolf’s ever was, though dogs also learned to lower theirs in submissive displays. Their coats grew softer, and colors were aligned with our ideas on proper attire. Sporting these predictable, often juvenile traits would be as much a part of their job as fighting wars, guarding kings, or more recently, finding suicide bomber victims buried at Ground Zero, a job people assume only a dog that looks precisely like a golden can handle since that's the breed posing with the fireman in the AKC's art collection.

For as long as we've tried to make nature fit our needs, we've had this optimistic belief that all happens for a reason and everything has its place. But nature, like humankind, is not so neat. Domesticated wolves evolved haphazardly in any number of directions. Simultaneously here and there, they branched into "landraces," or general types of dogs, before becoming the picture-perfect breeds we can't seem to live without today. These roughly similar animals often performed useful tasks for humans, taking on distinctive physical features sometimes related to their work and environments, but sometimes not. Size, strength, running speed, or coat thickness, for example, were vital concerns for specific tasks performed in particular regions. Selective breeding and geographical isolation combined to create a broad spectrum of dogs. Incidentals like coat color and ear style typically had no practical functions but were perhaps side effects of domestication.[31]

Yet humans, being superstitious, tended to magnify irrelevant details, just as they tried to impose racial stereotypes on each other. Even farmers, hunters, and warriors, whose lives depended upon dogs and who didn't have the luxury of finding the perfect pet, were not immune to seeing nonessentials as essential. Perhaps they feared that changing a single detail would upset a fragile balance, and they attributed abstract character traits like loyalty and trustworthiness to something as meaningless as markings. Cultural isolation also served to make dogs different in Egypt, China, and Spain, multiplying misunderstandings on how dogs should be bred to look. Vague likenesses in appearance among landraces weren't strictly governed by genetic barriers called "breed standards" as they are today. In fact, landraces were mixed and became even less recognizable when shipped across the globe for trade and conquest. Some lost their native ties to the places that had shaped them, and to their original tasks. Dogs were subjected to "gentrification," as one geneticist calls the movement away from practicality toward esthetics.[32] They were valued not only for their outward appearance but also for the class of people seen with them. Canines became luxury items exchanged between courts, commodities with reputations that may or may not have been warranted.

"I really do not understand," wrote Roger Caras, the former head of the American Society for the Prevention of Cruelty to Animals (ASPCA), "how a group of fanciers, whatever their breed, can think of coat length, texture, or color as more important than whether the dogs they are producing eat children or not."[33] Early on, the pedigree dog industry showed an uncanny ability to package and market pets according to the latest fashions. They could spin dogs in any direction, and the eternal quest for noble antecedents, blood purity, and formal perfection offered much leeway. Some people liked their pooches cute and cuddly. Others with exotic tastes preferred a more feral look and found their nobility, not in the dog, but in his ancestor, the wolf!

In a kind of reverse snobbery, the idea was to take what features the modern world had corrupted in dogs and restore them to their rightful positions. Ears went back up, noses grew again, and teeth descended to cartoon lengths that would frighten Little Red Riding Hood. According to the tastes of a few very wealthy canine collectors, the wolf was the essence of purity and the model for aristocratic living. The collie as we know it, for example, was created for the show ring in the nineteenth century and billed as the nearest living descendant of the wolf, a sham with no basis in science or birth records, but one that appealed to a target market. Queen Victoria favored collies of the old type above all breeds, and her royal imprimatur gave any dog by that name historical resonance and stimulated demand for an increased "wealth of coat."[34] J. P. Morgan was among many consumers to fall for the show ring version—a cross of several breeds, including the Gordon setter and the borzoi—paying as much as $4,000 per dog and starting his own royal kennel on the Hudson River, not to mention helping launch a fad that lasted decades.

Other dogs have been dressed in wolf's clothing. The German shepherd's imposing demeanor made it the wolf-boy of Westminster, and though DNA points to some backcrossing with wolves, by 2004 tests had shown closer kinship to his neighbors, the mastiff and the boxer a few cages down the aisle, than to either a herding dog (where the AKC has grouped the breed for years) or a wolf. The so-called Ibizan hound and Pharaoh hound were also bred to resemble ancient types, though their roots run about as deep as a bas-relief, probably no more than two hundred years. The Norwegian elkhound, another "primitive" dog, is an even older trick,[35] and the multicultural "American Indian Dog" is a pure fabrication. "Perhaps we have given too much space to old lore considering that we have little or no connection with the past in the wolfhounds now being shown," wrote show judge, James Watson, as early as 1906.[36] The large and sinister-looking Irish wolfhound to which he referred was once bred to outsize its ancestor, which legend says it drove to extinction on the British Isles, leaving legions of mental midgets parading in show rings or obsessing over birds and foxes. Wolfhounds went extinct themselves once their job was supposedly done, until the nineteenth century when they were miraculously "resuscitated" by crossing at least three different breeds—and still calling them purebreds.[37] Breeders of the so-called Irish wolfhound are gearing up for another comeback, as seen in a television ad where a fine specimen trails faithfully after a Lexus. I've passed both of these while dog walking in Central Park.

CHAPTER THREE

ROYAL PRECEDENTS AND RUFF DRAFTS

The doggy elite operates on two dimensions: looks and lineage, both of which have been shown to have some serious flaws. This is how dogs were segregated into commercial breeds, and this is how they are valued today. A far cry from the "canine Olympics" of popular imagination, dog shows are beauty pageants where judges base decisions on questionable pedigrees and random recipes scribbled, in large part, nearly a century and a half ago by English social climbers, then copied verbatim by Americans trying to invent similar honors for their own dogs, and for themselves. Each year, these high-profile events like Westminster and Crufts determine which dogs du jour deserve places in our hearts and homes, and for doing nothing more than looking and sitting pretty on official papers signed and sealed by established authorities.

"We live, I regret to say, in an age of surfaces," a social climber named Lady Bracknell observed in an Oscar Wilde play when the modern dog fancy was just learning to heel.[1] If only the fanciers would have done the same by admitting to shallowness, then leaving it at that. Regret accounts for the elaborate apparatus concocted to cover up tracks, extending the Victorian Age into the present day and making its obsessions our own. This quaint hobby of breeding and showing would be easier to swallow if so much energy didn't go into investing surfaces with substance and giving the whole affair an air of integrity. This distinctively *English* pastime of preferring dogs of fair birth and aspect to those of less certain origin with uncharted markings has been eagerly adopted elsewhere because it appeals to some lingering taste for formality and an inability to let go of the past.

Show ring judges on both sides of the Atlantic say they're interested in both form and function. But what function do noble brows and ancient bloodlines serve in today's world? Nowhere among the major powers is there such a strong attachment to primitive notions of tribalism and ancestor worship as in England, where prime ministers still praise countrymen for that *other* gift they've made to humankind, a wonderful royal family that serves no purpose but whose lavish lifestyle many subjects don't mind funding. Just as people use fancy dogs to look special, the English like to see themselves in their figureheads, and others want to see themselves in them. The acclaimed film *The King's Speech* owes its wild success to the latest version of the same scenario. Seductive is this image of two men alone in a room, one royal and the other mortal commoner, joking around and arguing on equal footing.

England is a fertile breeding ground for snootiness, a kind of cultural greenhouse for the rest of the world to whom it exports outmoded ideas on class and race that might have withered and died if not for their nurturing. The English have never had an equivalent of the French Revolution. They suffered their titled class to live and let them have their land. They've killed their fair share of royals over the centuries, to be sure. But English regicides have been motivated more by politics, religion, and personal tastes in rulers than by any grand scheme to eradicate an entire class of people. While Continental chaos reigned from 1789 onward, émigrés found safe harbor across the Channel until the storm blew over and they returned to Europe to assume their unrightful positions. It happened again at mid-century, a decade before the first large-scale doggy coronations were staged for all to admire. The island nation received the hated classes of France, Germany, and Austria with open arms and treated them as houseguests. An almost fairy-tale belief in princes and palaces kept the English living in the past while others were trying to modernize and get on with their lives. The popular appeal of class consciousness has not faded. English toadies (and their toadies' toadies around the world) still take time to memorize layer upon layer of social distinctions, then all the rules of protocol for greeting higher-ups according to their rank. Many secretly wish to move up the ladder themselves, sometimes even daring to try. This unchallenged expertise in the intricacies of inequality is a source of national pride, like a Frenchman's instinctive knowledge of old cheeses, and connoisseurs show no sign of breaking their crusty molds. The English have much of their identity invested in the belief that certain people are simply *born* better than others, and that if they're not, a little culturing can produce the most astounding effects.

"And a comfortable thing it is to think that birth can be bought for money," Thackeray remarked in a series of articles for *Punch*, a journal of satire known for sparing no one. "So you learn to value it. Why should we, who don't possess it, set a higher store on it than those who do? Perhaps the best use of that book, the Peerage, is to look down the list, and see how many have bought and sold birth—how poor sprigs of nobility somehow sell themselves to rich City Snobs' daughters, how rich City Snobs purchase noble ladies—and so to admire the double baseness of the bargain."[2] Thackeray's irreverent collection, called "The Snobs of England, by One of Themselves," became *The Book of Snobs* in 1848 at the very moment popular uprisings sent a second wave of unwanted elite packing its bags in a hurry to abscond to England—and barely a decade before the English began staging dog shows on a grand scale to further bedazzle the world with their breeding abilities. During the great century of upheaval and self-promotion—the nineteenth—noble makeovers were common and the British Legion of the Fabulous Few was growing more legion by the day. Social standing was courted precisely because of the illusion that it *was* so accessible, and joining the anointed was an early version of the American dream. In many ways, the English led the way to the future with science, industry, abolitionism, and the humane movement. But they also kept themselves, and their admirers, mired in the past. Not only was their entitled class tolerated, the proliferation of titles spun out of control from the reign of George III into the Victorian years. While the list of recognized dog breeds was growing by leaps and bounds, and throngs of entries within each canine "class" crowded ever-expanding exhibition halls, humans were herded and sorted along similar lines. From the humblest trades and civil services to the loftiest baronetcies and peerages, offices were enlarged, ceilings raised, and the range of decorations multiplied to meet a spiraling demand. The Industrial Revolution seems a trifle compared to what one historian calls the "honorific inventiveness" of the English.[3] Since the 1860s, awards within some categories of social superiority have increased by the thousands, even tens of thousands, prompting Lord Salisbury's remark that "you cannot throw a stone at a dog without hitting a knight in London."[4] Rock stars and socialists have clamored for royal recognition and gotten what they've asked for. A recent ruling has enabled even Americans of English extraction to apply for shields and standards and join what one British journalist calls "the Order of Elitist Anachronism."[5] They get a piece of paper and a visit to Buckingham Palace.

If only it were true that the larger a social club became, the less *anti*social it would be. But aristocracy has been up for grabs in England longer than anyone cares to remember, and it's just as snooty as it ever was. Heralds, or gatekeepers to distinction, were busy screening applicants at least two centuries before Richard III founded, in British bureaucratic fashion, a central office and badge dispensary in 1484. Since that time, what came to be called Heralds' College has been deciding who has the right to be called special and who has not. Heraldic shields have been drawn and "pedigrees," the same term used by England's royal-backed Kennel Club for canine honors, have been bestowed. The official Stud Book—dogdom's equivalent to a social register or a Peerage—was closed early on, unknowns were turned away, and the progeny of a spitz and spaniel was not supposed to be called "show quality."

But humans, unlike hounds confined to closed registries, have always had the chance to "breed up," provided they have cash in hand, a convincing case, and a nod from someone on the inside. Various degrees of nobility can still be negotiated, though only the highest of these are hereditary. Applicants undergo a rigorous examination before moving up in the world. Family trees are unearthed and roots dissected to make sure a person doesn't come, as one herald told me, "from just *any* social background."[6] Those deemed worthy of titles are awarded custom-made armorial bearings suitable for framing.

The composition of shapes and shades is as crucial as the choice of a family pet to people wishing to make the right impression. The coat of arms is a blank slate where self-image is inscribed and where it will remain for generations. A sort of hand-painted billboard, or a thumbnail on the Internet, it incorporates any number of symbols or icons from the real world and fantasy. Animals and insects invested with meaning, significant trees and shrubbery, mythical lion beasts of the land and sea, weapons, winged dragons, crescent horns, ermine coats, and unicorns—heraldry draws from many sources. Artists have tried over the centuries to accommodate the newly noble by squeezing in whatever corresponding attributes are checked off on their wish lists. Bravery, wisdom, fidelity, generosity, patience, fortitude, constancy, artistic talent, technical skill, or leadership ability are suggested by emblems executed in pigments no less laden with meaning. Tinctures of high-minded gold, hopeful green, mighty red, and royal purple are applied to elements and backgrounds. Even black wolves—whose background is noble or not, depending on one's personal taste—have made appearances on shields and standards, where they announce the bearers as fierce and vigilant protectors of underlings and who can be relied upon through thick and thin.

Dogs have figured far more frequently than wolves in heraldic design. They share the wild one's characteristic courage, but with a reassuring emphasis on loyalty. Selecting the right style of canine to represent a newly written family history used to be easy. Traditionally, heraldic dogs came in a limited number of forms, and the lack of selection would disappoint any modern-day catalog shopper. Old insignias offered three rough types that might be called landraces because they only vaguely resembled our picture-perfect breeds. The triumvirate inscribed on arms was hard to miss on shields or atop helmets, where canines served as crests and crowning glories.

The first of these was the massive and foreboding alaunt, a mastiff-type dog used in battle. Considered extinct but never a "purebred" by today's standards, alaunts were slapped on as heraldic emblems to signify characteristics like courage, strength, and fortitude. Remembered as dogs of war, they have a special appeal, and dogs billed as alaunts today are hokey recreations evoking romantic images of knightly battles and royal tournaments. They and their owners inhabit a geeky realm of Renaissance fairs and "Dungeons and Dragons."

Another dog that may not have existed as an easily identified type except as a heraldic symbol is the Talbot. This very old and resonant name has been affixed to everything from the earls of Shrewsbury and a town crest, to a good many English pubs and inns, and even an American line of women's clothing. The crudely depicted Talbot was, that same English herald tells me, a "half-imaginary hunting dog."[7] While dark knights of the order of the alaunt trace their pet bulldogs, boxers, Staffordshires, and mastiffs to a semi-fictional character, fans of foxhounds, beagles, and bloodhounds stretch their pooches' pedigrees back as far as Talbots. In fact, fanciers tried to include a breed called the "Talbot" in early dog shows. As a heraldic symbol, this hound linked families to qualities like courage, strength, prowess, and adeptness at the hunt.

The final dog to wander onto old armature can confidently call itself the greyhound, a type that has been around for a very long time. The lean and wispy wanderer remains, despite crossbreeding over the centuries, recognizable today. As a symbol, the greyhound runs more ethereally toward elegance and flight than brute strength, and as a hunter, this hound has gone after what it wanted in ways that others couldn't, snatching hare afoot and birds at wing and keeping royalty entertained along the way. Greyhounds coursed the noble stag with the equestrian class, as foxhounds did foxes so fashionably in years to come. They and their relations have been tied to the noblest families—even lesser aristocracy was once forbidden from keeping them around the castle, and for commoners they were out of the question—and the regal aura remains a major part of their appeal. "In its early days, only royalty with the rank of earl or higher were permitted to own the dogs" made social climbers drool when the *New York Times* announced that the Scottish Deerhound, a close cousin of the greyhound, had taken Westminster in 2011 despite a high rate of cancer.[8]

Canines continue making appearances in heraldic design, and in more ways than ever. Since the dawn of dog shows, breed clubs, and standardized pets—the very moment that human honorifics were also multiplying like rabbits—there's been a dramatic rise in the use of dogs as heraldic emblems. As that holder of the ancient office of herald informed me, there's been an "increase in dog imagery" since Victorian times, in fact "*very* much so."[9] The nineteenth century brought a much wider array of social honors, and the upwardly mobile decided they needed a better selection of animals to represent them. Crest-carrying members of the middle class needed distinctions of their own, and since there were so many of these, they needed more subdivisions to offset themselves from the hordes of fellow upstarts. Until that time, generations of social climbers had been content with tried and true symbols of pedigree. But a funny thing happened on the way to Madison Square Garden. The alaunt, the Talbot, and the greyhound no longer fit the bill, and the number of "good" dogs from which to choose grew by leaps and bounds. As our best friends were superficially diversified into easily identifiable commercial brands or breeds for show rings and front parlors of the newly rich, artists trained in the old techniques were suddenly being asked to master a broader range of canine shapes, sizes, and coat styles. The pure and classic art of heraldry became more complex as "heralds became more responsive to clients' wishes."[10] Foxhounds, whippets, bassets, beagles, cockers, King Charleses, and even Chihuahuas were crowded onto shields and standards. In recent years, newbie knights have requested further specialization. They want dogs not only depicted as their brands of choice, but to resemble their own personal pets Rover or Rex—which would be the canine equivalent of trying to make heraldic lions look like Tabby or Boots. Officials have naturally had to draw the line somewhere, and clients are often "disappointed" at unveilings, the herald tells me, by the lack of family resemblance.[11]

Some stabs at accommodation have been taken of late. A drawing of armature brandished on the website of the College of Arms illustrates to what lengths this office is willing to go to help folks turn dogs into mirror images of themselves. "The Arms of Dr. F. G. Hardy" were granted in 2006. Depicted is a striped-and-polka-dot shield with some frilly bits running down the sides. A heavy-looking helmet balances precariously above. Sitting atop it all in the role of a crest is none other than a black Labrador retriever, whose coat is not as fashionable as the yellow these days, but was the original shade worn by fetchers for the highest nobility ever since that breed was first conceived. It can be assumed in all safety that Dr. Hardy has at least one of these historically accurate status symbols curled up at his castle. That this heraldic dog is a Labrador is evident to anyone with eyes. What's interesting is the way it is presented. The Lab is seen in profile with something odd dangling from its mouth, perhaps one of the strands of string, tin foil, or plastic wrap the breed is famous for ingesting and needing surgery for removal—or possibly a cheesy pizza crust rescued from the gutter? The dog is seated, but its description is couched in the most archaic terms. "On a helm with a wreath Argent and Vert, Upon a Rock proper encrusted with Sea Urchins and Purpure a Labrador sejant Sable holding in its mouth a gathering of Bladder Wrack Vert," reads the caption.

This mouthful that only Monty Python could mimic should be translated for lay readers. "Sable" means "black" in heraldic terms, and so this is a "Labrador Sable." That's black Lab to you. "Sejant" refers to the animal's posture, as he is seated erectly with both front paws firmly planted on the urchin-encrusted rock that teeters atop the helmet. (A more traditional "Lion sejant" would assume the same position but with paws scratching and tongue extended like the bassist for the rock group Kiss.) The curious mass hanging from the dog's mouth turns out to be, not a half-skinned tennis ball or a masticated Frisbee, but the pièce de résistance. The "gathering of Bladder Wrack Vert" is a piece of slimy seaweed duly fetched for the master, one assumes, from great depths. Bladder wrack is known for its medicinal uses, so the doctor has chosen his symbols, and his water dog, wisely.[12]

Fanciers have gone to many colorful extremes over the years to show their dogs, and themselves, in some flattering light. Like purebreds that aren't as perfect as they look—or people who use pets to support their own family trees—dog shows, too, are a very mixed bag, indeed. Weird cannibalizations of old habits and new incarnations, questionable coronations where last year's ruler is deposed by the latest pretender, semisacred events with high ritual and high ratings—dog shows draw from sources ancient and modern. But like those photogenic breeds that brand-name loyalists can't seem to imagine in any other shapes, sizes, or coat colors, Westminster and Crufts (and the hundreds of dubious honors leading up to these supreme moments) might just as easily have taken any variety of formats along the way.

Considering how central dogs are to our culture, and how deeply feelings run about them, it should come as no surprise that dog shows, like the stars featured in them, are ad hoc creations with multiple origins. When did canine beauty pageants, also known as "leads" and perhaps "the last vestige of our feudal heritage,"[13] begin their long engagement? A common error reprinted in books and spread across the Internet stands to be corrected, because the oft-cited date of 1859 is misleading. Sharing the same year with the publication of Darwin's *Origin of Species* gives the dog fancy, in the minds of those who judge people and pooches by the company they keep, a sort of legitimacy that is not deserved. This accident of birth implies that artificial selections parading poofed-up and powdered in canine hit parades are somehow sharing the stage with survival of the fittest. As the health and longevity statistics on purebreds versus nonbreeds can testify, or the sliding scales that veterinary health insurance companies are applying to premiums, this couldn't be further from the truth.[14] Dog breeding and showing have had more to do with *social* survival of the owner than the survival of fitness as a basic concern.

The would-be first English dog show was, like many early events held in both England and the United States, devoted exclusively to hunting dogs of the gun variety. The most remembered show of 1859 in Newcastle upon Tyne was staged by a firearm manufacturer named Pape who took an interest in promoting the latest canine fashions to gentlemen of means whose sporting hobbies demanded nothing but the finest accessories, dogs included. Pointers and setters were featured in this and similar gun dog events across England and America throughout the 1860s and 1870s, and gradually other types were added to these productions prior to the first Westminster Dog Show of 1877.[15] A wider class of contestants in both nations arrived with new entries via railways from near and far, and an informal charity event, the International Dog Show, held in Washington, DC, featured a variety of breeds as early as 1863, as did P. T. Barnum's Great National Dog Show throughout the 1860s. Dogs were featured in the Centennial Exposition of 1876, and in the World's Fairs of England and Paris throughout the second half of the nineteenth century. The New York Poultry Society added dogs as a sort of side item in 1869, and the specialized dog show gradually emerged "for display of well-bred dogs, as it is in Great Britain."[16]

But getting at the roots of canine competitions requires going back further than the mid-nineteenth century to some of England's other favorite places for social exchange. For decades prior to the first famous show, informal gatherings were held in English hotels, where small companion dogs were brought to compare and contrast.[17] These staid, uneventful events were inspired by livelier foxhound shows that featured fully functional, working pack dogs of England's elite as early as the late eighteenth century.[18] Some of these prestigious foxhound shows are carried on today, the Peterborough Royal Foxhound Show being the fanciest. Healthy, athletic, spirited animals must be restrained by well-tailored handlers in red coats, white breeches, and black hunting caps, while spectators (men in bowler hats) laugh and applaud. Tails wagging enthusiastically, the hounds whine and howl at each other from across the ring before they're set loose to run around disorderly and catch treats tossed into the air. All around, humans and hounds carry on quite differently from their "improved" cousins, who heel and pose politely in solemn beauty processions of Westminster and Crufts.

Digging deeper for the birthplace of our grandiose canine crownings, we end up in, of all places, the humble taverns of old England. The English have long welcomed animals other than themselves indoors, unlike Americans whose public health paranoia decides which species get in. Canine company is not discouraged in establishments along the British Isles where food and beverages are served. There's even an official guide of favorite dog-friendly pubs where bipeds and quadrupeds scarf down bangers and lap up ale. Today's patrons and pets mostly belly up to the bar, but before organized dog shows, pubs were places to show off personal favorites. Impromptu gatherings were held for generations of pub goers of diverse social background, who brought their pooches along to share with fellow countrymen. "The aristocrat and plebeian were as brothers," commented Freeman Lloyd as he recalled the "democratic" dog shows of his youth not long thereafter, and the miraculous ability of Englishmen to overcome an inbred sense of class distinction—wishful thinking, perhaps.[19]

As another scholar of dog days past recalls, there was a time when a hunting hound was not remarkable until belonging to a nobleman, and then "the animal became ennobled, as it were." From ancient Wales, where dogs had "honour prices" that rose on a sliding scale from the lowest commoner's to the king's, which was most costly,[20] to the first shows at Westminster and Crufts, where a proper lady's Pekingese wasn't guaranteed to win but often trumped the rest in resale value and in puppies produced, there's been a tendency to want dogs for their social ties.

Before kennel clubs and "reputable" breeders priced good dogs out of reach for the average nobody, English game laws actually prevented commoners from being seen with animals that outclassed them. By the same principle, dogs descended the social ladder when they fell into the wrong hands, and in early dog shows, not just anyone's animals were allowed to compete with those of the upper echelon. Two hounds could be identical in every detail, but pooches with low-born owners could only compete within their "class." Even some farmers, who were supposed to value dogs for purely practical purposes, apparently bought into this nonsense, and it was widely believed, throughout the nineteenth century, that purebreds behaved nobly and only mongrels were capable of killing sheep.[21]

Another explanation for dog shows as we know them would be the old custom on English estates of commissioning tenants to rear or "walk" aristocracy's fine hunting hounds, animals which society's lower orders weren't good enough to own themselves. Masters knew their dogs stood a better chance of performing well in their elaborately staged hunting rites if hand-raised individually in the homes of their servants. Periodic match shows were held, competitions in which pups were judged on condition, temperament, and even appearance to some degree. Surrogate parents were awarded small pieces of silver plate for showing dogs worthy of their lord's imprimatur, a precursor to silver cups in contests to come.[22]

Aristocratic families developed their own strains of various dog types associated with their names, like vintage French families with their own personal wine labels. But again, these weren't breeds as we know them, at least not yet. General types were known by names like foxhound, pointer, or greyhound but lacked the demanding sort of digital perfection that would get them recognized by registries or noticed on better sidewalks today. The old ruling class, quite frankly, didn't need to advertise the modern way. Picture-perfect pets would have served no social purpose because everyone already *knew* who the owners were.

As England's socioeconomic landscape changed, more commoners could afford to carry better dogs in public and digital perfection could wait no longer. Urban pets needed to be instantly recognizable, and from great distances, as those formerly reserved for Lord or Lady So-and-So back at the manor. These new, accessible, standardized breeds were sometimes based loosely on old family favorites. They had a wide appeal for conferring as much cachet as well-bred horses but with less upkeep, and their social uses were invaluable. Nearing the end of the nineteenth century, social climber Gordon Stables appraisingly noted that dog shows had "to a very large extent, spread the taste for well-bred dogs, and there are very few ladies or gentlemen who care to be accompanied by a mongrel cur."[23]

Digging deeper, we find a less glamorous ancestor to canine beauty pageants, an embarrassing bone in family closets that makes even royalty seem no better than anyone else. Animal baiting and dog fighting are impolite subjects to breach in preshow pits of Westminster or Crufts where contestants rat their bichons and ribbon their Yorkies. Still, this relatively recent aversion to employing dogs in *other* capacities hasn't prevented fanciers from making the bulldog into one of the most popular breeds of all time. As we've already seen, dog shows have an undeniable heritage in blood sport events that drew English spectators of all classes to villages, towns, and cities across the realm where they occurred like clockwork for centuries. Ugly and brutal gladiatorial hobbies have a much longer history than those dainty processions fanciers know and love, and royalty played no small part in keeping them popular. Bulls, badgers, and bears were once standard fare in public amphitheaters throughout the kingdom, and it was often the upper echelon that set the tone for highbrow entertainment and examples of right and wrong. Lions, tigers, and other exotics were raised in royal menageries for command performances. Richard III even created an office called Royal Bearward to ensure fresh victims would be on hand at all times for impromptu matches. Elizabeth I craved cat fights and always enjoyed a good goring, encouraging her court and countrymen to do the same. So did James I, who hired a professional impresario named Edward Allyen to stage these odes to animal cruelty. A producer of plays and an actor, Allyen, like Charles Cruft, his spiritual heir, did what he was told.[24] Some early dog-show producers in the nineteenth century were actually "converts from the darker side of dogdom."[25]

By the nineteenth century, when dog shows took the place of cruder diversions, people of good breeding had decided it was no longer fashionable to see animals suffer in this style. Aristocracy and higher nobility became driving forces behind the humane movement that helped to put some distance between society's born leaders and certain "disreputable associations"[26]—and to prevent mongrels from being born. As soon as it became a crime to throw beasts into pits or chain them to stakes, high-born English scrambled to sever all ties, not with their shady blood relations who'd done the dirty deeds and encouraged bad behavior all along, but with society's lower orders who'd followed their example and were, it was suddenly being said, the only creatures capable of enjoying such base pleasures! Prim and proper Victorians were pleased to see a leading breeder of fighting dogs had renounced a vulgar vocation and renamed his frowned-upon establishment a "Canine Palace." The reformed English bulldog could now fight to regain the affections of a nation to whom it had heretofore been a hero. Meanwhile, sensitive sorts of the upper class had sworn off lion baiting, though they continued terrorizing foxes for fun.

Looking back on some of aristocracy's *other* strange animal hobbies to which respectable outfits like Westminster and Crufts owe at least some recognition, it's clear that not all ties to the past are flattering. Far from the sophisticated, high-toned urban affairs organized by modern kennel clubs, that famous event of 1859, held in the bustling commercial center of Newcastle upon Tyne, didn't take place in a stadium, a palace, or a pub, but in a more mundane locale for social exchange called the New Corn Exchange. The "dog section" wasn't very glamorous, but a novelty no one knew would last, a tawdry sideshow to a bigger beauty pageant devoted to—fancy chickens!

"The new feature of the addition of Sporting Dogs to the show of Poultry was a great attraction," reported the *Newcastle Courant* to a throng of local yokels with little else in the way of entertainment but the spectacle of unusual pets and the people who could afford to keep them.[27] Before the leisure class took to parading refashioned dogs across the stage, they warmed up on a few other species. In fact agricultural "improvement" took many forms in the nineteenth century. "Fancy fowl" were among several guinea pigs to get makeovers from England's landed gentry and higher nobility up to Victoria and Albert, who became avid collectors of beautified birds, pigs, and oxen.[28] The idea of crowning a farm animal might sound bizarre today, but "hen fever" had a powerful draw. The thought of a handsome hen or comely cow doesn't register with most pet owners, but in the years leading up to dog shows, the whole barnyard was being refashioned for appearance. Chickens were made chic with dazzling plumage and regal headdresses. Steers were status symbols with fine coats and massive fat that hung off enormous frames, casting them into striking angular shapes. Other species were subjected to the same taste for geometrical precision soon to work its magic on dogs, and those naive folk art paintings of rectangular cows seen in shops today are accurate reproductions. Beasts of burden as decorative objects? The pursuit of perfection had taken a wrong turn somewhere down a dusty country road. While genuine advances were being made elsewhere in agriculture, a kind of short-lived counterrevolution was under way in upper-class farming. That same retrograde pull, a drive in the opposite direction of progress that kept the new middle class fixated on predemocratic notions of good breeding and hereditary honors, had also corrupted farm animal breeding. It was almost as though members of the decadent upper classes, whose real influence was declining rapidly, were struggling to keep an upper hand in the only way they still knew how: as arbiters of taste.

"The object of the English fancier," noted naturalist William Tegetmeier, shifted away from food production and toward wasteful pursuits such as "the production of large globular crests perfectly free from white feathers." An eerie prediction of dog shows to come, fanciers of "ornamental fowls" became obsessed with "exactness of colour and marking." Large, edible breasts were no longer fashionable, and "reachy" birds were courted for their skimpy figures, long, aristocratic necks, and fragile limbs.[29] The term "mongrel" was applied to any animal that didn't measure up, and the more elegant and *useless* a farm animal could be made, the more social standing its owners gained from lavishing time and money on breeding, raising, grooming, and parading it around a pen. For practical purposes, status value had in many ways emerged victorious by the end of the Victorian Age. To enlighten Anglophile American social climbers across the pond who were eager to rise on the perfect heads of finer farm products, new publications offered instruction in proper pig feeding, feathering, and the optimal use of canine coloratura. *Country Life in America*, a monthly manual devoted to helping Americans imitate English landed gentry, offered advice on everything from window-box gardening and front porch design, to nature painting, catching brook trout, using the right soaps to achieve a rosy rustic skin tone—and "Dogs" just before the "Poultry" page of every edition.[30] When superior canines emerged as preferred pets for better homes and gardens, breeders wasted no time in revamping entire facilities to keep pace.[31]

Yet despite the many social benefits that well-bred animals showered on discriminating shoppers with their pelage and plumage, all was not well in the Land of Fancy. Beauty, as the French say, comes with a price, and that price is suffering. "The artistic manipulation of genetics," as one cattle historian calls the drift from practical uses to purely cosmetic concerns, brought the message, to anyone who cared to listen, that art could sometimes be immoral.[32]

Before the same lessons could be learned, and ignored, in the dog fancy, very similar downsides to inbreeding for appearance and pedigree were noticed among other beasts embellished for the stage. Bulls, it was true, could no longer legally have dogs set upon them in bloody fighting pits. But being valued like tropical fish for shape, size, color, and sheen was taking a toll. Infertility and illness appeared to be as rampant among fancy farm animals as they were in royal families. "Perfect" show cows and pigs were observed to be slow, sluggish, even stupid. Not unlike refashioned bulldogs in later years that could barely hobble around for the judges, massive bovine and porcine carcasses with less than reliable legging had to be wheeled in on carts to competitions, then airlifted on pulleys into the ring for observation.[33] Luxuriant skin that fanciers found attractive gave pigs difficulty in walking, and excess "leather" on faces led to the same vision problems seen in bulldogs, Shar-peis, bassets, and many dog breeds exaggerated for that style today. Birds that were tweaked "from the farmer's into the gentleman's fowl," Tegetmeier noted, had enormous top hats and heavy burdens. Not only did dandy birds not have enough meat in the right places to make them salable at market, they were "bred with tufts so large that they can scarcely see to feed." For the same reason, today's Wheaton terriers wander into lampposts on their way home from the groomer. Exaggerated crests on poultry presaged the over-the-top afros that would one day crown the heads of Dandie Dinmonts and bichons frises, or the foppish tufts towering atop so-called Chinese crested dogs. "Super-abundant feathers or comb" foretold our overstuffed golden retrievers with their conspicuously plush, impractical plumage. Certain strains of hen became as "delicate and difficult to rear" as any shivering lapdog with matchstick legs.[34]

Then there was that most peculiar fetish among fanciers, an inexplicable fascination with flush surfaces, the same trend that Edward Ash would call "the craze for dished faces."[35] As our best friends grew flat-headed and feeble-minded, Tegetmeier remarked that pigs were being "bred so 'dish-faced' that they have lost all profitable character."[36] Pugs followed pigs, and many dogs bred for "expression" in the ring would over time become virtually faceless, opening a whole new market for special disk-shaped kibble, like Royal Canin Pug 25, because these breeds can no longer even pick up food normally. These and many more freakish sideshow deformities were first imposed on the barnyard set, and dog show audiences also came to expect entertainment to the extreme.

"There are hundreds of dogs in Britain," explained an episode of the BBC's hit comedy series *Little Britain.* "The biggest, the Blue Setter, is as tall as the Houses of Parliament. The smallest, the Boodle, is invisible to the naked eye." Exaggerations aside, since these madcap amusements began, there's been a clear tendency toward exaggeration. Some dogs have grown so gigantic that they fall apart within a few years. Others have shrunk to be so fragile that the slightest stress leaves them lame. Certain breeds have backs stretched so thin that chronic pain is the only alternative to mercy killing. Though these deformities are as much the fault of the judges' interpretations of breed standards as the standards themselves, demanding rules invented for the earliest dog shows suggest the seeds of dog destruction were sown as early as the 1860s.

For no better reason than to multiply the ways to win, arbitrary categories were imposed for size, coat color, and any features that could be homed in on and heightened. Groupings by "Small Class" and "Smallest Dog under 3 lb." distorted stature on a whim. "Large Dogs," "Large Bitches," and "Large Variety Class" stretched the rubber band in the opposite direction. "Toys" proved that size, any size, still mattered, so long as it was exaggerated. "White Scotch," "Fawn Scotch," "Blue Scotch," "Black-and-Tans," and "White English" defined dogs by their coat colors. "Smooth-haired Terriers" and "Broken-haired Terriers" expanded the hair-splitting to include another concern irrelevant to dogs that no longer worked. "Small Black-and-Tans," "Large Black-and-Tans," "White Terriers under Six Pounds," and "White Terriers over Six Pounds" combined other obsessions. "Rough-coated Toy Terriers" created more opportunities for winning prizes.

Canine classes multiplied to dizzying heights, just as social honors were mass-produced in human heraldry. Fanciers spun meaningless distinctions from thin air, and even hunting and sporting breeds were subjected to demands that had nothing to do with utility or health, and everything to do with making show dogs jump through conceptual hoops on stage and giving their owners more reasons to feel special. A run on pointers in these early years led to ribbons being offered for "Large Pointers," "Medium Pointers," and "Small Pointers." The same distinctions were applied to bulldogs. "Spaniels" were segregated into "Large" and "Small," and bull terriers were divided into "Large," "Small," "Male," and "Female," to which more categories were added for weight. "Any Other Variety" made room for further improvement, and "Extra Class for Non-Sporting Foreign Dogs" seemed an afterthought, as did "British or Foreign Lap-dogs," and "Any Variety, Confined to Londoners" was snooty even by a snob's standards.

"In Variety over 30 lb. Mr. F. Gresham cleared the board," recalled one major player in early dog shows. "The other classes call for no comment." A final prize was offered for "Best Monster Dog"—which might have been awarded to all of the above.[37]

CHAPTER FOUR

EUGENICS, YOU, AND FIDO TOO

Performing live on national television can be stressful. Trying to coax your dog into doing the right trick at the right time can be downright daunting.

Several years ago, my lovely mutt Samantha and I were about to have our fifteen minutes of fame on *Good Morning America.* Sam had just won first prize for "best ball catcher" off camera the day before, and millions of viewers awaited the end of a kibble commercial when my rescue dog from an ASPCA shelter would single-handedly subdue a tennis ball with pride and panache for the world to witness, thus proving that humble mongrels could do anything their fancy "purebred" cousins could, maybe even better.

A longtime veteran of New York's annual *Great American Mutt Show* at public parks around the city, Sam was a mix of at least three different breeds, or perhaps no breeds at all. She'd earned her "recognition," as the AKC says of specimens it deems "pure," not in show rings, but on the agility field, where beauty is as beauty does and posing doesn't count. Sam had delighted audiences with her natural athleticism and an exhaustive list of difficult feats. She'd competed against a number of contestants for the spot on this latest televised affair and was handpicked over more likely candidates, in the public's opinion, for fetching with flair. My shelter dog of no "desirable" coat color had whipped the fancy pants off a black Lab everyone just assumed would win. She'd trumped a springer spaniel, humiliated a golden, given a shellacking to a setter, and effectively neutered a Portuguese water dog whose political connections didn't help him in the least.

Now all we had to do was wait for them to cut from that kibble commercial and show the world the stuff of which mutts were made. Sam and I awoke early that morning, both of us biting at the bit and ready to go on live television. The show's producer sent a limousine that brought us to the studio, where I learned we weren't going to have the full fifteen minutes of stardom, but a mere seven seconds, a possible recipe for failure. Sam was a born ball catcher, but unlike some of the more single-minded, single-purpose dogs programmed to repeat the same exact performance, my lovely lady, quite frankly, had other interests in life.

Sam and I nervously awaited our cue to perform. Adding to the stress, no one in the studio could say exactly when that confounded kibble commercial would end and my non-retriever's miraculous retrieving powers would be crammed into a few precious seconds of TV time. My task was to keep my multitasker in a heightened state of retrieving frenzy, to force her better instincts into an unnatural mold, at least until she went out live to repeat the performance that had impressed the judges off camera. I watched the monitors above, and someone handed me a basket of tennis balls. I was told to start throwing and not to stop, so that when Sam's defining moment arrived, she would appear to be acting seamlessly and effortlessly in her very best form. This was less about catching balls than catching the perfect catch on camera, and I began to feel like that sad sack in the Warner Brothers cartoon with a singing frog that only sang when no one else was around. I threw and threw and threw, trying to keep Sam's attention and prolong her will to play. She caught and caught and caught, giving each and every ball her best shot with stunning precision, leaping and grasping at least twenty electric-green orbs in midair with nature's own style, spontaneity, vibrancy, and verve—all but the one that went out live to millions of viewers across the nation.

A few minutes later, when the dust had cleared and all the balls had stopped bouncing, I learned that the only shot Sam had missed, at the very end when her interest was waning—the ball that rebounded off her teeth, ricocheted from the white picket fence surrounding the stage, and landed square in the audience—was in fact the one that really counted. We'd fudged our defining moment and there was nowhere else to go but home. Another kibble commercial started rolling on the monitors above. George Stephanopoulos cast a disapproving glare as we were ushered out the door, tails between our legs.

Does a dog need to have a certain look to behave in a certain way? Seeking some explanation for our present-day obsession with predictability, many are surprised to find the trail leads back to eugenics, that dirty word recalled with fear and loathing but a set of assumptions that have as much to do with pets as they once did with people. Few know that many of our core beliefs about bloodlines, appearance, and skill retain more than a tinge of those ugly theories that have made some people and pets seem superior for their complexion or ancestral profiles, and others inferior for having substandard markings or a checkered past.

Most upright citizens have officially sworn off applying eugenics to humans these days, but for some strange reason, they continue to breed and buy their dogs along old eugenic lines. Anderson Cooper was shocked and appalled on his show in May 2012 to report that forced sterilizations of "undesirables" were conducted by the tens of thousands in the United States until as recently as the 1970s.[1] But at home, he had a Welsh springer spaniel, a breed born to what AKC writer Freeman Lloyd once called "a doggie family that has existed in its approximately pure state for many hundreds of generations."[2] Despite its illustrious past, Cooper's brand of choice is now prone to a number of serious health issues and has an average inbreeding coefficient higher than that of first cousins.[3] Blood "purity" has worked against the springer, which has been subjected, like many breeds, to the same outdated theories of "better breeding" that get pups culled for having the wrong coat color, make "good" families feel superior to not-so-good ones—and get millions of innocent people killed for their ethnic or racial background. Sterilization, euthanasia, segregation, holocausts, and judgments at Westminster all have a common heritage in eugenics, and despite the fact that English isn't among the many languages that still use "race" and "breed" interchangeably, we have no excuse for not knowing or caring about this history.

Terrible but true: who among us, at one time or another, hasn't been guilty of stereotyping? And who among us has never let looks determine likability? Old biases aren't easy to shed. Perhaps the most obvious crime against progressive thinking can be found in our own backyards, where it's still socially acceptable to say, "I have a chocolate Lab at home," but not, "I only hire Latino/black/Asian/fill-in-the-blank maids because they clean better." Why is "We grew up with two goldens" in fashion, but "We've adopted a pair of Orientals" is not? What's wrong with "I have a *dog*" or "Two *dogs* are better than one?" I myself have no degree in statistics but question the myth that all pedigree German shepherds are loyal, smart, and trainable because one in a million qualifies for service work. Not all golden retrievers are heroes because one was depicted with a fireman at Ground Zero in a painting that hangs in the AKC's art collection, no more than all Americans are champion athletes because Michael Phelps won some gold medals.

The "science" of eugenics was founded in the mid-nineteenth century as a tool for keeping people in their proper places. "It is, too, a strange fact," wrote Gordon Stables, a firm believer in head shape as an indicator of character, "that the more highly civilised a nation is, the greater its care and culture of the canine race."[4] Based on a similar observation that fair-skinned folk with certain anatomical features were supposedly more attractive and intelligent than "darkies" (too repugnant, many thought, even to serve food on First-Class dining cars), eugenics devised an elaborate and complex system of color coding and measurement, an apparatus that grew more elaborate and complex with time. Focusing on a somewhat selective selection of mostly random and coincidental characteristics that conquerors and ruling classes had haphazardly amassed along their uphill climbs, traits certain groups just happened to share, such as blond hair, blue eyes, a taste for classical music, or a fondness for fox hunting—by-products of generations of inbreeding and upbringing only with their own kind—eugenic investigators compiled an exhaustive catalog of hair-splitting nuances to prove that races were, indeed, separate and unique. Some races, they felt, were essentially better than others, and mixing races—or "mongrelization"—was unhealthy and probably dangerous to all races involved.

The eugenic inventory of racial indicators grew so encompassing and complex that experts managed to convince many that their observations simply had to be true, if only because, it was thought, no sane person would have observed them if they weren't. The subtleties of human skin tone, the way the eyes were set into the head, the precise angle at which the jaw protruded, neck length, hair texture, nose curvature—the convolution of spirals in brain matter, the spaces between the toes, the distance between the navel and the penis—every detail was carefully gauged and painstakingly documented, then compared and contrasted in ways that somehow always seemed the most flattering to white, Northern Europeans and their white, Northern European descendants across the Atlantic (or people who looked like them). Superficial distinctions were exaggerated to the point that different racial or ethnic groups were said to have descended from separate prehistoric ancestors, a theory only recently disproved by DNA, not unlike the freshly debunked myth that not all dogs evolved from wolves. Embellished bloodlines based on outward appearance, and a rudimentary understanding of genetics that made heredity seem as simple as pigmentation in guinea pigs, were used to explain deeper character traits like morality, criminality, intelligence, and "feeblemindedness." Before long, eugenics had just about every aspect of human diversity neatly mapped, categorized, and evaluated based on looks or social ties. Anatomical and behavioral traits, even personal quirks, were correlated to family, class, race, and ethnic background, or to whether a person ended up working as a banker, baker, soldier, stenographer, poet, or piano tuner. Eugenics explained it all: infertility, spelling, dancing, neatness, insanity, gambling, gout, disobedience, double-jointedness, punctuality, "pug" noses on ill-born Irish, even ball playing.[5]

Among the many errors of eugenics were to misinterpret outward appearance, behavior, and culturally biased test results as indicators of other qualities; to confuse heredity with environment; to overestimate the role of individual genes in the inheritance of complex behaviors; to focus on human pedigrees instead of individuals; and to cling to an archaic belief in inbreeding for blood "purity," already proven as detrimental to half-mad, hemophiliac royal families as it would prove to be for fancy, "scientifically" bred dogs in the century to come.

Like so many attempts at improvement in the nineteenth century, eugenics dressed old habits in new garb. Ancient, quasi-mystical arts of physiognomy and phrenology, and a more recent discipline called craniometry, went into these dazzling demonstrations of mental gymnastics. What eugenics brought to the table was a protective layer of statistics and documents, modern additions of the nineteenth century that lent authenticity to the usual slants on race, class, and any other basis for bias. The arcane assumption that head shape indicated personality or intelligence was now provable with an extensive set of precise measurements. Skulls could finally be placed side-by-side in glass display cases at natural history museums as updated reliquaries to be interpreted as eugenic high priests saw fit. Primitive, gut reactions against outsiders and oddballs because of the way they looked, acted, or dressed now had the blessing of observations showing darker-skinned people did, in fact, tend to be dishonest—because they didn't blush, which they couldn't, at least not visibly, being darker-skinned—incontrovertible proof that they were born with something to hide. In the same vein, the medieval notion of "blue blood," based on the fact that bloodlines tended to be more visible on fair-skinned aristocrats than on darker-skinned workers, Africans, Jews, or Arabs—whose own blue veins were, indeed, less visible because they had darker skin—now had the blessing of a host of new parameters for defining race and inevitably showing fair-skinned testers in the fairest light. National types, patriots declared confidently, could now be clearly defined and separated from outsiders—"race," until quite recently, meaning national origin—giving them carte blanche to discriminate at home and dominate abroad through conquest and colonialism.[6]

The Third International Eugenics Conference, one of many events such as "Fitter Family" and "Better Baby" contests held around the country, was organized by the American Museum of Natural History in 1932. The exhibit sought to prove that talents were inherited traits. Featured was a lineup of rectangular fur samples from various animals, not unlike color swatches in clothing catalogs, or allowable coat colors in breed books today. Visitors were invited to step up and feel each sample to test their "sense of elegance in fur feeling"—perhaps to recruit those with promising careers as Westminster judges?[7] The most unsettling part about an unflinching history of eugenics is how socially acceptable this brand of "science" was, and remains, in mainstream opinion. The History Channel—which a friend of mine calls "The Hitler Channel"—has spent decades pounding into our heads the same stories of the Third Reich's ruthless campaign for racial purity and shaming this barbaric tribe for its crimes against humanity. Viewers could have learned more by hearing that it wasn't a son of the Fatherland but Darwin's social-climbing cousin, Sir Francis Galton, who first gave this sort of behavior the respectable name of "eugenics" in 1883. Not only was Galton not chastised for finding a new defense for Britain's traditional ruling class and imperial rule—and inspiring racial purges in the century to come—he was knighted for his mental gymnastics.

Wherever it caught on, eugenics seemed to make respectable society more respected and the powerful more powerful. Across the Atlantic, it was the Rockefeller Foundation, not the Ku Klux Klan, that financed Germany's early racial "research." The caricature of the right-wing eugenicist is a tad racist because Americans of all political persuasions developed eugenics far beyond the wildest dreams of the cash-poor English. Involuntary sterilization laws were enacted by Indiana Hoosiers and hoity-toity Connecticuters three decades before Hitler thought to take our example and modeled his own final solution on ours. Systematic "purification" was widespread, institutionalized, and enforced by legislation from coast to coast by the time the world caught on, and America's eugenic mission would extend deep into the twentieth century. Basing a person's value on appearance, pedigree, and some narrow definition of intelligence was very much the norm, and disseminators of racial bias weren't marginal or war criminals but upstanding members of society, often the best and brightest leaders of our most venerable institutions. Promoters of profiling were doctors, lawyers, legislators, politicians, literati, Nobel Prize–winning scientists, and even a few Jews who figured among the major proponents. Courses in eugenics were standard fare at the top Ivy League schools attended by America's finest families, who funded the fight against "racial degeneration" and campaigned for "social improvement," lowering birthrates among "defective classes," and restricting immigration to white, Northern Europeans (or people who looked like them). Like the Rockefellers, the illustrious Harriman clan was a major benefactor of eugenic research, inspired by the father's Anglophile hobby of breeding race horses. Thoroughbreds born to the House of Harriman were also among the earliest importers of those Labrador retrievers we can't seem to imagine in more than three preapproved shades today.

How did eugenics finally lose its mass appeal and cede its social standing? As the late historian of science Stephen Jay Gould remarked, it wasn't any of the blatant inconsistencies, obtusely unscientific methods, or strong notes of self-serving prophecy that finally did in eugenics among people of good breeding and taste. It was those unavoidable horrors of World War II, still dramatically reenacted on the Hitler Channel, that showed where these ideas led when taken to their logical conclusions. This sudden unveiling inspired Americans and English to open their eyes and publicly disavow all ties with the movement they'd only recently raced to embrace.[8] Still the question remains: How could morally upright bipeds have gone along with eugenics for as long as they did?

While concerned scientists and watchdog groups are on constant guard against returning to bad habits of the not-so-distant past and treat the growing field of behavioral genetics with suspicion, little effort has been made in the dog fancy, a creation of the eugenics movement and heir to its misguided principles, to purge dog breeding of pseudoscience, to make it more a science than an art, or to bring beliefs current with knowledge and the values we profess to hold dear. The 1828 edition of Webster's dictionary defined "cur" or mongrel as "a degenerate dog; and in reproach, a worthless man."[9] Rather than apply the lessons learned and redefine what "better breeding" might mean in this day and age, the dog fancy behaves as though nothing has changed since the nineteenth century, and that nonhuman animals aren't subject to the same laws of biology as humans. Parties entrusted with the welfare and improvement of our best friends—kennel clubs and the scientists on their payrolls, breed clubs and their memberships, puppy mills and "good" breeders alike, a colossal dog industry invested in business as usual, and the local vet who keeps politely silent about everything—many experts continue to support unethical and counterproductive breeding practices by misdirecting our attention, not to how sick, stupid, or aggressive golden retrievers are becoming, but to how pretty they've managed to keep the coats.

Despite major strides made in universal suffrage, desegregation, affirmative action, and human rights, little has changed in the realm of dogdom, where random features like skin, coat, or eye color, skull shape, nose length, and social background are routinely linked to deeper character traits. "Breediness" carries weight not only in the selection of show dogs and house pets but also in more important choices of candidates for useful, no-nonsense tasks such as therapy, assistance, and search-and-rescue work. Behind casual claims to breed superiority—loyalty, intelligence, trainability, beauty—is the kind of talk that's illegal in some places if the subjects are human but a sobering reminder that breedism, the barefaced promotion of eugenic stereotypes, is pure racism.

A passing glance at the sacred scrolls called breed standards, those elaborately detailed guidelines used to select which pups to breed and which to bucket, and the everyday expressions used in the ring, shows just how deeply entrenched eugenics still is. Preserved are retrograde terms like *degenerate*[10] (as in "degenerate coat color" for washed-out mutts, or "degenerate races" of half-breed humans), *undesirable* (esthetic features not "allowable" in the ring, or individuals whose lifestyles don't "conform" to classist notions of normality), *expression* (used by judges to describe that *je ne sais quoi* they see in champion material and lifted directly from physiognomy, and *essential* (any random trait believed to be a sign of blood "purity"). Traditional terms for mixing races—"mongrelization" and "debasement"—have been applied to humans and dogs alike. Such offensive language continues to obscure judgment and misguide selection of show ring champions, house pets, and seeing-eye dogs, and hardly anyone seems to notice or care. Parallels between eugenics and dog breeding abound, not just in the carefully controlled phraseology of official standards upheld by the AKC, but in the dog fancy's tools of measurement, and in the cockeyed results handed down as lessons to unsuspecting children. The "wicket," an adjustable device used for gauging a dog's height in the show ring, is frighteningly reminiscent of contraptions used to measure skulls and noses of "the Negro type" or "the Jewish type." The idea of a "tramp," or stray mutt, sounded cute enough in Disney's *Lady and the Tramp* but was, in fact, a legal term used by eugenicists to describe one category of "undesirable" forced to undergo involuntary sterilizations.

The division of dogs into easily identifiable types was far more calculated than human cataloging. The beasts we can't seem to imagine in any other shapes, sizes, or coat colors were deliberately invented for commercial and competitive purposes. Standardized breeds were designed to look unique and indispensible by giving contestants more ways to win prizes in the ring, and consumers more opportunities to show their own breeding, taste, distinction, and spending power on pavements. Once the pantheon of prize-winning material was put on display in show rings, pet shop windows, front parlors, and public parks, fanciers soon forgot it was as contrived as a Sears Roebuck catalog, that the diversity was as artificial as Heinz 57 varieties. "Show" golden retrievers were little more than Irish setters in a different coat color, but like eugenicists with their racial indicators, the dog fancy first stopped breeding for function in favor of form, then backtracked and assigned unique personalities and skills to their creations!

The confusing array of standardized, branded, recognized terriers currently available for purchase and the source of so much family pride provide an excellent example of how inventive the dog fancy has been. Contrary to popular lore and breeders' advertising claims, "improved" breeds of the terrier type were invented for the stage and sidewalk. Any that aren't purely fictional works are, often and sadly, working dogs made physically and mentally incapable of performing their traditional tasks. Ancient types were reshaped into cartoon replicas of their useful ancestors, and soon everyone but farmers and hunters without the luxury of gullibility forgot the whole operation was a theatrical hoax.[11] Whether any of these repackaged terriers ever had practical uses—none of them ever did in their "improved" forms—is immaterial to fashion hounds trying to display something special at both ends of their leashes. Those rare eccentrics who still use dogs for more than posing in a heel position, on the other hand, such as seasoned hunter and hound historian David Hancock, who was interviewed in the BBC documentary *Pedigree Dogs Exposed*, are struck by the absurdity of believing the tilt of an animal's ears or coat color are indicators of any one individual dog's essence, much less the owner's. "And then there are those who swear by this breed of terrier or that," Hancock writes with disbelief, "as if every single human from Devon or Durham had similar qualities."[12]

Not only has the sort of thinking that makes tolerance of yellow, brown, and black Labs seem like a sign of diversity not been helping dogs, this catalog selection has worked against the *genetic* diversity needed to keep populations healthy, smart, and functional. Selecting dogs, often from the same litter, for distinctive but irrelevant features like fur texture or ear style has led to many of the health problems we're seeing. "Some have suggested that there are too many breeds," writes Kevin Stafford of the Institute of Veterinary Animal and Biomedical Sciences at Massey University in New Zealand, "and that breeds, such as terriers . . . with similar functions and type should be crossbred to produce fewer breeds with much greater genetic variation."[13] At the same time, it should be added, dogs are routinely neutered, killed, or in some way disfavored for having heads or coat colors not "typical" of their races, but their very lack of uniformity is often a sign of the diverse heritage that purists try to cover up.

Broad categories of hunting, sporting, guarding, fighting, farm dogs, and so on—animals whose traditional uses over hundreds and thousands of years have left them with tendencies toward certain pronounced temperaments and talents—have been dissected and color-coded for the stage, then given catchy brand names like golden retriever, yellow Lab, and fox terrier. The modern fancy isn't entirely to blame for this unnatural drive to differentiate within strictly defined parameters. Before dogs were sorted and segregated for a mass market into easily identifiable molds, general types skilled in tracking, retrieving, or flushing out game were used in ritual hunting exploits of upper-class sportsmen. For centuries, finer families swore by the superiority of their own private labels of greyhound or foxhound, not breeds by today's standards but strains that often had distinct coloring that identified them as belonging to noteworthy kennels. Legends of their exploits were handed down at arm's length from one earl to the next and kept alive in small social circles. Opinions went unchallenged within the league of gentlemen because no one else was in a position to contradict, not the hired help or local tenantry, who were only too flattered to tag along. It went without saying, but was frequently said, that lower-class mongrels and their Cockney owners could never, even if given a chance, outperform highbred hounds and their highbred humans. As for "foreign" types, many English continue to resent the invasion of Continental pointing breeds that are, as Hancock notes, "accused of lacking style."[14]

Americans saw themselves as rightful inheritors of English-style eugenics. No less of their identity was invested at the other end of the leash where they could distinguish themselves from anyone without the means to be seen with pets that might as well have had price tags tied to their collars. Dog shows and breed registries were slower to thrive in the United States than in the UK, owing to the brief interruption of a civil war, but no time was lost in catching up, and by the twentieth century, the AKC and Westminster were purveying widespread snootiness almost as well as the Kennel Club or Crufts. Having no royalty for sponsors, the closest to the genuine item was Freeman Lloyd, that imported English image consultant who helped Americans forge their alliances with "pure" blood through pet ownership. Lloyd presented the fancy's eugenic mission unflinchingly in an essay on "correct conformation" for the *American Kennel Club Gazette and Stud Book* in 1943. "As a matter of fact," he instructed, "the head and face of a dog, like those of human beings, are usually an accurate gauge of character, and the art and science of phrenology may be applied to the former as well as to the latter."[15] A similar *Gazette* article penned by another established expert appeared in 1947, despite the grim lesson the world had just learned on which way this eugenic madness led. "What is important is the creation through competition of a better breed," the article commented, explaining the importance of breed standards in dog shows—and sounding like a manifesto for social Darwinism.[16]

"But in the parlance of the Old Virginia Gentleman, he must be treated like a white man," was the dog advice to sportsmen in a self-help manual called *The Gentleman's Dog: His Rearing, Training, and Treatment*. For author C. A. Bryce, MD, this meant "something more than crusts and kicks and sleeping on the ash-pile," treatment more befitting a man of color, we can safely assume. "You cannot expect to raise a decent self-respecting dog unless you think enough of him to give him comfortable, clean, and well attended sleeping quarters."[17] Like many dog authors wearing two hats, this doctor doubling as a canine aficionado helped impress upon Americans the resemblance between well-bred pooches and well-bred people. Like Dr. Stables and others, Dr. Bryce clearly believed that better addresses, good marriages, and segregation were ways to prevent mongrelization or miscegenation in *both* species. And yet breeding within a gene pool restricted to members of certain preapproved colors, combined with environmental input from the right people, even the most devout eugenicist knew, were no guarantees of superiority. Freeman Lloyd, a hunter, hound historian, show ring judge, and canine art collector, stressed the role of an expert eye in handing down final judgments after inbreeding "the best to get the best." Determining the *very* best required the seasoned taste and knowledge of a proper white gentleman with discriminating taste, a man like Lloyd himself. The English arbiter, whose writings introduced aristocratic Labrador retrievers to Americans, explained the need for balance between inner and outer dog that could only be determined by men who knew better than they, especially in his own personal breed of choice. There were springer spaniels, Lloyd cautioned, and there were "'springers' whose 'long' pedigrees appear well on paper, but whose appearances proclaim 'a nigger in a woodpile.'"[18]

In hindsight, golden retrievers, yellow Labs, and Anderson Cooper's brown-and-white blue blood begin to look like blond-haired Hitler Youth to unseasoned neophytes lacking Lloyd's expertise. Until very recently, the fancy has held the reins on canines, enjoying virtually unchallenged authority and absolute power in matters dog-related. The show culture and its priorities have dominated breeding, not only determining how champions and house pets should look but also influencing in subtle ways the choices of candidates to lead the blind and sniff out bombs. For generations, kennel clubs and their associates have made up, like eugenicists of old, a powerful circle that enjoys society's utmost respect and operates free from meddlesome outsiders.

But nonmembers have been bolder of late. At the risk of seeming impertinent—or being called an animal rights extremist—a fun exercise for simple spectators with a fondness for dogs might be to step back and consider the dogs themselves, or at least wonder what's been done to improve them as our servants. After a century and a half of tinkering with former hunters, herders, guarders, and multitaskers, is it really so unreasonable to ask the experts for a progress report?

Looking for signs of improvement, the first item to strike an untrained eye might be the utter lack of resemblance between modern-day show breeds and their ancestors who performed specialized tasks that helped humans survive and flourish for thousands of years—jobs they stopped doing the moment they stepped into show rings. A standardized springer spaniel looks nothing like its said ancestor, a general type of dog bred, not to conform to any specific look or to win prizes, but to help hunt birds. *Downton Abbey*, the series about an aristocratic family that debuted in 2010, features a yellow Lab that looks little like the breed did as recently as the early twentieth century.[19] Show people defend as their raison d'être the careful preservation of "traditional" types, "correct" form, "pure" blood, and "ancestral" lines. They claim to protect the sacred union of "form and function," but the two were only ever related in very general, commonsensical ways, and not decided by a long list of demanding rules like breed standards, which are constantly subjected to new interpretation by judges. Show champions, and their offspring we keep as pets, haven't done any real work in ages, and their looks show it, say those rare eccentrics who refuse to breed nonfunctional dogs with chests too barreled to fit into fox holes, or absurdly plush coats and theatrical drapes of skin that impede movement and hinder vision. Yet kennel clubs, breed clubs, conformation judges, breeders, and assorted fanciers—the ones *supposed* to have all the taste and knowledge about dogs—seem to have a poor faculty even for pure esthetics. As for function at this end of the leash, it has been known for some time that show ring judges typically have no practical experience whatsoever with the former herders, hunters, guarders, and sentries they're evaluating. They do not hunt. They are not shepherds. They don't tend to be policemen or soldiers.

"Both the appearance and behavior of modern breeds would be deeply strange to our ancestors who lived just a few hundred years ago," says evolutionary biologist Greger Larson.[20] Meanwhile, mere amateurs with an eye for artifice are struck not only by the extreme differences in appearance between the old and "improved," but by the radical break from breeding practices considered sound for centuries before this sudden attraction to "scientific" breeding in the nineteenth. Traits traditionally along for the ride became essential. In fact, the less dogs have been needed to perform useful work in recent years, the more intensely they've been scrutinized for formal perfection and blood "purity." For eons up to the eve of dog shows, contenders for real jobs were continually outcrossed, not chronically inbred, to various degrees depending on their tasks. Prior to commercial repackaging and the cult of novelty, dogs weren't sold as promising puppies (or put down as instant failures) based on their markings or relations. They were selected much later, as adult individuals with observable skills and temperaments.[21] Humble farmers and idle upper-class sportsmen alike knew that utility, whether this was the master's survival or his pleasure, depended on a proven ability to perform.

Critics of the fancy say measuring our companion species against beauty-pageant ideals can, at best, distract from more vital concerns like health and ability. At worst, they say, eugenic breeding standards can overtake and ruin entire populations of traditional types. A Dog Health Workshop was sponsored in 2012 by the Swedish Kennel Club, which has historically focused more on health and utility in dogs than show ring conformation. Included was a series on "Selection for Behavioral Traits." According to speaker Per Arvelius of the Department of Animal Breeding and Genetics at the Swedish University of Agricultural Studies, "If nothing else, more focus on one thing when selecting animals (for example, 'beauty') by definition means less focus on something else (for example, health, temperament)."[22] Animal rights extremism, or common sense?

Erik Wilsson, of the Swedish Armed Forces, which employs dogs for no-nonsense military uses, was also on the panel for behavior and breeding. Though Wilsson considers breeds (or preferably, "populations" of distantly related dogs) more reliable than random mixes for his purposes, he adds that breeds as defined by kennel clubs are no guarantee of quality. Outcrossing—mating dogs to those not listed in official stud books, closed for years to new blood by the AKC and England's Kennel Club—is vital to health and utility. Combined with reliable temperament testing and selection of individual dogs regardless of ancestry or appearance, breeding can sometimes produce better workers. But strict inbreeding for superficial uniformity? "I think exhibitions have only added bad things to dogs. Selecting for efficiency will get a functional anatomy although they may differ in size, color, etc., details not relevant for their work," Wilsson concludes.[23]

"Give any show ring enough time," writes Patrick Burns, traditional Jack Russell man, hunter, scholar, and vocal critic of kennel club practices, "and it will ruin any breed of working dog—it always has and it always will."[24] This would explain why farm dogs, police dogs, war dogs, racing dogs, sled dogs, and many other useful types are not typically even AKC-registered. This is why some breeders who, because of a kennel club's vast influence or for whatever reasons want its support, are said to outcross on the sly to keep their stock healthy and functional.[25] Employers of traditional border collies, Jack Russells, and many breeds eventually split into "working," "field," "show," and "pet" versions, have kept their dogs bred in separate lines, out of show rings, and safe from a judge's gaze. But irrelevant concerns have influenced even the most useful dogs. Executive director of the US Police Canine Association Russell Hess recalls a time before looks and pedigree had infiltrated police work. "Most of our dogs are imported and not bred in the USA," he comments sadly on the unfortunate results forty years later. Originally "departments used dogs received by donations and never purchased animals. Many dogs looked like a German shepherd but never came with registration papers and frankly these would outperform registered dogs costing several hundred dollars."[26]

Even in choices of appearance that may or may not be along for the ride, outside critics say that dog shows reward precisely the opposite of what they should. David Hancock mourns the loss of traits he has found helpful in dogs, and all because of some inexperienced judge's idea of "expression." Current preferences in color-coding and shape in eyes, he feels, are unfounded. "Dark eyes are considered highly desirable in nearly all pedigree breeds of dog and yet the keenest-eyed working dogs I come across are invariably light-eyed." Eye shape, too, is subject to dispute among hunters on the field and poseurs on the stage. "I always find that perfect oval eyes are the healthiest, yet round eyes are actually desired in some pedigree breeds." As for ear essentials: "I suspect that prick ears are the natural shape for all dogs and that in pursuit of breed conformity we may have impaired one of dog's most important senses."[27]

Some hunting preferences, like service dog prejudices, may well be based on personal tastes, but many outsiders to the fancy agree that "expression" can work against utility. "The behavior exhibited in the show ring is standing," writes Janis Bradley, founder of the San Francisco SPCA Academy for Dog Trainers. Breeding "true" for behavior, Bradley cautions, has always been a difficult task, with a wide margin of error. Success becomes all the more unlikely when it's not even a priority.[28] Unfortunately for the dogs, show ring performance doesn't stop at standing. In as much as behaviors have ever been heritable, or remain as "superficial reminders of the ancestral working dogs," according to renowned biologist and dog-sled racer Raymond Coppinger, the tendencies displayed on stage might possibly work against pets and working dogs alike.[29]

"Animal rights extremists" concur on this. "Dogs that carry their heads and tails erect catch the attention of judges, and thus tend to win shows," writes Stephen Budiansky, author and science contributor to the *New York Times*, *Wall Street Journal*, and *Washington Post*. "Those are also the marks of a dominant, hence aggressive dog."[30] The reverse may also be true. A study conducted by Kenth Svartberg at Stockholm University in 2005 concludes that the very traits desirable in pets such as playfulness and nonsocial fearfulness, are undesirable in the show ring where many of the breeding dogs are chosen.[31] Either way, aggression has become a serious problem in the cocker spaniel (cocker rage syndrome), the springer spaniel (springer rage syndrome), and the gold standard of eugenic perfection, the golden retriever. First stripped of their original functions, some breeds have been made so sickly and disturbed by inbreeding for looks alone that their usefulness, even as decorative household items and symbols of family pride, is in jeopardy. So severe are their problems that behavioral geneticists hope to find in these sad but beautified beasts the genetic component to aggression that continues to elude them.[32]

Could it be that any improvement in dogs has been made *in spite of* shows and *without* the breed standards that champions manage to meet and somehow survive? According to Kevin Stafford, the extreme anatomical features awarded prizes—and very much inherited through extreme inbreeding—prevent normal mobility, communication, and socialization, leading to a host of behavioral problems and affecting a dog's performance in any capacity.[33]

None of this is news to observers outside the show culture, and the obsession with breeding true for looks but not behavior has even led a few insiders to risk the fancy's wrath. "Personally," wrote Roger Caras, former Westminster host and judge and president of the ASPCA, "I consider it a terrible lack of responsibility for a breed standard not to include standards for behavior and temperament."[34] That was 1982. "Rightly or wrongly," wrote canine geneticist, breeder, and dog show judge Malcolm Willis in 1995, "it is a fact that dog breeding in most countries is dominated by the show-ring," where he hoped that breeding would one day favor sound health, temperament, and utility "regardless of physical beauty." Willis was writing from a university located, ironically enough, at Newcastle upon Tyne, site of the legendary first canine beauty pageant of the nineteenth century.[35]

The year 1995 was also when the American border collie, descendant of a highly specialized, tightly wound, single-minded, energetic but extremely useful type of dog never meant for show rings, homes, or any environment but the wide open country, was recognized by the AKC. After a long and bitter fight with the US Border Collie Club—"dedicated to preserving the Border Collie as a working stock dog" and "opposing the showing, judging, and breeding of Border Collies based on their appearance"[36]—the AKC gave up on trying to seduce with prospects of blue ribbons, silver cups, and sidewalk glory. Following a familiar strategy after failing to induct resisters into the fancy's hall of fame and failure, the AKC redirected its patronage to a new and separate club composed of fanciers inexperienced with working dogs and more receptive to the dubious honor of approval.

Back in England, where this traditional farm dog had evolved over centuries as a roughly similar "collie" type, Willis still yearned for some sign of improvement in 1995. "Although it was decided that a working test would remain for KC registered dogs before they could become full champions," Willis remarked, worried like a flock facing that herder's inescapable stare, "the sad truth is that few Border collies have taken this test and still fewer have passed it. With such failure to attend to essential features, it will be only a matter of time before the ill-named *Show* Border collie will have lost its ability to work."[37] More than a decade later in 2008, the year of the BBC's boycott of Crufts, England's Kennel Club felt compelled to backtrack and assign usefulness to dogs bred for looks from the time they were standardized. As though to show the world their refashioned version of the border collie was still "fit for function" despite generations of favoring form, officials set out to reform field trials with "some alterations that will make the test more relevant to what it aims to assess—a dog's herding ability."[38] Prior to that, not a single sheep had been sighted on those virtual fields as green as AstroTurf, and not many border collies have been seen since sheep were added to the equation. During the first three years of improved English trials, only nine dogs qualified to take even this limited test of ability.[39]

Meanwhile, in average homes on both sides of the pond, pet owners swayed by romantic tales of a pastoral figure now deprived of pastures either end up abandoning their silken two-tone replicas for being too difficult to manage, or pride themselves on cramming what remains of their uniqueness into completely inappropriate environments. It's not uncommon to find these hardwired misfits staring blankly at walls, or trembling and drooling with pupils dilated. "Noise phobia" is said to affect at least 50 percent of pet border collies. Many are prescribed Xanax. Ten percent suffer severely, and the breed has become a subject of study—again, on the genetic basis of mental illness.[40]

Not all purebreds are overactive or brimming with enthusiasm. Others, according to outside agitators and extremists, have swung to the opposite extreme. Many replicas bred for the stage and sofa, it is said, have had their senses dulled and spirits broken to the point of lethargy. Fancy dogs seem uninterested, and uninteresting to all but the judges who praise them, the scientists who study them, and the hobbyists who buy them. Some breeds appear to be sort of stupid, leading critics to that political hot potato called "intelligence."

"The dumbing of America has gone far enough," the *Washington Post* wrote in 1994 in defense of the more traditional border collie, whose patrons were fighting *against* AKC recognition. "Yes, we have gotten used to falling SAT scores. . . . But we must draw the line somewhere. I say we draw it at dogs."[41] The concern goes beyond border collies, according to a study of thirteen thousand dogs conducted by Kenth Svartberg in 2006. The *Telegraph* reported that "the mental and physical agility of many breeds is being eroded." Defining "intelligence" by a number of characteristics, including sociability and curiosity, testers concluded that dogs bred for looks, especially show dogs, were succumbing to "introversion" and "boring personality" in just a few generations. Pedigree favorites were "less responsive and not as alert or attentive," more a source of concern among scientists than judges or hobbyists. Was this an example of form following function? "Perhaps the genes behind attractive looks could also be closely linked to those that cause fearfulness," said Svartberg.[42]

Golden retrievers and yellow Labs could be the new dumb blonds, not due to pigmentation but because they've been inbred for coat color. Holding off on the sort of overblown generalizations that legitimized eugenics, another study, at Aberdeen University in Scotland (birthplace to goldens, Labs, and other sporting dogs turned couch potatoes), defines "intelligence" in terms of spatial awareness and problem-solving abilities. Distinct differences between breeds and mutts were observed. "With a pedigree as long as his tail, you might expect the pure-bred pooch to trounce his mongrel cousin in an IQ test," reports the *Daily Mail*. "But it seems all that breeding may be for nothing. For when it comes to intelligence, scientists say the crossbred wins, paws down." Researchers found that mixes were far better "on the ball" than pedigree dogs. Mutts were also cleverer at locating the proverbial bone, cloaked with a tin can before their eyes, than many pedigree dogs that didn't "even realize it still existed." These and other tests led the Aberdeen team to predict mongrel talents could easily translate into not only equal but *superior* performance for police, seeing eye, herding, and house pet work, if only these disadvantaged curs would be given a chance. Reverse prejudice? Seven out of the ten best problem solvers at Aberdeen were crossbreeds. The top dog wasn't a border collie, or a springer spaniel for that matter, but an eyesore of a "collie-spaniel cross called Jet, which scored full marks."[43]

Translating the dog's traditional skills (or what remains of them) into contemporary uses, recent trends for service animals have been no less revealing. The retrieving tendency, for example, is needed for assistance work where the drive to happily pick up fallen objects comes in handy to persons wheelchair-bound. Sufficient size is also important for bracing the disabled or pulling vehicles. Golden and Labrador retrievers often fit the bill, but so do Labradoodles and Goldendoodles, says Jenny Barlos of Assistance Dogs of America.[44] An individual dog's intelligence and temperament, she says, not breed as defined by kennel clubs, ultimately determine who gets the job. "About 50 percent of the dogs that pass our initial evaluation do not make it to final training and I think that's about average," says Barlos. "The dogs that make it through initial evaluation are very few also." In the greater scheme of things, it might seem that the heroic qualities attributed to goldens and Labs across the board are overextended. The minuscule number of high-profile individuals that even qualify to qualify are exceptional, perhaps negligible. A keen and lifelong desire to learn and work are essential, says Barlos, though admittedly some breeds with familiar faces in the standard shades are disproportionately represented. "AKC registration is not important to us," Barlos continues. So why are so many goldens and yellow Labs seen visiting hospitals, nursing homes, restaurants, and cruise ships? "They have a friendly public perception while having full access with their owners," Barlos remarks. Perhaps it's time for some affirmative action in the dog world. Animal Farm Foundation in upstate New York has not only been placing "pit bulls" ("We keep this in quotes," it says) as family pets but also training and placing them for assistance work. At least one has become a search-and-rescue dog.[45]

While tasks like assistance, drug sniffing, and finding land mines demand exceptional skills and temperaments that *may* be found in certain breeds and nonbreeds alike, no-brainer therapy jobs are also subject to profiling. I've come across boastful owners of many a purebred prouder in recent years to add the title of "certified therapy dog" to the list of honors used as evidence of blood superiority. Everyone these days seems to be sporting a therapy dog on the sidewalk runway, and I myself am considering growing whiskers and applying. But according to Kelly Gould at Karma Dogs, which specializes in using rescued animals to help children with emotional problems, if species matters, "the breed has nothing to do with it."[46] Karma has had success with purebreds and mutts of all varieties. Certain breeds do tend to be smarter than others, says Gould, but that isn't key to therapy work. "It's the unconditional attention and bond that kids make with the dog that matters." As the wisdom of the ages has always taught without the glamour of show rings and rigors of beauty standards, success comes down to the individual dog's disposition and ability to leave the past behind for a second chance. Not only do dog shows tend not to improve dogs in this capacity, no matter how cute they look on television, perhaps they spoil them for other careers. A group of ten retired show champions, chosen by judges as best representing their breeds and prodigiously bred for consumers addicted to the scent of blue blood—applying for therapy work because what else could they do now that they'd lost their looks?—failed their training and evaluations across the board at Karma. Veterans of the stage had been rewarded all their lives for a very different sort of performance, leading spectators to believe formal perfection automatically fit them for any function. But standing and posing had left them too set in their ways, or perhaps their careers as therapy dogs had been sabotaged at birth. Many dogs are being "overbred," Gould explains, careful to add that it was a nice gesture to try and give these former champions a break but sorry it didn't work out for them. Regardless of breed, only "one out of ten dogs pass our test the first time," says Gould. Pedigree and standardized appearance, it seems, have not been relevant, except perhaps in negative ways. One of Karma's best success stories, a six-month-old chow mix with behavior issues, was turned around and made into a model canine citizen. "When his vest is on, he knows it's work time," says Gould. Goldens and Labs, based on her experience, are "kind of dumb" and not always the best "breed ambassadors."[47]

So maybe breed is relevant, after all, if only to know which dogs, as a rule of thumb, to *avoid*? There may be no solid-gold 100 percent guaranteed way to improve dogs, a thought guaranteed to strike terror into the hearts of purists everywhere. But like it or not, one likely route to making dogs a bit smarter, healthier, more emotionally balanced and useful could be to ignore breed standards and pedigrees—and *mix the races!*

Overbreeding for either form or function, it turns out, can result in losing both. Many purebreds are getting too "pure" for their own good (and ours). A tragic example is the German shepherd, one of the top working breeds throughout the twentieth century. When not being deformed for show rings and homes, many German shepherds have been made soft and unreliable in the field. As we've seen, police departments in the United States are dropping these dogs, but so are departments around the world. Attempts are being made to cross them with other breeds or to replace them altogether with a Belgian Malinois, even in their land of birth, Germany, where they've been a source of national pride.[48]

Useful traits in overbred golden and Labrador retrievers are also being salvaged, and an unapologetically *mixed* heritage may spare them the sad fate of the German shepherd, with its vanishing skills and declining health. US and UK fanciers haven't been keen on discussing recent developments, but for a variety of demanding services including assistance and seeing-eye work, the hybrid golden Labrador retriever has been found, by growing numbers of experts beyond the show ring, to be more reliable than either side of its family tree.

"Golden Lab" shouldn't be confused with the latest yuppie affectation on Manhattan sidewalks, where the yellow Lab is made to sound more expensive. Not even the Queen of England calls her yellow Labs "golden." In fact, golden retrievers weren't even called "golden" until the twentieth century, when the fancy decided to up the ante and make "yellow" dogs sound fancier. If people are going to be pretentious, they could at least get their facts straight. The golden Lab proper is a true hybrid that goes against the rules of pedigree breeding, a rough type selected for ability, not looks, a dog that would go unrecognized by name droppers but for the colored vest. A practical solution to excessive clinginess in goldens and excess enthusiasm in "nice but dim"[49] Labs, the new and improved version is no freak exception but a growing trend. Guide Dogs, a major provider of working animals to the UK, reported in 2010 that 47 percent of their success stories were golden-Lab crosses. At last count, in 2011, 55 percent of all the dogs they used were either golden-Lab or Lab–German shepherd crosses (and only 30 percent and 9 percent, respectively, were "pure" Lab and golden).[50] Similarly, but on a smaller scale, Guide Dogs of America reports that in 2011, among graduates successfully placed in jobs, 25 percent have been golden Labs, an increase of 23 percent in just one year from 2010.[51]

Final proof that best friends can break their molds, and a sign of dog days to come: search and rescue dogs, themselves rescued from death row in shelters, and many of these mixed breeds, are heroically overcoming every disadvantage life has dealt them. "When it comes to selectivity, Harvard has nothing on these pooches," says a 2013 article on dogs trained by the National Disaster Search Dog Foundation.[52] Federal Emergency Management Agency–certified graduates, animals once abandoned as useless, are rising to challenge every cliché on desirable appearance, family history, and environmental influence. Yet despite the marvelous talents and personalities of these and other exceptionally smart, temperamentally balanced, trainable, and *useful* animals, fans aren't holding their breath for an appearance at Westminster or Crufts anytime soon. Golden Labs and less calculated crosses aren't likely to be "accepted," "approved," or "recognized" because they don't conform to the eugenic standards of any one breed. As hybrids, they aren't bred from eugenically "pure" bloodlines.

It may be possible to breed a better dog, however narrowly or broadly that is defined, but this isn't likely to be accomplished within the dog fancy's eugenic tradition where practical concerns are compromised by conformation. In any event, and whether they're black, white, or parti-colored, the needs of truly useful, working dogs can be too much for the average dog owner to handle, and the golden rule for finding the perfect pet may be simpler than imagined. For the vast majority of canine consumers hoping to live out virtually those legends of heroic ancestral deeds, who believe that pedigree papers give them possession of unrivaled talents hidden behind coats of arms borne by noble beings whose forebears supposedly lived in palaces, who crave convenient formulas and precise measurements for "predictability"—when all they really need is a nice companion who won't bite the kids—there's that one-size-fits-all advice said to come from the ASPCA, though its origins have been lost with the wisdom of the ages:

If you can't decide between a shepherd, a setter, or a poodle, get them all . . . adopt a mutt.

CHAPTER FIVE

A FRICKIN' MENAGERIE

Rounding a corner in the far West Village, I led my daily trio of crazy terrier mixes toward a remote dog park on the bank of the Hudson River. This might have been a calm and uneventful afternoon. The sun was out. The air was clear. The area was quiet and pleasant, with well-kept houses, some of the oldest in New York. Flowering vines crawled up ancient brick facades. Quaint, shady side streets with narrow walkways didn't have enough traffic to interest even the muggers. I felt safe in an upscale neighborhood that everyone knew was "good," though the caliber of my crew was questionable to all we passed.

In fact, there was no telling what might happen next with this wild bunch of ill-bred curs. For people who craved the myth of predictability, the mixed breeds I was hired to walk didn't bring comforting feelings of familiarity. They had no recognizable brand names. One nondescript specimen, judging from his long and cottony but substandard speckled coat, appeared to be a Wheaton gone awry. Another random mutt had a head that didn't seem to fit, and a tail that looked Crazy-Glued to no good end. My third mixed bag had an awkwardly long torso and wiry hair, pointing to the possibility of some bastardized dachshund. My disorderly crew was not what fanciers had in mind, but shared one distinction that might have saved them in a purist's eyes. I could state with near-certainty that each member of my pack had a few ounces of genuine Jack Russell blood coursing through his veins. Oskar and Sebastian had the right body. Max had the right head. They all had the right attitude. I often fantasized about bringing them to the AKC on Madison Avenue and asking for certification. Surely, these three half-breeds had enough Jack among them to qualify for one pedigree. . . .

My daydream of a world without border collies was shattered, and my leadership challenged, the moment these feisty mongrels caught wind of another dog across the street. Throw a few terriers into a mix and you're asking for trouble. They were practically foaming at the mouth, trying to get at the strange dog they'd never even seen before. Normally, what set them off were skateboarders and raving lunatics, or well-dressed yuppies wearing headset phones and speaking to the air. These things launched them into a rage, and understandably so. What was it about this dog? My own mutt at home, a shepherd mix who defied description, liked to save her venom for the bulldogs. Whenever we were promenading and encountered this bizarre style of dog with the flat, motionless face, glaring bug eyes, and perpetually exposed teeth, my Samantha always got upset. The animal across the street that had riled my ruffians didn't look like a bulldog at all, but he'd managed to strike a nerve. From deep within three misleadingly cute and cuddly frames emerged one hellish sound so ferocious that it chilled me to the bone. These dear, sweet little darlings wanted blood, and they didn't care how "pure" it was.

Across the charming old brick street, in front of a time-weathered, Federal-style house with peeling shutters and a mossy facade, was a pet more typical to this neighborhood in recent years. Since rents had skyrocketed and most of the interesting people had been exiled to up-and-coming Brooklyn, mutts had been moving over for their social superiors in the Village. Corporate couples with three-headed baby strollers took over those narrow walkways, and indigenous dogs were displaced by prestigious pedigrees trotting alongside with names like Airedale, Cavalier, Labrador—and the specimen before us that day, the lofty golden.

It's a proven fact that when neighborhoods are gentrified, the dog populations change accordingly. A 2008 study in Toronto mapped that city by pet preferences.[1] Predictably enough, the higher the income, the more likely people were to have golden and Labrador retrievers. Less affluent areas were left with their lesser breeds, perhaps "pit bulls" or dogs of no recognizable variety. Stationed across the street on this elite block of Manhattan's Greenwich Village, planted on a corner of this most sought-after locale in all of New York, was the final word in doggery, an AKC aristocrat with papers to prove it. The golden was universally accepted as a breed apart, even by fanciers forced to settle for purebred dogs of other colors. Standing there, in his kingly coat of golden fleece, was one of humankind's proudest achievements, a gold standard against which all inferior types were measured, a pooch in a superlative shade and the polar opposite of the mangy mutt. A few yards away and straining at their leashes, my disadvantaged terriers did not like him in the least.

Curiously, this dog appeared to be oblivious, which both I and my terriers found alarming. Any pup so young should have been alert and enthused, ready to exploit every sight, sound, and scent on the pavement. Instead he posed handsomely like a statue in lustrous garb, a lion's mane on a beast supposedly invented by a true lion of the British Isles called Lord Tweedmouth (another name that Monty Python could have coined). Firmly mounted on perfectly shaped feet, "round and cat-like," as the English standard demands, he stared into the distance nonchalantly through his ample upholstery at something of another world. He did not make a sound, and as my pariahs lunged and snarled with teeth bared in passing, I noticed his eyes were sad and sunken, red and vacant, the sort that say an animal isn't quite right in the head. This poor, privileged pup was trapped inside that gilded coat, inbred to a ghastly extreme. I suspected he was living his life without friends or enemies in a pure, hermetically sealed environment. My scraggly regiment of rejects also knew there was something awfully wrong with the animal, which stood there confused and despondent. They wanted this dog dead—and he could keep the coat.

Looking upon the pitiful creature, I became almost as outraged as my charges. What kind of madness had inspired the aberration before us? Why select for a particular coat color and foot shape but ignore an essential like the brain? Less than a century ago, determined to get dogs right, fanciers set about working on "the conversion of a domestic animal into a living advertisement of man's eccentricities," as canine critic William Arkwright complained to the British Kennel Club. Creators of this and many other "purebreds" seemed to enjoy nothing more than "promoting the length of ear at the expense of flesh."[2] Canine monstrosities, like circus freaks, attracted crowds. Show dogs performed tricks, usually without moving at all. Their colors changed as though by magic, and eyes waxed and waned on command. Legs stretched and retracted like rubber bands at the wave of a wand. How far would the wolf in every dog have to go to please the people? How many hoops would be placed in his path?

Dogs eventually given the name "golden retriever" weren't yet available to the general public when Mr. Arkwright wrote his critique of these new dog shows in 1888. An early model, in a darker shade that would be disqualified today, was the property of an elite group of landed aristocrats who still used their dogs for retrieving birds. Their coats had not yet grown to their present length, which is so ridiculously long and luxuriant that moving through brush without tripping or being entangled would be quite a performance, indeed. At that time, it wasn't the golden retriever that occupied center stage but rather the new and improved collie, a dog of similar coloring that had caught the fancy's fancy. After only a few years in the ring, this breed had strayed far from its progenitor, a hardy working dog whose predominant coat color had been black like coal—thus the name "coaley," so the story goes.[3] Audiences weren't satisfied with a roughly similar type of dog proven for generations as tried and true, an individual with variable coloring but a solid character and a unique set of talents. In no time at all, show business transformed this animal into a breed and turned the coat from black to "golden sable and white."[4] A humble herder and hard worker became a big, fair-haired fur ball with "an enormous head, an enormous coat, and enormous limbs."[5] This theatrical version would become "Lassie" in the next century, and heroes never wore black.

Consumers wanted identical copies, and so the breeders refashioned the collie to look more like the trendy dogs of the day. To maximize the response and broaden the appeal, they gave him the pointed head of a borzoi, a snooty sort with a Roman nose known to be on an intimate footing with royalty. They took this revamped head with a beak that made the dog look like an anteater and screwed it onto "the clumsy bone of a St. Bernard," a recent arrival on the social scene being used to guard elegant country mansions. Not content with having made the traditional collie into a Frankenstein composite of other show types, "they have commenced to graft on to the breed the jaw of an alligator, the coat of an Angoran goat," Arkwright remarked as if judging a bad work of art.[6] The noble herder became a laughing stock among many farmers, but the city folk liked him just fine.

Arkwright may have been right on the mark about collies. But he failed to understand that making things appear as they were *not* in real life was the whole point of show business. Where was the fun in reality? The fancy came into full force during the golden age of circuses, freak shows, and world's fairs. Audiences had acquired a taste for illusion and demanded that dogs be something more than just dogs. Collies weren't the only animals being reissued as theatrical versions of their former selves.

As we've already seen, enterprising showmen showed their showmanship by rebuilding the bulldog, a type that was deliberately crippled to assume the tough stance of another animal altogether, the bull he once fought in the ring. Those extreme skin folds were only added as decorative flourishes years after the fact, retroactively given the elaborate purpose of allowing the bull's blood to flow neatly down the face. Old engravings of bulldogs show no such feature. It is a common tactic in the fancy to invent intricate, technical-sounding reasons for breeding dogs to look striking on stage, though the elaborateness of these explanations are often grounds for suspicion. Other dogs would step into the limelight and be remade for dramatic effect.

Today's so-called "fox terrier" was no different from our so-called "Parson Russell Terrier" until quite recently when he was given a laughably long nose to draw attention to what these small diggers *used* to do for a living before being thrust into the arena. A Pinocchio story if ever there was one, this tale of exaggerated snout size was pure fantasy because no dog ever needed this appendage to hit pay dirt and corner a fox.[7] Pushing the envelope for other breeds, skulls have kept enlarging to keep the crowds coming back. The dachsy's back has grown to absurd lengths relative to its ever stumpier legs, giving the judges something more to measure.

The German shepherd was invented in the 1890s as a symbol of Teutonic purity, but changed dramatically when he became a show dog, and even more when he was recast for the silver screen. Audiences were so impressed by his role as Rin Tin Tin that breeders crushed his hind legs and froze him permanently into the statuesque pose that everyone knew and loved. Lassie go home. Perhaps to distract from the dog's wolfish demeanor and Nazi ties, and to make him look more like a war hero, front legs were left straight, as though planted firmly on a rock like a sentry. Hind legs were bent and lowered unnaturally to the ground, which produced a dragging effect when he tried to walk but kept the body in this inclined position. The ultimate effect was that of a dog gazing out over some imaginary valley below. Audiences continue to expect this pose today, even though keeping it causes endless agony to the dog himself. The iconic stance of Rin Tin Tin played no small role in giving the German shepherd this crippling deformity of the hind legs.

The German shepherd, or "frog dog," recently made a comeback in New York City, where he was painted in stars-and-stripes and hauled out as a statue of a search-and-rescue dog surveying the crater of 9/11 in exactly the same pose, complete with rock. But dog show people aren't alone in overdramatizing for appearance. Men who have employed dogs for more traditional purposes, such as hunting or tracking, are also sometimes guilty of stretching the truth on the usefulness of certain exaggerated features. The long and droopy cartoon ears on the bloodhound, for example, which hunters still insist are needed to somehow trap a scent securely from a passing breeze, are likely not as indispensible as we've been led to believe. "Consider this," says hunting writer Patrick Burns. "Most professional Search and Rescue dogs, where human life is in the swing, are not Bloodhounds or any other type of long-eared 'wrinkle beast'—they are German Shepherds or Retrievers, Malinois or Border Collies."[8]

The fancy treats dogs as works of art or entertainment. Flesh and bone are sculpted in surprising and scintillating ways, esthetically pleasing to some people but never intended by nature.

Cracking the whip at the helm of creation like a ringmaster, changing the outward forms of the animal kingdom at will—this is the work of fanciful minds who, for all their imagination, still insist on predictable, assembly-line perfection. Not only are some cookie-cutter dogs packaged to look as unlike heinous wolves as possible, they're often not allowed to look like dogs, either.

"Don't let us turn them into dogs," wrote a Pekingese fancier in the 1930s when these queer little bug-eyed beings were the darlings of high society. Let them have butterfly ears, cat tails, monkey faces—let them be anything but those dirty mongrels that roam the streets, picking through garbage, and acting rudely toward their lion-coated superiors. Give them, instead, "grotesquely enormous eyes, like some weird Chinese monster of another world."[9] Let them be anything, so long as they're not dogs. Until very recently, when fanciers were confronted with irrefutable evidence of a dog's shady past and his true relationship to the wolf, it was still possible to imagine all sorts of stories. Family trees could sprout from any crack and grow in all directions. The more reasonable theories held that if a dog was not descended from a wolf, then he likely came from the fox, coyote, or jackal, or some combination of the three, which would still be less odious than pure *Canis lupus*. Over the centuries, other animals would be added to the menagerie. Dogs would be expected to mimic them like multiple personalities.

As we've seen, it was widely believed that dogs had mated with different species to give them their wide variety of outward forms. Apparently, they'd been delivered undiluted from God in biblical times and must have interbred with bears at some point to become the larger breeds and crossed with foxes to become smaller dogs of the terrier type. One pre-Linnaean treatise, Topsell's seventeenth-century bestiary, *The History of Four-Footed Beasts*, discussed real animals side-by-side with unicorns, dragons, sphinxes, and satyrs.

The entire animal kingdom has been mixed and matched, as it was in ancient times when beasts were imagined in the most unlikely combinations. Gorgons in Greek mythology were believed to have wings of gold, brass claws, boar tusks, and serpent skin and fangs. Chimeras had fire-breathing lioness heads, goat heads, or snake heads. Hindu Garudas were both man and bird. Ganeshas had elephant heads and human bodies. Indian Buddhist lions had canine heads. Pegasus was a winged horse. Cerberus was a dog with three heads that worked in unison, like my terrier trio, to guard the gates of Hades. Prior to modern classification based on the more plausible theory of evolution, the sky was the limit and people had ample room for wild imaginings. "There is a four-footed beast called the sea-wolf," Topsell explained to bedazzled readers who hadn't traveled far from home. "This beast lives both on sea and land."[10] So-called "sea-dogs" appeared as heraldic symbols for centuries, like the strange pair of canine hybrids with fish scales on their backs seen on the Stourton family crest from 1790.[11] "The Arcadian dogs are said to be generated of lions," Topsell also recounted in his bestiary, which included many monstrous mixes.[12] "The dogs of India are conceived by tigers, for the Indians will take divers females or bitches and fasten them to trees in woods where tigers abide."[13] Similarly, on mastiffs, Caius wrote, "They are sayd to have their generation of the violent Lion."[14] Over four centuries later, Lloyd suggested this legend of a cat-dog was still alive and well by describing the Staffordshire terrier as having "tiger-like muscles, with the prowess of a lion."[15] Bulldogs, the Staffordshire's cousins, have been admired for heads that resemble either tigers or lions, depending on the observer. Frightening as the thought may be, ancient myths have influenced the way we see dogs and the way we force them to breed true to form. Fact merges with legend, and separating the two, at this late date, can be quite difficult. That tall tale from the early nineteenth century about the bulldog having his paws sawed off during a baiting session may, in fact, be traceable to some forgotten belief in tiger-dogs.

"Thus come these valorous dogs," Topsell explained, "which retain the shape and proportion of their mother." Cats crossed with canines were believed to be powerhouses and champion fighting dogs to owe their strength of body and character to the feline half. Alexander the Great himself, according to Topsell, who recounted the legend, was impressed by these unions and became an avid arranger of matches with tiger-dogs "to try what virtue was contained in so great a body." Perhaps mastiffs, these champions were set against bears and boars, it was said, and finally a lion, the most powerful beast—the *king* of beasts—in the royal menagerie. To Alexander's amazement, even the supreme predator was no match for the tiger-dog, which latched onto the lion's snout—as a bulldog might have seized a bull—and wouldn't release despite whipping and prodding. Several strong men failed to loosen the tiger-dog's grip, so the legend continued, and Alexander ordered them to cut off his tail but with no effect. A leg was severed, then another, and another, until "the trunk of his body fell to the ground" with the tiger-dog's mouth still attached to the lion's snout. Even after decapitation, "the bodiless head still hung fast to the lion's jaws." What a performance! "The King was wonderfully moved and sorrowfully repented his rashness in destroying a beast of so noble spirit, which could not be daunted with the presence of the king of beasts."[16]

Lions, tigers, and bears—any animal was nobler than the lowly wolf. We ought to know better today when a species is defined as an animal that mates with others of its kind to produce fertile offspring, as dogs and wolves are still very capable of doing. Yet we can't seem to shake our habit of expecting dogs to be something more. This age-old tradition of seeing canines as composites of other species is stuck somewhere deep inside our brains. Any number of impossible unions are drawn into the fancy's fantasies. Any species is fair game. Much of the animal kingdom has been pickled and preserved in the literature and, more importantly, in the breed standards, the very recipes that still determine how pets are bred to look. Breeds like the collie are, indeed, shaped into alligator-goats, and this is just the tip of the unicorn's horn. Myth has become reality. Shar-peis and chow chows are produced in "bear coat." Pugs are available in "fawn." The Catahoula Leopard Dog is known for its feline spots, and bulldogs are expected to have "tiger-like shortness of the head" and keep their famous bullish stance.[17]

Sick or strange as it may seem to make one species look like others, a recurrent theme provides a partial explanation: an animal is often confused with its enemies. Perhaps dogs are wearing bits and pieces of other creatures as trophies of war or coats of arms. This might be said of any breed that sports a tawny cape resembling a lion's. Rhodesian ridgebacks, also known as "African lion hounds," have coats in a leonine shade, and their body shape has often been seen through a lion lens. Marco Polo is popularly quoted as saying the Tibetan mastiff was as "tall as a donkey with a voice as powerful as a lion." The short-haired mastiff wears what the fancy still calls a "tiger head." The long-haired version has a "lion head."

Laboratory experiments gone bad, sideshow freaks, fantastic creatures born of poetic comparisons, perhaps on the island of Doctor Moreau, today's official breeds are odd assemblages of so many bits and pieces. While Victorian zookeepers were busy crossing lions with tigers and horses with zebras, and domestic interiors featured elephant feet as umbrella stands and goats' heads as lamps, the dog fancy was mixing and matching species in styles that are still very much with us today. Stitched together with the parts of other animals, purebred dogs aren't treated so much as living, breathing, sentient beings as they are crafted to be like furniture or decorative objects. Many a gilded lion's paw has been attached to a chair and table. Rhinoceros horns and deer hooves have managed to find their ways onto settees, divans, and chandeliers. *Objets* have been decorated with fish scales, dolphin heads, and bird beaks. Who hasn't heard of a "claw-foot" bathtub or a "wing-back" chair?

Dogs have been designed in precisely the same way. Fur is called "feather" and any extra is "furnishing" in the show ring—or is it a show*room*? The longer growth on bellies of setters, long-haired pointers, cocker spaniels, and other breeds is called "fringe," and ears are known as "leather." When discussing bone structure, the customary term is "timber," and excess flesh is "lumber." Several dwarf breeds with a deformity called achondroplasia are said to have "benched" or "Queen Anne" legs. Bulldogs and collies are done in "tortoise shell," perhaps to make them look like inlaid snuffboxes. Labradors, boxers, cocker spaniels, Gordon setters, and others are expected to have "chiseled" heads. Greyhounds, on the other hand (or foot), have long been admired for their "snake" heads and "drake" necks. Shar-peis have "hippopotamus" heads, while those on papillons and Pekingeses are made to resemble "butterflies"—not to be confused with the "butterfly" nose featuring a patchy coloration that was "decidedly objectionable" to the Bulldog Club of America in 1914. A spotted snout is also grounds for disqualification for the Labrador retriever, though he is expected to have an "otter" tail. Queen Elizabeth's corgis don't look anything like their working ancestors, with the faux "fox" heads sewn on in recent years, and other breeds have "bull" necks, "ewe" necks, "goose" necks, and "pig" mouths. Long-haired strains of certain breeds have "bear coat" and shorter versions wear "horse coat." Poodles are groomed in a number of styles including "fox," "lamb," "lion," and "Teddy bear."

The very term "pedigree" comes from another animal, because a family tree resembles a crane's foot, or *pied de grue*. But whether cannibalized canines are works of fine art or butchered messes that look kind of creepy, it's difficult to deny that they're inbred, groomed, and mutilated to look like mythical beings. Dogs are given the same decorative flourishes as inanimate objects manufactured for esthetic effects. Humans have historically seen nonhuman animals as reflections of themselves, like the figures on heraldic shields or the logos for the Lions Club, the Elks Club, the Loyal Order of Moose, or the Mickey Mouse Club. From among the many creatures we've chosen to mirror ourselves, certain themes recur more often than others. Added to the schizophrenic circus is one of the lion's few contenders among the "noble" animals, the horse with its known ties to equestrian classes. Greyhounds, Italian greyhounds, Afghans, borzois, whippets, wolfhounds, and the like are valued for their equine form. Terms for dog anatomy in the ring are often borrowed from the horsey set, and one hoity-toity strain of foxhound is said to wear a "saddle mark" upon its back.

In the fancy's unending quest for the perfect pet, more often than not the focus has been on individual parts rather than the whole. Animals, vegetation, dinnerware, rare jewels—there's no limit to what can be done. Chow chows, for example, are said to have "diamond" eyes (due to turned-in eyelids, often requiring surgery).[18] Ears and tails figure prominently in the standards and can be a breed's defining characteristics. The Pembroke Welsh corgi has "small, catlike ears," while those on the Frenchie, as we've seen, must be "bat" and not "rose." "Tulip" ears are allowed on some breeds, cocker spaniels were once required to have theirs "vine-shaped," and "trowel" ears complete the allegory of an English country garden. Fox terriers are made with "button" ears that are semi-prick. Ears that stand completely erect are more wolf-like, and some people prefer them cute and floppy. Breeders in the nineteenth century tried to package limp ears as a sign of trainability and loyalty, though upright ears might have served dogs better for the hunt. Cropped Doberman pinschers still manage to intimidate man and dog alike with their devilish horns. A "pit bull" with ears sculpted by a razor inspires pedestrians to take the other side of the street. But if a Boston terrier, his civilized cousin, doesn't have ears erect, he stands to be corrected. For ears not "prick" enough, blowing a horn in the show ring has been another way to get their attention.

This question of mutilating the ears to cancel the effects of breeding or domestication—using a knife to restore a more feral effect and create a more natural-looking dog—remains a subject of bitter debate in the dog world. The British fancy banned cropping early on when the monarchy declared that no dog could compete in such an altered state. Unless a breed was born with upward ears, it couldn't have them. Sir Edwin Landseer, the great dog painter, refused commissions from barbarians who'd butchered their animals in this way. The distinction between "prick" as opposed to "drop" ears is mainly an esthetic matter now, though you wouldn't think so to hear people still defending the archaic custom of cropping. Shorter ears were once a practical matter for fighting dogs because they gave an opponent less occasion to grab and tear. Whether they were worn in the pit or on the battlefield, long ears were liabilities. "We do not, however," Thomas Bewick wrote in 1790, "admire the cruel practice of depriving the poor animal of its ears, in order to encrease its beauty."[19] Animal fighting has been illegal in most Western countries for many years now, and today's war dogs tend to be used as scouts, sentries, trackers, and explosive detectors, not as fighters. Still the attachment to tailored ears has remained strong in pets and show dogs remade for looks alone. A group of nostalgic purists in the nineteenth century appeared before a British judge to argue that, although the mastiff could no longer legally fight lions, tigers, or bulls, his life still depended on having ears so carved up that they might be served as chateaubriand.

Tails are attached to the less noble end of the beast, where they've caused endless controversy. It is universally accepted that the greyhound must have "a tayle lyke a ratte."[20] But whether these extremities should fall naturally on other breeds, or be shortened to stand erect like a finial on a china cabinet, is open to debate. Over the centuries, there have been many theories on stubby tails. "When wolves are in danger of being taken by hunters," Topsell explained in 1607, "they bite off the tip of their tails."[21] There was also a medieval theory used to justify the practice of docking. In yet another confusion of the species, it was widely believed—owing to a misunderstanding inherited from the Romans—that the tail had to be cut off for health reasons, because when it was removed, long, sinewy strands resembling "worms" had been found.[22] What better way to deworm a dog than to cut off its tail? Docking was seen as the best way to battle these parasites, though anyone today ought to know that a tail is not a worm but very much a part of the dog, something to which he's grown attached.

Still the esthetic preference for stubbiness has been defended on practical grounds. A long tail on a spaniel, or any other dog that hunts low to the earth in heavy brush, might be torn and infected, defenders argue. So they cut it off. Too much tail could blow a dog's cover as it rises from tall grass, alerting the birds to his approach. So they cut it off, even from dogs never destined to hunt. Small terriers are said to need diminutive stumps to burrow into fox and badger holes without becoming stuck like Winnie the Pooh in the honey tree. The idea is to leave just enough of a handle for the hunters to grip and pull the dog out before he's torn to ribbons. So they cut it off, from hunters and house pets alike. Along similar "practical" lines, a tax on dogs in Norman England no doubt played a role in our present-day taste for sawing them at one end.

The wording of the law was such that an owner's responsibility was to pay only by the number of tails the tax collector counted—a rule not unlike the one imposed on New York hot-dog vendors, who must pay their suppliers, not by the number of dogs left at the end of the day but by how many buns.

Interestingly enough, old English game laws once required the tails of commoners' dogs, the usual suspects for poaching, to be cut short, the intention being to *disable* them from hunting. However the question of docking is sliced, depriving animals of body parts has typically not been for their own benefit. On land, tails are used for balance. This is why dogs have them. In the water, a tail doesn't operate so much as a ship's "stern," a term used in the fancy, as it serves as rudder. On land or at sea, a Labrador retriever needs his "otter" tail no less than an otter does. Mutilating dogs was once defended for the benefit of humankind, though today this archaic custom is purely for show. A rugged-hunter-turned-lapdog doesn't require surgery to sprawl across a living room sofa. Nor does he need a historically accurate behind to be seen in public. Fanciers want to preserve the pointless custom of docking certain breeds on the pretense that long tails are easily bloodied and broken, when all they really need to do is be more careful when slamming doors. These same fanciers defend the practice of breeding unnaturally long ears on golden retrievers and cocker spaniels, even though these are prone to infections, proving that at the end of the day their true concerns are esthetic and not practical.

Dog snobbery has little to do with practical uses of our long-time companions and lots to do with memorizing the proper terminology, like those breed connoisseurs on the sidewalk, to show a level of refinement superior to the uninitiated. The essence of the French bulldog was once compared to "the exquisite quality of Bordeaux, the glorious vigour of Burgundy, the exhilarating sparkle of champagne with the culminating satisfaction of an 'eau de vie' of purest Cognac."[23] The Frenchie and other breeds such as the so-called Coton de Tuléar actually come in a shade called "champagne." Similarly, as buzzwords go, the logo chosen for the Westminster Kennel Club in the 1870s was the profile of a champion pointer imported from England deemed to have a perfect head and a coat in "lemon and white," an expression still in use today. "Orange" can be found within the spaniel spectrum. The "rich chestnut" patch of color on the forehead of the Cavalier is a noble birthmark known as the "Blenheim spot," referring to both a famous battle and an English castle. Among other tasteful expressions dog enthusiasts should have under their belts is "Belvoir tan," sported only by hounds in a hunt of the highest caliber.

After lemon and orange, "apricot" is another favorite flavor of dog, as in the "apricot poodle." Ladies of leisure used to having high tea might prefer their poodles in "teacup" size. Chow chows come in "cream" and "cinnamon." Many breeds are "dish-faced," the Old English sheepdog was once said to have a "china eye," and some breeds have "tea-pot" tails.[24] "Blue" is a Wedgwood favorite but utterly foreign to mammals. Nonetheless, stare long enough and you can almost see it in the coats of chows, Australian cattle dogs, Kerry Blues, and aristocratic Great Danes that come in "pure steel blue." The color possibilities are endless. *The Encyclopedia of the Dog*, an important etiquette manual for the upwardly mobile, displays the coats allowed for each breed in small rectangles like fabric swatches from a J. Crew catalog. French bulldogs can be ordered in fawn, pied, red-brindle, or black brindle. Pugs come in silver, apricot/fawn, and basic black.[25] Chessies are available in "deadgrass," and Wheatons resemble rolling fields of the purest grain. Shar-peis come in "sand," since one of the main attractions to those bountiful waves of infected, rotting skin has been their resemblance to a rolling desert landscape. A breed can be "harlequin," "particolored," or "flowered coat," so long as its standard allows, or even "piebald," like fancy chickens, horses, and pigs once were.

"Yellow" Labs became socially accepted when the Duke of Windsor showed a penchant for a weave quite rare at the time. "Dark chocolate" is a newer term—what child would want a "liver" Lab? The age-old "black-and-tan" still applies to several breeds, a classic two-tone coat appealing to experts who've mastered the art of wine snobbery and graduated to beer. "Mouse" is within the tasteful range for the Weimaraner, "a snob sporting dog," Roger Caras recalled, "developed and jealously guarded by the one of the biggest collection of snobs the dog world has ever seen."[26] Then there are the vizslas, Weimaraners of a different color, described by a dog trainer friend of mine as "dumb as they are red."[27]

Fruits and spices, tulips and roses, alligators and goats, horses and hippopotami, bulls and bears, bats and mice—by far the most common disguise for dogs is, if we are to believe the Saturday morning cartoons, their polar opposite. The term "cat foot" appears on the AKC's website at least 127 times. The word "lion" occurs some 401 times and, in the vast majority of cases, refers to dogs rather than anything they might chase if given the opportunity. This odd habit of making dogs look like cats, or anything else for that matter, predates the standards and the modern fancy itself. Canines recalling the king of the jungle were around long before Britons adopted the lion as a symbol of their pride, or Romans and Chinese were grooming their lapdogs to look like lions. The English idea that lions were noble likely came from their Norman invaders, who'd borrowed this from the Byzantines, who in turn had been inspired by the Greeks. A look at the endless quest for a feline form reveals, once again, not only a tendency to point out surprising similarities between different animals, but a conscious effort to turn these observations into idealized "points" in the breed standards that determine how dogs must, in fact, be made to look. In one of many species mergers, a kind of feline fetish has developed, and this has affected dogs deeply.

Mythical lion dogs of China and Japan called "Foo Dogs" and "Shishi dogs" no doubt played a role in making the ideal so sought after. Whenever the owner of a Lhasa apso, shih tzu, or some similar breed praises a pet for its catlike aloofness, or for un-doglike habits like climbing on backs of chairs and lounging in windows, the ancient belief in feline-canine fusions rears its hybrid head. The single-most far-reaching distinction made in today's breed standards, the detail most likely to qualify or disqualify canine contestants in the ring, is whether the feet are of the cat or hare variety. Dozens of breeds are dissected in this way. Tibetan mastiffs, Shetland sheepdogs, pugs, coonhounds, and Chihuahuas—these and many more are judged by the degree their feet resemble a cat's or a hare's. The Dogue de Bordeaux "trots like a lion," and the proper footwear for the golden, a lion among lions, should go without saying.

"No living thing is capable of expressing in its face and bearing so much contempt for the world at large," explained the London *Times* about the snooty appeal of the Pekingese or "lion dog of Peking" in 1914.[28] The taste for dogs done in this high-class style is so old and widespread that it's difficult to know where to begin. For untold ages, breeders have strived to make dogs resemble the beast royale. The pug was once known as the "hairless lion dog." The chow chow, says the AKC, is a "lion-like, regal breed" with its ample mane and catlike aloofness.[29] The Tibetan spaniel has been billed as "the dog for cat people."[30] Closer to home, the Boston terrier looks no less feline. Papillons, Cavaliers, Japanese Chins, and long-haired Chihuahuas have been deliberately bred to look like little lions. "Shih tzu" literally means "lion dog." Löwchen means "little lion dog" or *petit chien lion*. The Maltese was once known as "the little lion dog of France," and a breed that was neither lion nor French—and probably not even Maltese—was first listed in the United States as the "Maltese Lion Dog" in 1877. The Lhasa apso was once known as "the barking lion sentinel dog."

A closer look reveals a long list of breeds, some that even professional fanciers don't suspect, clearly lionized in one way or another. The early twentieth century saw a short-lived fad for something called a "Danish Lion Dog"—perhaps a Great Dane? On American Eskimo dogs "the coat is thicker and longer around the neck and chest, forming a lion-like ruff," reads the AKC standard.[31] Setters have a "cat-like crouching attitude," according to a famous breeder.[32] "The Leonberger was originally bred to resemble a lion," explains that breed's ultimate purpose.[33] Winnie the French bulldog, with her domed skull, arched back, and round paws, would look more catlike still if only her ears were "correct." While smaller dogs are common candidates for lionization, any breeds valued for their feline appearance or demeanor should be considered "lion dogs." One need only look at old artworks to see hunting and war dogs traditionally portrayed with ferocious grins, lionlike feet, claws and teeth, and powerful tails.[34] Breeds with any of these traits, including compressed faces, strong jaws, abundant wrinkles, manelike hair with golden, tawny, or reddish coloring—or the overblown coats on golden retrievers—are born from the same tradition of making animals look like something they're not. No other species has played a larger part in this metamorphosis than the lion, so highly prized that the fetching price for the world's most expensive dog to date—sold in 2014 to a Chinese property developer scrambling for status symbols—was the $1.9 million gladly paid for a very lionlike Tibetan mastiff puppy.[35]

Dogs that aren't inbred for some feline effect are altered cosmetically. The Löwchen's look is due more to his creepy hairdo—called a "Löwchen clip"—than how he came out of the womb. Tibetan terriers, terriers only in name, are groomed to the same end. The bichon frise has a mane sculpted in the lion style that became fashionable in Italy during the fourteenth century, and many breeds are traditionally shown with a lion clip. One mastiff was actually reshaped and passed off as a lion by a Chinese zookeeper in 2013, until it barked and gave itself away![36] A royal crown and a lion's pride—whether having a mane makes these pets look noble, or ridiculous, is a matter of opinion. Topsell explained why this particular garb could be so revered in the animal kingdom. "The hair of some of them," he wrote describing, not lion-dogs but real, honest-to-goodness lions, "is curled, and some of them have long, shaggy, thin hair, not standing upright but falling flat, longer before and shorter behind." This could easily be the description of a well-groomed Löwchen. "And although the curling of the hair is a token of sluggish timidity, yet if the hair is long and curled at the top only, this portends abundant animosity."[37]

The formula for a top-heavy aristocrat with a seventies man-perm could also describe a poodle. Viewed as effeminate today, thanks to the outlandish bouffant it often sports, this breed was originally a rugged and respected hunter. Poodle-like dogs have been around for a long time. As seen in engravings, they once wore thick, curly, but shapeless coats, helpful when hunting birds in marshlands and without all the sculpting that's done today. The over-the-top afros and funny pompoms sculpted around legs and hindquarters *supposedly* to keep vital parts warm hardly just happened to fit the same lion mold as so many other dogs throughout history, and were added for reasons at least partly esthetic. Similarly, the Portuguese water dog, a White House resident during the Obama administration, is often recast as the Lion King and ends up looking like one of those enormous topiary bushes at the entrance to Disneyland. Any breed with a lion clip becomes a kind of cartoon animal. As with ear cropping and tail docking, the elaborate and intricate "practical" reasons supplied for breeding, mutilating, or grooming animals should be treated with skepticism. In light of the overwhelming evidence, a more plausible explanation would be that a good many dogs have been forced over the centuries to look unreal or exotic, like other species altogether, or anything else in the whole wide world, so long as they don't look like wolves—and very often not like dogs, either.[38]

CHAPTER SIX

THE MIDAS TOUCH

Unseasoned dog walkers would have turned away and gone on straight to their next gig rather than confront the snarly forces behind that door. Sight unseen, inside the unlit apartment were two bellicose Boston terriers, sisters with the endearing names of Marge and Eunice, but whose behavior was anything but cute at the moment. It didn't take a dog whisperer to guess they were at each other's throats.

Fighting dogs can be intimidating to anyone who doesn't know how to handle them, and being shielded by a thin piece of steel and a series of expensive locks is a small comfort. Unable to witness the bared teeth and shooting blood, the squeamish would still be daunted by the muffled sound of high-pitched screams, a pretty good sign that fur and flesh are being torn. The frenzied scratching of paws on hardwood floors, the gnashing of teeth and locking of jaws, and the occasional thud of two bodies united in rage suggest two animals engaged in mortal combat. This was a situation I encountered daily. The deal was to brace myself and intervene as quickly as possible, get through that door, grab those bickering Bostons, and pull them apart before their scheduled walk turned into an emergency visit to the vet around the corner with a crimson trail along the way. Taking good care of Marge and Eunice was about more than letting two dogs relieve their bladders: it was a matter of damage control.

What was all the fighting about? The whole fiasco was pointless really, which didn't stop it from happening every day. Unnatural aggression is one of the many side effects of inbreeding in fighting dogs, which the ancestors of Marge and Eunice were. These weren't "bad" dogs, just badly programmed. Tightly wound terriers like these tend to respond mechanically, like Pavlov's dogs, to what sets them off, with limited thinking between stimulus and response, which is why they can be such ruthless, even foolhardy hunters. Many other small terriers—the only true terriers according to some hunters—were designed to insinuate themselves into fox holes and not mind having their faces torn off once they hit pay dirt. Is that a sign of intelligence? Electronic-locator collars are standard equipment, so when they bury themselves alive, as they often do, they can be found and dug up before it's too late. Such a lack of forethought is a far cry from the way wolves methodically stalk their prey, sometimes for days, before the pack moves in for a kill. Nature rewards those who avoid injury—and as long as no one's starving, what's the hurry? Wolves may not even finish eating right away, but sometimes dance and play around their victims, which is more in line with human table manners than stuffing one's face and losing it in the process.

The pedigreed pair of Boston terriers were no credit to their ancestors. The slightest jingle of my keychain was enough to catapult them into a bloody rampage against what they knew not, a senseless diurnal fury that was tough to contain. I'd been nipped a few times while trying to protect them from themselves, though none of their anger was directed at me. Having known the frisky, snorting sisters with their weird, alien-antenna ears for years, I'd seen their sweeter side. These spirited spitfires were all over each other because they loved me *too* much. Competing for my affection, before I could cross the threshold and dispense that precious commodity, was no different from the way more balanced dogs might fight over other vital resources, like food or water—flattering for me, and good business for the vet, but unsuitable for apartment living.

Marge and Eunice's mom and dad, away all day in their respective office cubicles, were painfully aware of their dogs' slight behavior problem. "The girls," as they called them, put on the exact same performance each time they too tried to enter. These weren't supposed to be guard dogs. On the contrary, one of the original selling points for the breed was the claim that it wouldn't bark too much around the house (the American Kennel Club never said anything about them trying to kill each other if someone came to the door). Marge and Eunice were an overly enthused welcoming committee. The prospect of a visitor was simply too exciting for them to handle with their inbred temperaments and exaggerated under-bites, and corrective surgery wasn't very promising. Several years prior to my arrival that day, a trainer had been hired to take some business away from the vet. But my clients couldn't bring themselves to take his professional advice and keep these littermates, together since birth, in separate rooms all day waiting, first for me to come and walk them, then for their mom and dad to return in the evening. Forcing close siblings into utter and inconsolable solitude for six or eight hours at a time, they'd decided, was simply too cruel, even if it meant the girls could no longer savage each other. The trainer was promptly let go. The dogs went on ripping and gnashing for years to come, and the owners accepted this nonsense as normal for the breed. The battle resumed like clockwork when I arrived, but despite all sights and sounds to the contrary, and no matter what the neighbors down the hall might have thought, these dogs absolutely worshipped each other. Ears were shredded and tails abridged, but Marge and Eunice always reunited after a hard day of fighting. Curled up at the foot of the parental bed, they spent hours licking each other's wounds and celebrating their mutual love—tough love, but love just the same.

I hurried to unlock that door and burst into the dark apartment grabbing them by their matching pink rhinestone collars. Once their wild rage had all but evanesced, Marge and Eunice were left standing dumbly, with no idea of what they had been fighting about. I cautiously loosened my grip, gauging where their heads were before setting them free.

Contemplating an intricate weave of love bites as I hitched the two dogs and led them down the hall, layer upon layer of scar tissue on war-torn backs of black and white, I had before me a breed not much older than a century. Difficult to believe, the strange creature we've come to call a Boston terrier was once the all-American dog, the most popular breed in the nation—that is, until it was bumped for the German shepherd, who had to move over for the cocker spaniel, who conceded to the beagle, superseded by the poodle, who then got ousted so the cocker spaniel could enjoy another moment in the sun before being demoted by the Labrador retriever, who reigns supremely in homes across the country. The Boston's rise and fall shows how radically pet preferences and the precise ways we expect dogs to look change for no apparent reason, at least no good one, like any other passing fashion. The Boston no longer enjoys the honor of being on the AKC's list of top ten for registrations, though the breed is showing signs of new life. Dethroned and living in marginality since the 1930s, this dog returned as a favorite accessory again in the 2000s. The breed is said to be a blend of virile English bulldog softened with hues of the Frenchie and highlighted with flashy accents of the sporty but sterile and deafness-prone English white terrier (now extinct, for obvious reasons).

The Boston terrier made its debut in the 1890s as the "American gentleman" breed, referring to both the owner *and* the dog.

This was the AKC's gimmick for promoting its new invention. Here was the club's own signature model of nonmongrel, a type that it took a direct role in developing and marketing for a rapidly expanding pedigree dog market. The Boston has been billed as the well-dressed gentleman dog for over a century, and the question of how the fancy managed to pull the wool over the eyes of canine consumers is worthy of an entire book. "Gentle," the AKC's famous dog man Freeman Lloyd once wrote, describing not Bostons but aristocratic greyhounds and thoroughbred horses, was "a name reserved in a chivalrous age to noble actions and good blood."[1] Thinking of animals, whatever their breeds, as aristocratic took no shorter a stretch of the imagination than believing in social registers and family trees, which Lloyd obviously did. A common variation on "American gentleman" was "Black Satin Gentleman," more to the point, since the breed was chronically inbred to wear a coat resembling a tuxedo, regardless of a dog's gender.

The Boston terrier was the ultimate confusion of species: a dog tailored to look like a human being. The coat, as we've already seen, is the main attraction on pedigree pooches, the most likely reason for choosing one breed over another. Could there have been a more fitting costume for the American gentleman breed than evening wear? Set against this elegant attire, the bespoke Boston's facial expression was "indescribably human," according to one authority,[2] a remark that appealed to prospective pet buyers in search of something more than a run-of-the-mill mutt to represent their households. Getting the dog to look this way wasn't easy, and the breeders resorted to some colorful extremes to give the Boston the right cut. As we've likewise learned, this was not the first Procrustean move made against our best friends.

For centuries, dogs had been inbred, groomed, and mutilated for any combination of distinctive looks. They'd been assembled ad hoc as patchworks of body parts with coats, legs, tails, necks, heads, and ears inspired by trophy lions, tigers, bears, birds, snakes, hippopotami, and the rest of the royal menagerie. They'd been born Crazy-Glued to vegetation and inanimate objects—ears made to look like roses, vines, ship sails, and buttons, tails resembling chrysanthemums, eyes like almonds, and everything short of having silver spoons in their mouths.

Dogs picked up a number of items along their way to our hearts, but few people today realize just how much the wolf lost when he moved into the house of *Homo status conscious* and became what one evolutionary biologist calls "*Canis over-familiaris.*"[3] A domestic dog's ability to communicate with others of its kind, for example, was impaired without those subtle variations in coat coloring added by nature to enhance body language. Ridiculously plush, curly, or monochromatic fur—or gaudy markings that signaled spending power—flat and immobile faces, inexpressive eyes, glaring teeth, goofy long ears, and stubby or "screw" tails all severely limited what dogs could "say." Refashioning these poor animals to the point of disability would make it difficult for them to state their intentions to each other, resulting in misunderstanding, fear, and the sort of unnatural aggression that Marge and Eunice displayed daily with their frozen faces and bug eyes. The wolf was stripped of his very practical attire when dogs were designed to signify something altogether different: their owners' wealth and social standing.

This custom of forcing dogs to bear the symbols of our pride, this habit of dressing a wolf in man's clothing, has a long history. The human form had also figured into the dog's anatomy by the 1890s, and the Boston's black-and-white coat was hardly the first attempt to impose a dress code on unwitting status symbols. Nor would it be the last. Naturally spotted or piebald coats distinguished early canine landraces from their lupine ancestors, but long before the standardized breed called a "Dalmatian" was invented, upper classes inbred spotted dogs to wear flecked ermine robes like their patrons, or the trimming on royal crowns. The modern fancy preserves the anachronism in Dalmatians, knowing very well that the look is responsible for congenital deafness in the breed, and that severe depigmentation in animals is linked to nervousness, not to mention the frenzied responses a loud pattern elicits from other dogs.[4]

More recently, in the 1950s, the Duke of Windsor tried to pin the "gentleman" title onto his prize-winning pugs by masquerading them in starched white shirt collars and bowties they wore to formal events.[5] The collars were detachable from the pugs and no harm was done, but the "shirt" was actually woven onto the Boston terrier. This white portion of a Boston's markings is due to "Irish spotting," a not unusual pattern for many breeds and not itself necessarily linked to congenital deafness. But like the white areas on a Dalmatian's spot-blighted ermine coat, too much "shirt" is a sign of trouble, and even Bostons born with more "perfect" markings are deafness-prone.[6] (Marge and Eunice were spared this defect, luckily or unluckily, depending on how well their walker handled those doorway dramas.)

An animal skin on a human back raises enough sidewalk protest these days. Seeing the opposite on a Boston terrier should raise as many eyebrows. Yet it was this dog's unusual coat that saved the breed from oblivion on the rag heap of threadbare, no-label mongrels. After a grueling debate in the 1890s over whether to allow the "gentleman" into the registry and baptize him a "purebred," the powers-that-were decided at the eleventh hour to pass the two-toned tyke through the door and into the pantheon. The Boston's markings were the deal breaker. Despite the not infrequent deafness handicap, that familiar coat is the very item that established the dog as a breed apart, the Boston's original claim to distinction.

Once again, it all comes back to humans. "Black tie" was conceived, not by a dog breeder but by a Savile Row tailor in the 1880s. His Royal Majesty the Prince of Wales had new clothes, and word traveled across the Atlantic to a group of dapper dudes residing in a place called Tuxedo Park, an early gated community and gathering place for Anglophiles calling themselves "The Bluebloods." From that point forward, any man pretending to the title of "gentleman" would need to dress the part. Thus, the name "tuxedo," which soon stuck as far as Boston, and the dog born wearing one.

Anything that made upwardly mobile Americans look lordly was alright by them. The English still enjoyed the upper hand at the end of the nineteenth century. Cultural subservience was a way of life for card-carrying members of America's upper crust who could afford the best English clothes but were painfully aware that they could have all the money in the world and still not measure up. Men could disguise themselves as gentlemen, but without *breeding*, they didn't hold a candle to their English masters. Buying pedigree dogs was one way to get some. While freshly minted moguls self-helped with etiquette manuals and season tickets to the opera, sent their children to British-style boarding schools, and perfected their wardrobes and accents along foreign lines, tapping into their social insecurity was like shooting fish in a barrel for the AKC. New money was visibly nervous. Convincing it that a "purebred" dog with a traceable bloodline was somehow superior to a mongrel with no past was not very difficult.

But like the self-styled American gentleman who felt a bit awkward in his newly tailored suit, the AKC was still learning its craft. The Crufts dog show, the most prestigious of many competitions held in England each year, was not as old as Westminster with its English-sounding name, but was already a role model for grand American events of this kind. The AKC itself was modeled after the English Kennel Club, though it could boast of no royals on its board of directors. Most of the breeds in American dog shows, moreover, had been either invented or "improved" by the British. They came over on steamships with their standards ready-made, and native fanciers were only too eager to continue improving upon them at home. Breeders, breed clubs, the AKC, and its show-ring judges followed the old recipes faithfully because they still lacked the self-confidence to decide what, exactly, a champion looked like without the expert advice of foreigners. Owning an English breed was like rubbing elbows with royalty. The downside was that dogs competing in American shows were often left at the mercy of visiting English judges whose disapproval could be devastating.

Some Americans felt they were above showing deference to the English. They decided to go that extra mile and solve their problem in a bluntly American way—they went to England and bought the store. Self-made magnates, when they weren't collecting foreign castles, monasteries, and statuary in the nineteenth century, were importing entire kennels from the British Isles, piece by piece, including staff and studs. The strategy assured that no one, not even English judges, could question their standing in the ring or out. So it was that J. P. Morgan's unassailable collies, which he extracted from deep within the hills of Scotland, gave him that added edge back home. The yachtsman of Wall Street slept soundly in the knowledge that his dogs were the finest in the land, at least until another enterprising American with the same idea imported some collies and beat old man Morgan at his own game.

England's dog fancy, America's role model, was also a product of social insecurity. The nineteenth century was an uneasy time for old ruling classes. Aristocrats in Europe and the British Isles were still smarting over the French Revolution when the first dog shows were held. Many of their relatives, after all, had been altered by Procrustean blades of another kind, and socioeconomic change was no less a threat to their way of life. The impoverishment of the old nobility, transfers of land and money to a rising commercial class, and the continual democratization of political institutions were cause for alarm to the powers-that-were. England was not spared the effects of a nonviolent revolution. Shifting status in the fashionable drawing rooms of London brought feelings of instability in 1849 and inspired the first *Who's Who*, a list of England's first families compiled to remind people who they were (or weren't). *Burke's Peerage* and *Burke's Landed Gentry* let them know exactly where they stood. Preserving the past became something of an obsession in the nineteenth century when the old ways were changing and the future was up for grabs. A rising interest in genealogy, human and canine, combined with a morbid obsession with taxidermy in the Victorian years were supported by the eugenics movement.

Across England and Europe, a dying class of impoverished or downsized nobles, often left with little but their titles and taste, was determined to keep a fragment of its former glory by salvaging the glamorous position it still held in popular imagination. It was no coincidence, for example, that a member of the short-lived line of Tweedmouth barons presented the family retriever, a later standardized version of which would be crowned "golden," to the AKC when this clan was already in decline and selling off the Rembrandts[7]—and about to leave the Scottish estate in ruins as a shrine for annual pilgrimages to hundreds of identically coated canines.[8] Property and privileges went up for auction, but nobles could at least preserve the *idea* of aristocracy and some respect for tradition by becoming the authoritative experts on "good" bloodlines. A family name could live on, if only through dogs, long after the end of the line.

Pedigree dog enthusiasts have to blush when they're reminded of the important role that aristocracy played in repackaging outmoded ideas of lineage and breeding for modern canine consumers.

Dog fancying was, in no small way, a form of crown worship. The English fancy was not more than a few years older than the American imitation, but unlike the AKC's founding fathers with names like Belmont and Mortimer, the key British figures in those early years had pedigrees stretching deep into the past. The royal imprimatur of Queen Victoria gave England's Kennel Club much of its prestige and helped establish a central authority when any would-be dude in a smock thought he could hold up his dog as a "champion." The first breed clubs often had kings, queens, princes, princesses, dukes, and duchesses serving on their boards to make sure that only animals with the proper look and the best blood—subjective ideals though these were—got through. Men like Sir Henry de Trafford, Lord Derby, and Lord Orford were prolific purveyors of breeds, many of which were "preferably called after the breeder."[9] The Kennel Club itself was ruled by the Prince of Wales and his borzois, as it is steered today with HRH Michael of Kent and his black Labs at the helm. Aristocrats were the figures whose preeminence made them the natural consultants when breed standards, the rules which still determine a dog's outward appearance, were first committed to paper. Where else could the fancy turn but to members of the old elite, who knew better than anyone how to breed "the best to get the best"? So many prototypes had been created or kept by their own ancestors and continued to reside at their enviable family palaces and estates. Overseeing a soon-to-be *closed* Stud Book was a way of guarding the door, of keeping canine bloodlines "pure," of preventing mismatings between members of unequal social stations, and of upholding standards of beauty in a world that seemed to grow uglier by the day.

"'Royalism' probably led him to own the same variety as the King," wrote Lady Wentworth in *Toy Dogs and Their Ancestors*.[10] Breeding and showing were no royal jubilee for the dogs themselves, despite the vow to "improve" them and to "further" their "interests," according to breed club charters. The whole appeal of pedigrees was as it remains today: no outsiders allowed. Animals logged into a closed Stud Book—in other words, one of those *closed* populations that account for vast numbers of congenital canine illnesses today—were, like their noble patrons, the products of incest. They were mated to their own fathers, mothers, brothers, sisters, and close cousins, a practice that continues to the present day when no new blood is allowed to contaminate the elite. For having been taken under the arm of an inbred aristocracy and its growing legions of imitators, chosen members of the new canine upper crust, not surprisingly, would suffer from crippling deformities and defects similar to those endured by royals. Breeds would develop hemophilia and a host of congenital illnesses. Such is the price of nobility.

Heritable conditions aside, all this talk of breeding must have pricked the ears of Americans aspiring to the good life and yearning for social distinctions of their own. Rather than shun the old ways and avoid unhealthy breeding practices, and despite all their talk of equal opportunity and meritocracy, they rushed to embrace the madness of the past. Millionaires were a dime a dozen in the States by the 1890s. Hordes of self-made men were scrambling to set themselves up as breeds apart, to "stabilize" their offspring, and their dog breeds, like England's old upper class. While the American fancy was busy "improving" the dogs they'd purchased abroad, society was struggling to put together its own homegrown human aristocracy and then training it to act the part. But without real royalty to decide who was better than everyone else, chaos reigned.

Thus, the need for higher authorities. Ward McAllister, a blueblood of Anglophile Southern stock, tried to shorten the list of American family names that mattered to a finite "Four Hundred." The club by that name didn't last very long, but became the symbol of the shameless elitism of these times. The exclusion movement took other forms as well. The first volume of the Social Register, for example, was published in 1886—eight years *after* America's own canine *Who's Who*, the AKC's Stud Book, first closed its doors to nonpedigrees. A number of gentlemen's clubs, modeled after ultra-elite London establishments, also opened their doors during these years, if only to close them to outsiders. The Knickerbocker Club, the University Club, the Union Club, J. P. Morgan's Metropolitan Club—and the Westminster Kennel Club, whose members gave these other clubs as home addresses when signing its charter[11]—made insiders feel special for having been admitted, and much of the appeal of "improvement" came from disapproving of others.

The Leash, one of several ultra-elite clubs that still exist in Midtown Manhattan, and so private it doesn't have a website, was founded in the 1920s "to promote interest in the thoroughbred dog and to study and apply principles of scientific breeding."[12] Besides being a speakeasy, The Leash was a sort of refuge from a changing world where anyone with a few thousand dollars might feel worthy of owning the best purebreds. Founding members included the most discriminating dog collectors and exhibitors, and ritual hunters of the highest breeding. Many were AKC directors or delegates, breeders, and show-ring judges from the days before the entire business was swamped with plebeians. Much like an English hunting resort for trans-Atlantic wealth, the old Goodwood Estate, which still caters to its clique of "like minded people"—and is home to a Ralph Lauren clothing boutique for humans and hounds, the "first European club shop"[13]—the Leash was and remains a haven for society's uppermost crust of like-minded gentlemen (and, in time, ladies).[14] Here members can feel safe applying eugenic principles of old from posh wood-paneled clubrooms lined with silver cups, leather chairs, and fox terrier friezes their ancestors enjoyed.

But American families would have to ripen before being offered medals by the *Légion d'honneur*. The cleverest way to gain a superior standing was to found a dynasty and ensure the family name irreproachable *hauteur* for generations to come. The surefire path to snootiness was a trip to England or Europe to shop for aristocratic studs to breed with heiress daughters. The strategy was not unlike importing canine champions, and by 1909, more than five hundred of these matings had been arranged. "Before long, many of the remnants of Europe's royalty, some of them exiles or wastrels, and some completely bogus," writes the author of *America's Gilded Age*, "were auctioning themselves off to the highest American bidder, and the wives of Ohio grain millionaires, Chicago slaughterhouse tycoons, and New York street railway magnates" were parading their corn-fed daughters with hefty price tags.[15] These were business arrangements plain and simple, and both sides profited. The rich Americans guaranteed themselves absolute respect at home, ensuring that their descendants would forever walk the earth wearing regal auras no one would dare to question. Their own flesh and blood got to mingle with royalty, and a coat of arms often came with the deal. The titled Englishmen, for marrying beneath themselves, got to keep the family castles that were likely inches away from public auction. They also received an added bonus. By agreeing to commingle common blood with their own, families chronically inbred for centuries received life-saving doses of hybrid vigor unavailable in their restricted social stations at home. The Americans turned their girls into ladies.

Going straight to the source was also the advisable strategy for self-improvement in the Land of Fancy, and many American dog investors wasted no time in traveling abroad. One can only imagine the thrill of victory felt by liquid Yanks who'd scoured the British Isles for founders of canine dynasties and brought them home to win trophies. A special illustrated section of an English high-society magazine called the *Strand* seems to have been detached in 1894 by one of these tuft-hunters and carried back to the States, where it currently resides in the AKC's collection. According to the insert, pedigree people were gathering in London to compare notes on their pedigree dogs. The Duchess of York's dachshund was said to be a "tiny Prince whose birth not long ago was heralded with acclaim throughout the breadth of the dominions." The Shah of Persia's stately Afghan made an impression with its high breeding, for "in his veins flows blood bluer than any other dog in the world."[16] Rich Americans didn't mind begging for similar models from the same breeders when stud shopping abroad.

Also known as Judith Neville Lytton, the author of *Toy Dogs and Their Ancestors* had some illustrious ancestors of her own. Lady Wentworth was the great granddaughter of Lord Byron the poet, and born to a family responsible for a type of toy spaniel corrupted, she said, by the modern fancy and its crass commercialism. Nobility, it seemed, was selling itself cheaply and dogs had "been 'improved' out of all beauty." Lytton saw silver cups and blue ribbons as mere trinkets for social climbers. The entire business, in her eyes, was fixed. Breeders and breed clubs, she claimed, were racketeers that had "the glitter of challenge cups and medals wherewith to dazzle," and Lytton looked upon the fancy with the sort of attitude that only a person of gentle breeding can express so disdainfully. Yet she took pity on the Americans arriving in droves on pilgrimages to pay homage at the altar of aristocracy. Unsuspecting visitors with large purses, she warned, were being duped. "It is a dealer's business to foster ignorance, and America has been taught to admire wrong types"—whatever that meant—"so that we may keep our best dogs and yet please our customers with indifferent ones." Inferior dogs—however these were defined—were being "rushed through as champions and shipped to America out of the way, where they are immediately boomed as marvelous sires and undefeated champions."[17]

Socially insecure Americans probably were being taken for the royal ride. But if the newly rich were easy prey to foreign swindlers, genuine aristocracy was no less eager to follow the transnational pet set wherever it migrated. Pedigree honors could be won on both sides of the Atlantic. The world's grandest grandees, when they weren't congregating in London and showering their borzois with champagne in the best hotels, were flocking to New York where adulation and solid gold cash prizes awaited. Upon their arrivals, the *New York Times* often commented ironically on the quaint notion of aristocracy, human and canine. But many Americans took nobility, and its dogs, quite literally when both debarked. "The general judgment is that the class of the sporting dogs is very high," the *Times* remarked on the Westminster Kennel Club show of 1902. "The Prince of Siam has signified his intention to visit the exhibition to-day, and Lord and Lady Algernon Lennox, the latter of whom is a field spaniel enthusiast, have also been invited."[18] So intimately were well-bred dogs linked to well-bred people that it was difficult to distinguish one from the other. "Rolph, a Danish boarhound, weighing 106 pounds, which is the grandson of Prince Bismarck's famous Satan," arrived in 1880. "It is entered by the Baron Carl von Tena, who has only recently arrived from Germany, and is staying at the St. Denis Hotel."[19] As in England, where impresario Charles Cruft was keenly aware of the prestige that big names lent to his events, the American fancy went to great lengths to court "society's upper crust" at home and abroad for its New York shows. Soon "the aisles were filled and the society feature of the show was scarcely secondary to the attraction in the dogs themselves," the *Times* observed with disbelief.[20] America's homegrown best and brightest, though *un*titled, were seen descending from carriages and entering "richly-dressed"[21] through the very same portal as Europe's *entitled*. Any man owning an important pedigree dog was referred to as "gentleman." Female fanciers were all "ladies." Both were announced in the papers by their full names along with a clearly displayed "of" linking them to their hometowns as though these were feudal estates. "Lizzie Adele Josslyn, of Pittsfield, Mass.," the *Times* recorded, "has entered a German mastiff named Strolch, bred by Prince Karl of Prussia, and she marks his value as 'priceless.'"[22] A certain "Mrs. Benjamin Guinness of Douglaston, L.I." had a prize Peke named "Pekin Pu Tay II"[23] that conjured up memories of the Imperial Palace. The redoubtable "Miss May Bird of Hempstead" owned wolfhounds, as did the czar of Russia, and "Mr. and Mrs. Champion of Staten Island" possessed *champion* dogs that were described with an amusing typo as "*Pomp*eranians"[24] (italics mine). There was even a family of fanciers called "the Breeds."

Official announcements were designed to either amuse or intimidate readers of the social columns. Arriving in old Madison Square Garden each year for common folk and their mutts to admire were "high-bred" dogs, "high-class" dogs,[25] and "high-priced" dogs.[26] There were "noble" breeds, "aristocratic dogs," "blue-blooded canines," "prominent dogs," "dogs of noble parentage,"[27] dogs of "exalted station,"[28] and "dogs worthy of respect."[29] The less kind among the columnists called them "spoiled beauties"[30] or "fashions in dog flesh."[31] These newfangled, standardized breeds came and went like the latest hat styles. "Poodles are still quite fashionable among aristocratic people," readers were advised in 1884.[32] Then came French bulldogs a few years later with those weird bat-shaped head ornaments for ears. Show dogs had very distinctive looks, but Westminster organizers couldn't be so choosy in the beginning about which ones they allowed to compete. In fact, a kind of open-door policy was in effect until Americans could afford to be more exclusive. "Pedigrees are not required," it was admitted in 1878, the year of the second Westminster competition, "but where two dogs are equal in merits, the one with an authenticated pedigree will be placed first."[33] Much to the frustration of the natives, this rule left many local dogs at a disadvantage and gave the imports the edge their owners thought they were born deserving. The preference for pedigrees also came as a small reminder to those *un*titled Americans that, no matter what the individual merits of their dogs or their own personal accomplishments in life, lowly birth had branded them and their dogs as forever second-rate to the *en*titled.

The American fancy was a mixed bag, to say the least. But it seldom lacked the genuine article. Real nobility graced New York's port and attended the noteworthy shows whenever it could. Unless beckoned by other aristocratic duties of the surf or turf, titled fanciers could be counted on to show their faces, and their dogs' perfect skulls, against a sea of inferior specimens. When attending in person was physically impossible, they sent their famous pooches to represent them as canine ambassadors. The best shows were not about being seen with dogs—that was for pedestrians, and these people seldom *walked* anywhere. Typically, someone was hired to escort the animals in the ring, and their owners didn't need to be present at the shows. Everyone knew of these foreign dogs' presence, and their status rubbed off on the locals said to be in the same "class." Even if the canine contestants were delivered with masters in absentia, dog shows were never so much about dogs as they were about people. Nor was the true sport of these events supposed to be in winning the sordid coin—that, too, was pedestrian. "The idea of such persons struggling for $20 or even $50 prizes is laughable," the *Times* explained about contestants in the first great New York show, "although they are all doubtless eager to secure the blue ribbon . . . nearly every exhibitor is a gentleman or lady owner, and above the necessity of breeding for profit."[34]

Prizes were for prestige and recognition—and for reminding people who they were or weren't. Promoters counted on audiences buying into this snootiness and were only too eager to go out of their way to collect notable dogs for their viewing pleasure. They waited hand and foot on aristocrats attending only in spirit but lending their dogs for the public's edification. "It is expected the Princess Louise will send some specimens from their private kennels," the *Times* remarked in 1879, "and the club will send special agents to Ottawa for them."[35] Then in 1880 came the announcement: "Sir William Vennor's private secretary arrived on the *Britannic*, bringing with him the string of champion bull-dogs, bull-terriers, and black and tan terriers. . . . Sir William, who has once before visited this country, was unable, on account of pressing engagements, to sail on the *Britannic* himself."[36] Dogs belonging to an invisible king, queen, or czar always outranked the rest, even if they didn't necessarily win. When a member of Victoria's brood arrived without its mistress, there was no shortage of *frisson* on the docks. "One famous dog, bred by Her Majesty, the Queen of England, will be on exhibition, and valued at $20,000,"[37] likely referred to Victoria's champion deerhound named "Hero,"[38] but could have meant any one of her illustrious collies named, in succession, "Noble I," "Noble II," "Noble III," "Noble IV," and "Noble V."[39] Queen Victoria kept hundreds of dogs in her kennels at Windsor Castle, including a Maltese, a breed said to be of ancient lineage on the verge of extinction, a fellow fading aristocrat Her Majesty rescued for posterity, or so it was said.

Dog shows were meeting places where commoners could rub elbows, if not with nobles, then with their dogs. After pooches with aristocratic patrons who might or might not show came the hordes of non-noble fanciers bent on increasing their social chances. "One gentleman—Mr. William L. Bradbury of Nason, Va.—exhibits six 'basket' beagles, recently imported and of very excellent breeding," said the *Times*, boosting American morale.[40] A pair of old English sheepdogs actually *born* in England and valued at $2,500 were said to have "won a long string of ribbons abroad."[41] Ticket sales responded favorably to these cameo appearances of dogs with old pedigrees now in the hands of self-made men.

Dog shows were not just for entertainment. They offered a way up in the minds of social climbers, and the appeal of belonging to an elite was about as irresistible as that of the sparkling jewels in a royal crown. Winning a competition, or simply having a dog worthy of entering, was like receiving the approval of a king or queen. Everyone wanted a piece of royalty, and by 1892 this elite was already becoming so large that measures had to be taken to rescue it from commonality. "Superintendant James Mortimer has discouraged owners of second-rate dogs"—whatever that was meant to mean—"from entering the product of their kennels, and the Westminster Kennel Club has added a most convincing argument to Mr. Mortimer's persuasions by raising the per capita entrance fee from $2 to $5."[42] When authorities weren't maintaining high standards for the canine caste system, they were trying to keep commoners from acting the part. The question of proper human behavior became crucial at dog shows with doors that opened wider each year. These were places where good form and good breeding were put on public display. Well-dressed and well-mannered high society attended so that the rest of humankind could see how things ought to be done. But the audience was not always anxious to imitate, and neither were the dog owners, who often showed a lack of refinement. Concerned parties feared that without a basic respect for higher powers, shows would soon degenerate into sordid scenes no better than the animal-baiting events of old.

Cheating was, in fact, still rampant at the turn of the century in both American and English competitions. Entrees were often given fake names and birth dates, and some were entered as different dogs in several shows. Animals with substandard markings were dyed. Undesirable spots were painted over with boot polish, and desirable ones were sketched in. A famous forgery uncovered at the Crufts show was a wirehaired fox terrier whose coat had been altered with alum, a product once used to whiten human skin when paleness was in fashion. Another involved a poodle whose eyes were enhanced with belladonna, a substance used to dilate women's pupils when that look was de rigueur.[43] "I have seen spots on the Dalmatian's tail very artistically put on with nitrate of silver," Gordon Stables reported. "And I know of a case where a very beautiful top-knot [a sprig of hair on the top of the head] was glued on the cranium of an Irish Water Spaniel."[44] More recently, in 2003, a Pekingese won best in show at Crufts after having undergone some gruesome corrective surgery to help it breathe, but the dog wasn't disqualified because the alteration was made for survival and was not *cosmetic*![45]

Bad behavior at dog shows caused concern in some circles. Across the Land of Fancy went a call for order and pleas for the respect that was due these supreme examples of the canine species. Judith Lytton's prophetic *Toy Dogs and Their Ancestors*, read in both England and America, was as much about toy-dog breeding as it was on etiquette and fair play. Many pages were devoted to proper comportment. Lytton complained that her own countrymen, and women, when they weren't shamelessly selling poor replicas of England's heritage at inflated prices to unsuspecting tourists, were setting bad examples on a global stage. Her strongest objection went to the so-called "ladies," crass types she said had crashed the gates and won respectability with their ugly dogs. "So bad a name do lady fanciers get," wrote Lady Wentworth, using the term "lady" cautiously, "that, as far as the outside world is concerned, one might just as well become a professional card shark as a dog fancier!"[46] The *New York Times* added a similar footnote to the 1892 Westminster show. "Some of the men who have dogs on exhibition," it was conceded, "are about as bad as the women."[47]

Thus the almost comical solemnity that reigns over Madison Square Garden each year when the boxing matches and rock concerts have cleared out. The final decisions of today's show-ring judges are surrounded with as much high ritual as a papal blessing of the animals. But however hard authorities have tried to keep dog showing a dignified occupation for ladies and gentlemen, the impulse to continue opening the door and raising the volume has always had the last word. Early on, a cry for democratization came from within the fancy. "Kennel clubs were held up as vulgar breeding institutions," the *Times* reported after the Westminster show of 1878, "where dogs are dealt in for profit, and complaint was made that in the struggle for prizes individual breeders have no chance with them."[48] Already by 1893, the *Times* recorded "Nearly One Thousand Pleading for Prizes,"[49] and that number would grow by leaps and bounds. Expansionism was by no means an American invention. From the time of the very first competitions in England, promoters saw opportunities for profit and growth. Democracy always sells. So does aristocracy, and dog biscuits baked "By Appointment to Her Majesty the Queen," like the ones manufactured by an American entrepreneur named Spratt who helped to make Crufts a premier venue. From the start, and despite all pretenses to upholding higher causes, dog shows have been about selling things and putting on a good performance, and various gimmicks have been tried to enlarge the number of spectators and paying contestants. Charles Cruft, a clever impresario, went so far as to include several separate categories of stuffed taxidermy dogs so he could boast that his event had more classes, and class, than any other in England. Like aristocratic owners who might attend events in spirit only, dogs could be entered as mere husks of their former selves. Cruft, the father of the modern dog show, who was called "the British Barnum," spared no expense in showing Queen Alexandra herself in an opulently furnished viewing box of her own, forcing spectators to wonder whether Her Highness or the dogs were on display. The logo Cruft chose for his prestigious show was a crown—set above the head of a Saint Bernard.[50]

What was good enough for royalty became a minimal requirement for those highly born in the realm of dogdom. Back in New York, the owners of pooches a cut above the common riff-ruff took Cruft's example and displayed their animals in as comfortable settings as the queen's, as though these were their natural habitats. Between all the drama of showing and judging, ticket holders were invited to squeeze down crowded aisles of private cages and admire their occupants up close. Not far away from the jarred embryo specimens displayed at the first Westminster show, "some of the exhibitors asked and obtained permission to decorate the houses of their pets. Mr. Haines, of this City, and Mr. Baldwin, of Newark, both of whom exhibit Yorkshire terriers, will have their boxes lined with velvet. Others will doubtless follow their example."[51] Others doubtless did. "The kennels provided for these handsome animals were unusually spacious," the *Times* reported from the main floor in 1883, "and they had to be, for some of the specimens exhibited were hardly smaller than ponies. Among these big dogs there was not much attempt at ornamentation. The animals themselves were sure to attract sufficient attention without the aid of ribbons, rugs, or tapestries. Some of the apartments for the smaller dogs, however, were gorgeously furnished with carpets, curtains, ribbons, and even mirrors."[52]

The fancier the breed, the more ostentatious the natural surroundings. Many of the small and toy breeds were modeled after useless court dogs, and their owners played this to the utmost. "Some of these are housed in royal fashion, and bask all day among silks, satins, and velvets," the *Times* noted in 1892.[53] Aristocratic lapdogs, like those ethereal palace sleeve-dogs of ancient China, couldn't be expected to live just *anywhere.* "The toy dogs," said the *Times* article on the Ladies' Kennel Association show of 1903,

> as is usual with a crowd, attracted, in anything, more interest than any other class. Those delicate little animals, whose health must be preserved in glass houses, were gazed at with wonder and amusement. One of the most elaborate of the toy dog houses was a long, palatial like edifice chiefly of glass, with white woodwork. Within were four Japanese spaniels reclining and sleeping upon silk cushions, each one in his separate compartment. Blue curtains adorned the miniature windows, while to complete the luxury of this dog home four electric light bulbs suspended from the arched ceiling supplied the proper amount of light. Mrs. R. T. Harrison of this city was the owner of this elaborate dog house, with its tiny inmates. J. E. Dickert of Toronto showed two little toy terriers enclosed in a house partitioned off in the style of a stateroom. The dogs' bed, with curtains to draw before it, was elevated about eight inches above the floor, and a box stood handy to assist the pets to clamber up and down as they chose.[54]

Smaller animals with limbs as fragile as their family trees were displayed like so many doggies in the window—or perhaps as laboratory samples pressed between glass to be scrutinized by a judge's microscope. "Some of these pet dogs are entirely covered with glass," read the story on another ladies' show in 1901,

> the front portion being arranged like a door, which is shut when the faithful attendant believes it is time for the delicate specimen of canine flesh to take its nap, and at the slightest suggestion of a cooler breeze the silk cushions and mufflers are brought into

> requisition. The extravagance to which continued devotion to pet dogs can go was illustrated in one section of the pet row, where a colored maid stands patient guard over her delicate charges all day long, occasionally taking them out, combing their hair, and rearranging the pillows with as much care and attention as though serving a human being.[55]

Spectators could safely assume these very public interiors for dogs mirrored their owners' private lives. That was the whole point. A palatial home, replete with expensive furnishings, the latest technological advantages like electricity, and full-time "colored" servants, was the American dream. From the early years of the pedigree dog cult, having a purebred, whether large, medium, or petite, curled up in the front parlor enhanced not only the owner's self-image, but the place that person held in society's esteem. Behind the sleek glass surfaces and transparent motives of showing off dogs, however, all was not well in the Land of Fancy. One of the uglier instances of cheating involved a Boston terrier entered in a New York show and fed ground glass by a jealous competitor. The poor thing died before it could become a champion.[56] Not all pedigree dog owners, it seemed, were ladies or gentlemen, no matter how opulent their natural surroundings or high-bred their animals.

Still, the fancy has never shied away from trying to live up to its name. Dog shows have always been glitzy events, part royal pageant, part circus, part Renaissance fair, and part society freak show. "DOGS HOLD HIGH CARNIVAL—SOCIETY VISITS ARISTOCRATIC CANINES IN THE GARDEN," the *Times* heralded one event in 1892 with its gaudy processions, bright banners, and box seating.[57] Dogs with dramatic coats were shined up for the crowd and paraded around the ring in heel positions with tails raised proudly like royal standards. Some were clipped to look like kingly lions and escorted to center stage. Trumpets sounded to prick up the ears on breeds earning points for their prickiness. Every conceivable method was tried to keep the number of snooty entries rising and the audience coming back in droves, even stuffed and pickled dogs for public viewing.

Sometimes the fancy got too fancy for its own pants. "A big band of music was thought of but was abandoned. . . . It was found that every time the band started up every dog in the place joined in refrain, to the distraction of the musicians and the disgust of the audience."[58]

CHAPTER SEVEN

ARISTOCRACY FOR SALE

Marge and Eunice, the bickering Boston terriers, managed to compose themselves before we reached the elegant Art Deco lobby of their apartment building. Upstairs and behind closed doors not five minutes earlier, they'd been engaged in mortal combat, but my encouragement as their chaperone was forcing them to act more sensibly. The two snorting sisters put on their public faces, paused briefly until I stepped forward, then slowly and self-consciously exited the vintage 1920s elevator lined in black patent leather. Like old friends, they passed magnificent columns of the finest black-and-gold marble and floated across an expanse of black-and-white parquet that mirrored their white bellies and white calla lilies spraying from alabaster vases set into alcoves along the walls.

Boston terriers have traditionally been called "tuxedo" dogs because of the design on their coats, but the interpretation could swing the other way. Why should markings be sexist? These girls could have been prim and proper debutantes gossiping about suitors at a cotillion, while skirting across a ballroom floor. Instead of evening jackets, the black patches might just as easily have suggested ladies' shawls draped over the shoulders and coming to square points on both sides. Black was cut sharply by solid white on the forelegs, creating an effect of long gloves rising over the elbows. Angular heads were neatly compact, with black hair pressed closely to the skulls like conservative hairdos, and foreheads were sliced symmetrically at the center with thin white blazes, as though reserving spots for tiny tiaras or royal crests. Pink rhinestone collars glimmered on slender necks, but neither jewels nor markings were boldly indiscreet or "flashy" as they say in the show ring. Sharp fangs, protruding from under-bites and recently in use upstairs, were hidden from view as the breed standard required and public decency demanded.

Back in the Roaring Twenties, when the opulent Art Deco building of Marge and Eunice was constructed, Boston terriers were moving into a world of respectability. The breed was thought to belong in homes where nothing bad ever happened, spacious apartments and cavernous townhouses where black-and-white parquet pooches fit in with the decor and their owners' sense of decorum. Here was a dog whose day had come, "our little aristocrat of the dog world," proclaimed Edward Axtell, an early breeder, in *The Boston Terrier and All About It: A Practical, Scientific, and Up to Date Guide to the Breeding of THE AMERICAN DOG.*[1] This wasn't the first "purebred" born on our shores, to be sure, but it was the first useless canine house pet like court dogs of old, a companion animal suited to a class of people learning to frown upon practicality as a poor person's concern.

In many ways, the Boston signaled its owner's own arrival. Pulled from the rabble and polished to a state of inbred perfection, the "Black Satin Gentleman" had only recently risen from the depths of anonymity to live with the folks on the hill. "Although first fostered by coachmen, butlers, and grooms," a writer for the American Kennel Club's *Gazette* sighed with relief in 1924, "the aristocratic appearance and demeanor of the Boston Terrier soon was noticed and he quickly won a place in the house instead of the stable."[2] To a growing number of patrons, this dog was exactly where it was destined to be, and the metamorphosis from pariah to parlor poseur made for a classic Cinderella tale with powerful appeal to a nation of social climbers struggling to put their own pasts behind them. Following the paw prints of close relatives, English and French bulldogs, these pups with their impromptu pedigrees had been snatched from unworthy hands like pearls from swine, rescued from the midden heap, airlifted from the masses like misplaced royalty. They were precision "fitted to take their rightful position as an important member of the family in one of the homes of the 'Four Hundred,'"[3] one book brimmed with enthusiasm, and soon established residence among society's "upper ten," commented the *Gazette* as it narrowed the number of worthy owners still further. "You Can't Keep a Good Dog Down," sang the new arrival's praises as one might ring in a new peer of the realm. "Although of Humble Origin, the Boston Terrier Has Instincts of a Gentleman."[4]

An American success story, the improved-upon pooch was "equally at home in the drawing-room as in the stall," and with that "indescribably human" expression, he was seen eating people food off china dishes, attending "subsequent teas and other functions," and accompanying "Mrs. Ritz-Carlton" on her rounds about town. So well received was the handsome canine caller that leading aficionados and connoisseurs of other species were opening their doors to a dog that added "volumes to the general smart set up of the équipage."[5] Like the Dalmatian, for centuries a complement to stately processions, this bird of a similar feather was tied to the equestrian class, perhaps more intimately for riding *in* the carriage rather than trotting alongside. Here was a commoner ennobled, a mutt with a name for himself, a dog turned show dog. Apart from the occasional boo-boo on an Oriental rug, the well-bred terrier of Boston could be taken anywhere, and in formal wear at all hours of the night and day, a less than subtle hint that both dog and owner no longer needed to *work* for a living.

Miraculous transformations are seldom as elegant and effortless as society's new arrivals would have us believe. Nor did the overdomesticated dude reach loftiness overnight, though he did have some help. The Boston's record speed in achieving the "reproductive uniformity"[6] required for breediness must have impressed Henry Ford, who was also trying to get Americans where they wanted to go on a grand scale. The drive for assembly-line perfection and brand-name identification was born of a sense of urgency so strong that the AKC declared its eagerness to "recognize" the Boston Terrier Club in 1891, two years before club members even had an exact dog whose "interests" to further! "I would like to admit the Club," explained a member of the Stud Book Committee before the Boston was fully calibrated, "but it appears we have to take the dog, too."[7]

Why bother inventing yet another pedigree house pet when the English were supplying a standard selection of classics that were tried, true, and color-coordinated? Because Americans were, quite frankly, tired of looking abroad for their self-esteem. Deciding that approval from afar was something they could finally forgo marked a coming of age for self-made Americans. Whether or not they even liked dogs, purebreds were basic fixtures for finer homes and vehicles, but why go all the way to London when they could run off their own? For as long as social climbers could remember, England had enjoyed a virtual monopoly on the world's most noteworthy types and held the cards to their breeding standards, making locals feel they were along for the ride. "The English do things better," Anglophile *Outing* magazine stated as its position on the growing divide over whether to go on imitating or choose another destiny. "There has been a conflict, sometimes bitter, between those who adhere strictly to English ideals and standards and those who would press into recognition the American changes."[8] Foreign show-ring judges, it was true, had been invited to lend an air of glamour and authenticity to local competitions. They decided who had the best dogs, but hosts on the receiving end didn't always like the rulings of ungracious guests who obviously hadn't taken time to survey the social terrain.

That violent split over Frenchies, a few years after Bostons were born, was fueled by the same resentment at arrogant experts. "Perhaps some of these, like Mr. George Raper," one English critic said of his countryman behind that row over rose ears, "think nothing of 'running over to New York' to judge a show there, returning to take a few British shows, and then 'running back' to fulfill more American or Colonial engagements in other countries."[9] Antipathy was brewing as early as 1881 when the *New York Times* reported the decision "to have all American judges making decisions even on dogs of the British Isles" at a major event.[10] Assigning a "thoroughly Americanized"[11] Englishman to referee shows across the country kept contestants happy for a time, though headlines like "English Experts to Judge"[12] intimidated, and "English Judges Stir Dog Fanciers" hardly did justice to the hurt feelings of one group of ladies when aliens failed to see the virtues of their bulldogs, Pomeranians, and Japanese spaniels. "It has been several years since dogdom has been so disturbed and upset as it has been by the decisions of the English judges," the *Times* noted with concern.[13] Perhaps British loyalists were content to go on aping their oppressors, but rising numbers of disgruntled hobbyists wanted to end their reliance on foreign dogs and declare a second independence.

This wasn't a class struggle but a struggle for some class. American consumers were desperate for status symbols to make them proud to be American, but prouder still for being prouder than *other* Americans who didn't have them. The Boston terrier seemed to fit that bill. Where could rebels take their case for recognition?

The AKC wasn't the only dog authority in the world, but it was the US breed registry with East Coast society's ear. Elders of Madison Square were in a perfect position to solve the national identity crisis. They were soon to have the final word on coat color, and memories of their social ties in these early years would live on long after the Whitneys and Rockefellers had left the show rings, leaving the AKC with a legacy to shield it from the ugliest scandals and making it the only dog authority most people have even heard of today.

Keepers of the keys to good breeding were poised to tap into delusions of grandeur through pet ownership, and in a single stroke of marketing genius, the AKC exploited the growing resentment over foreign influences and, at the same time, social insecurities at home. The AKC was doing some soul searching of its own. Originally an elite social club founded for the enjoyment of the ultra-rich, it was turning into a business, a proper corporation that sold not so much quality as the *concept* of quality through breeding. Sponsors of the dapper dog made the same career move as clothing designers today who expand from impractical, limited-edition couturier catering to a select clientele to off-the-rack items for a mass market always eager to imitate. Americans wanted a chicken in every pot and a car in every garage, and having a pedigree pooch in every parlor was not unlike owning a Model T, a working man's stab at leisure vehicles. While the world waited for the Boston Terrier Club to produce a dog worthy of its breed club's name, the AKC took a keen interest in cultivating the half-bred hound into something presentable. Versed mainly in English types that arrived from great distances prefabricated with breeding instructions included, the elders kept an arm's length and provided advice and support in every step of the mutation from mongrel that anyone could have into purebred everyone would want, from mutt into must-have.

"This was the first new breed to come before the Kennel Club," the *Gazette* recalled in 1924, "and with all the pride of a mother over her first born, the club intended to be assured that the newcomer was eugenically perfect."[14] The Boston terrier was the AKC's protégé, its own private label, a signature brand to promote for decades. The breed would generate a fortune for the registry in its formative years. "In 1891, the Boston Terrier was an experiment," the *Gazette* explained. "But once recognized as a regular breed, its fortunes ran parallel with those of the AKC. It became a firm financial friend of the governing body and during many years it has been, through the registration fees, a large, if not the largest, contributor to the treasury of the club."[15] That organization's rise from small shabby-chic offices lined with dull filing cabinets, to deluxe digs on Madison Avenue currently housing one of the finest canine art collections in the world, owes a heavy debt to the sustained success of the two-toned tyke.

Now if only Americans could agree on what, exactly, it meant to be a "gentleman," or a "lady" for that matter. Breediness was never born in a vacuum, and the question of who, or what, deserved special privileges needed to be answered. Dogs were valued for reflecting their owners' social standing, and vice versa. Who should have the pleasure of looking down on those with nothing in their laps: Mrs. Ritz-Carlton or her driver? The initial impulse was to say: both. Axtell the commercial breeder proclaimed universally in 1900, "I think this breed appeals to a wider class of people than any other breed, from a man of wealth who produces puppies to be given away as wedding presents or Christmas gifts, down to the lone widow, or the man incapacitated for hard work." Axtell and his ilk packaged the Boston terrier as a product of industry and thrift, a kind of local boy made good and a way to earn some extra cash. "A Boston without a good tail is almost as worthless as a check without a signature," he cautioned aspiring entrepreneurs once the brand became official, and average Americans were encouraged to become what we would disapprovingly call "backyard breeders" today. By taking part in a more open and democratic production of prizewinning pedigrees, any man, woman, or child of any social station, it was said, could at long last achieve breediness on their own, heaping prestige on their households and helping to "fill the pocketbook," "gladden the eye," and "keep the wolf from the door."[16] All it took was a modest investment—and a small registration fee per pup payable to the AKC—to transform humble kitchens, garages, and toolsheds into royal kennels.

So who would it be: Mrs. Ritz-Carlton or her driver? Fanciers couldn't have it both ways—or could they? For reasons as conflicted as human motives are, all this talk of graduating from stable to carriage didn't kill this dog's democratic draw. As with canine crowning and breeding for blood "purity" and elitist "perfection," aristocracy and meritocracy could at best cohabitate uncomfortably like the two-toned markings on a Boston's back. Following a pattern popular since the invention of constitutional monarchy, the idea was never to do away with English-style snobbery—God forbid—but to salvage its spirit for future generations to enjoy. It was no accident that Anglophile gentlemen, born-and-bred rich kids affiliated with Harvard and the Harvard Club, were first to step up and sponsor a breed that didn't, technically, exist quite yet.[17] The true order of their concerns was revealed with their intention to secure "recognition as a distinct breed"—whether this meant the breed club's gentlemen or the ideal dog they hadn't yet produced was unclear—"and this we can only do by proving that we have one."[18]

The AKC greeted the applicants with open arms when they asked for recognition, sympathizing with their cause and nurturing their vision of a house pet with no other purpose than to be born meeting its standard. The Stud Book Committee's first task in ushering them on the path to perfection was to choose a name for the club and the breed it would be called upon to produce. Self-promoters had introduced themselves as the "American Bull Terrier Club," a variation on an established English breed and club, both of which would be taken by someone else in 1897. "Boston" made more sense, with a newer but noble ring, suggesting dyed-in-the-wool WASPiness and hinting at Mayflower descent. Dropping this name in public places would anchor any owner instantly in history—who would want to be associated with a *Cleveland* terrier? Aristocratic pets were tied to the land, and not just any location, another tactic borrowed from the English, whose own Kennel Club was carving up the Land of Fancy into West Highland, Shetland, Lakeland, Yorkshire, Airedale, Staffordshire, Norfolk, Norwich, Sealyham, Pembroke, Cardigan, Ireland, Wales—not to mention England, Scotland, and the border in between—each of these alluding to places, breeds, breed clubs, and corresponding coat colors.[19]

The AKC's role in deciding the breed standard for the Boston terrier—years before it assumed control over standards for any breeds it registers and shows—should put to sleep supporters' usual argument that only breed clubs, not the registry, have legal ownership of the standards and reforming them is not the AKC's business. Securing sponsorship from the right class of people, inheriting an arbitrary set of features based on pure esthetics (and odd ones at that) selected with complete disregard for health and sound construction—the most calculated makeover could still fail if unsavory items from a canine candidate's social background reared their ugly heads. The dog desirous of the AKC's imprimatur had an embarrassing bone buried in his family closet, and that bone was *English.* "It is supposed that this dog was imported, but nothing is known as to his breeding," Watson recalled, "though he was undoubtedly of the half-bred bull and terrier type used for fighting."[20] The problem was, *too much* was known of this dog's breeding, and a change in ear style was not going to do the trick.

"Our little aristocrat"[21] was, indeed, recently descended from the fighting dogs the English had bred for centuries, and early photos bear an uncanny resemblance to what any law enforcement official or man on the street would call a "pit bull" today! In fact, the American lapdog would probably be sharing that name were it not for the purebred whitewashing received just over a century ago. Common sense suggests a good many more dogs of the bull and terrier type must have been arriving before "Hooper's Judge" was selectively enshrined as Dog Adam in the AKC breed history. These animals, and their owners, were probably up to no good. As with the Pekingese breed and nobility's "Fabulous Five," propped up as pretenders to a dynasty of lion-dogs on British soil and remembered only at their best addresses—later found never to have mated[22]—we may never know the whole story about America's court dog. The breed's luster fades in light of the fact that these dogs likely became popular in the Boston area because humane laws pertaining to dog fighting were more stringently enforced in New York at the time.[23]

"To come down to the hard-pan truth, the dog was originally a pit terrier," Watson was forced to admit. "That was his only vocation as a man's dog, and it would be impossible to find one man in the club who would now make use of him that way. That day is past entirely and the only thing to consider is the future of the dog."[24] The way to sever this dog's "disreputable associations,"[25] the fancy wanted buyers to believe, was to change his associates and his address. A Boston couldn't be a court dog unless he was accepted as a house pet, and so all the standard clichés were rolled out to flatter prospective pet owners by insisting that a large part of inheritance came from environment. Like purveyors of golden retrievers who swear that no dog with ancestors from a Scottish estate would ever bite, and owners who proudly predict *their* goldens would "show the burglars where to find the silver"—meaning *their* family has a set worth stealing—early promoters claimed Bostons wouldn't disturb anyone's peace by barking because they weren't guard dogs. Bostons were said to be affectionate, "the most intelligent, observing, and discriminating of all breeds," the clichés unfurled. They were easily housebroken, had "peculiar reasoning power," and were guaranteed to "grow in grace," provided they kept the right human company. The "gentleman" dog was a perfect "companion for ladies" who could walk this refined creature with pinkies extended and a parasol in the other hand. "Boston Terriers are not aggressive to other dogs," a Dr. J. Varnum Mott argued, "hence the injuries sustained as a result of fighting are very few and far between."[26] This guy obviously had never met Marge and Eunice with their war-torn coats.

If, indeed, some dogs were aggressive, it was due to unsavory social ties. And who would choose to be seen with an ex-con canine but a man who was himself a criminal? The taste for violence indulged in the fighting pits of old, explained Freeman Lloyd, the AKC's official British accent, was unique to the lower, subterranean classes. "It is strange that miners, generally, are affected with these rough, and often wicked tastes," read the *Gazette* article, buttressed by ads for kennels placed prominently in the margins. "Some there are who say that such men, spending most of their time without the benefit of sunshine, become addicted to the darker and lower amusements."[27] According to Lloyd's theory, society's dregs lacked the benefits of fresh air, scenic landscapes, better company, and flattering light—unlike the upper classes that swore off animal baiting but kept the terrier half of fighting dogs for civilized pursuits like fox hunting. Meanwhile, dog fighting was declared unsporting, but the bulldog in the Boston stood on shaky ground.

Rule number one from the Social Climber's Handbook: once you're in the front door, slam it shut before any unrefined relatives come sniffing around. Bulldogs were reformed gladiators from defamed leisure activities. They'd barely gotten as far as the parlor by the excess skin on their exaggerated under-bites and, in many minds, were still on probation, when their close cousin the Boston came knocking for recognition. Crossbred with pug court dogs, as Bostons would soon be softened with hues of the fashionable Frenchie, bulldogs were still struggling with some shady family history. They'd been granted entry to better homes where they lounged like "a Pug of high degree lolls in a draper's window, beside a large black cat,"[28] but they sat there uneasily, and the cat looked nervous. Bulldogs had been crippled to a snail's pace, perhaps to reassure people that they were no longer a threat. But an extremely gaseous nature, due to the poor design of the torso, made them awkward around the house, and constant flatulence meant they often slept on the front porch. Owners who didn't shut them out slept with one eye open for an animal they didn't fully trust, despite the fancy papers, the unlikelihood of strenuous activity without heart attacks, and constant assurances of "predictable" behavior.

The bulldog's position was at best precarious, and this was not the time to be digging up questions of breeding. Its club no more wanted to be associated with Bostons than the Boston's club wanted to be associated with them! "Especially bitter were the members of the newly formed Bulldog Club of America," the *Gazette* recalled, and having fair-born patrons from riding circles only cushioned the blow when the gentleman dog ran into a hurdle on his way to purebred standing. "In the recognition of the Boston they thought they saw a menace to their own respective breed. In a small way the antagonism was increased through a press campaign which attempted to show that the bulldog, as a breed, was unfit for gentle society." The sudden appearance of a close relation from the old country, but from the wrong side of the tracks, was embarrassing bulldog backers who were quick to retaliate by calling the Boston—and by implication, any owner—the "savage animal."[29]

Separating the terrier from the bulldog in animals of this type was a delicate operation because "our dogs of guilt," as Roger Caras called fighting types of old, had a shared heritage and bore a striking resemblance to one another.[30] In fact, former fighters had been lumped into the same canine class for years at the dog shows. "Round Heads," the name given to pregentrified Bostons, were often mixed indiscriminately with bulldogs and bull terriers, and any member of this clan would be labeled a "pit bull" today. "Lovers of dogs for their own sakes," on the other hand, said the *Times*—meaning, for the prestige they lent to respectable households—and amateurs of these "business dogs" strolled down separate aisles before competitions began. Softer, civilized breeds, the canine dudes, were segregated into different doggy neighborhoods at the shows, and viewers were advised on which blocks of cages were best avoided. Blunt-skulled bullies didn't occupy those elegant "apartments" so "gorgeously furnished with carpets, curtains, ribbons, and even mirrors."[31]

Conspicuously displayed apart from poofed-up hairballs that could be "annihilated in a single kick,"[32] bulldogs and their relations kept to themselves. Their cages were Spartan and securely locked, not to keep thieves out but to keep apparent monsters in. "The vicious-looking bull-dogs kept up a continual snarling," the *Times* reported,

> and there was no doubt some reason for the "dangerous" notice over their kennels. Nobody ventured to pat them on the heads; visitors were content to look at them from a safe distance, and reflect upon what dangerous and unfriendly-looking brutes they were. There were some fine specimens of bulls, but none of them were troubled with beauty. Their little mashed-in noses

looked pugger than ever as they drew up their upper lips and said suggestively to passers-by that they would like to take hold of their legs.[33]

Just as segregation served to keep different canine classes in their proper places, the way to change a dog's identity was to change his address. The bulldog already had a foot in the door when the Boston came knocking, because Americans' constant fear of not imitating the English had convinced them to give the brute a second chance. To be linked to finer property was, by definition, to cease being stray and disorderly, and the Boston was in dire need of a niche of his own. An early breeder of pure-white Round Heads had shown it was possible to harness his dogs' inborn aggression for nobler pursuits, namely, for chasing strays off finer farm land. "And woe to any kind of vermin or vagrant curs that showed themselves," Axtell warned all trespassers.[34] Good dogs knew their property lines and they stuck to them. In fact, one of the AKC's sales pitches was that "the Boston is not given to wanderlust, like so many of our other breeds. He seems to feel that 'there's no place like home.'" What dog would want to leave a good address but one that didn't belong there? "Never once have I seen them astray off the estate,"[35] a supremely pretentious writer for the *Gazette* described Bostons inhabiting a fashionable stretch in New York's very horsey Westchester County. As with other luxury breeds linked to desirable spots, saying a dog felt no need to roam implied the owner had a well-stocked estate from which he should never wish to wander. The notion that good dogs kept better addresses, as we've seen on other stops across the Land of Fancy, was as old as aristocracy. Gordon Stables restaked that claim for pets "looking pleased and happy, and but seldom caring to leave their own well-kept lawns, unless to make a rush at a stray cat, or bark at a butcher's Collie."[36]

Disagreements over whether to accept the Boston terrier into the pedigree pantheon were finally resolved with the AKC's guidance. "Then, as a good canine citizen, the Bulldog Club fell into line and welcomed the little stranger," the *Gazette* recalled that fateful year of 1893 when, after fierce resistance, the new dog's future looked made in the shade.[37] "The two old standard breeds of world-wide reputation, the English bulldog and the bull terrier," Axtell elaborated, "had to be joined to make a third which we believe to be the peer of either, and the superior of both."[38] The Boston terrier assumed his position in the window next to the cat and became the number-one breed in the United States and Canada for many years. Perhaps the initial reluctance was to be expected. "The answer probably lies," the *Gazette* explained, "in the fact that in those stirring times the American Fancy was young. And young blood always is hot blood. Also it lacks the ability to form accurate and correct opinions."[39]

The AKC acted as chaperone and peacemaker to assure the hurried inbreeding, and the ad hoc selection of traits that made Bostons a breed apart from the rest paid off to the benefit of Americans hoping to be taken seriously on a global scale. It was in everyone's interest to set aside differences on coat color, tail shape, and so on, and show the world America's newfound breeding abilities. The homegrown aristocrat walked the same path as the bulldog and "was taken into the house on trial. His manner proved, though his birth might have been humble, that his instincts were those of a gentleman, so in the house he remained."[40] Once the dog became a permanent fixture, the Boston Terrier Club united under the banner of one universal standard. Axtell and other breeders, industrial and cottage industry, had the blueprint they needed to start production on the gentleman dog with a view to produce prizewinners.

Boston terrier became a household name, and a host of ancillary products sprang up bearing the image. Mass-produced dog food, off-the-rack men's suits, Studebakers, Camel cigarettes, playing cards, poker chips, gas-heating systems—not to forget those ever-popular Buster Brown shoes—the image of that weird creature with the Botox face, surprised stare, and alien-antenna ears added to the perception that big brand names were more reliable than the "heterogeneous types."[41] Standardization was the way of the future, and brand-name recognition had as powerful a draw as eugenics. "Do many of us truly assess the suitability of a breed," David Hancock asks, again with disbelief, "mainly because of its role in marketing a brand of toilet paper? I'm eternally grateful that T.V. programs like *Dallas* and *Dynasty* don't feature Kentucky Mousehounds or our quarantine kennels would no doubt be packed with them now."[42] And what about using basset hounds to sell Hush Puppies (and vice versa), or more recently in 1999, Mitchell Gold equating English bulldogs with six-pack abs, leather sofas, and Soho loft spaces?

When he wasn't busy conquering foreign markets and capitals, the Boston terrier helped wage a campaign to win hearts, wallets, and handbags at home. Over the course of the next century, the AKC managed to convince about half of American consumers not only that it was alright to keep dogs as house pets but that newfangled purebreds—those with the AKC's good housekeeping seal of approval—were infinitely superior to the animals that had evolved side-by-side with humans for eons, faithfully fulfilling some of our most basic needs without presenting any registration papers or symmetrical markings at the door. Turning perfectly fine companions into surplus luxury items with gaudy extras was supposed to be the modern way, but in many ways, it was a return to primitive habits of tribalism, ancestor worship, and ritual display, now neatly packaged and available to anyone with the right price. To a sensible person living in an informed democracy, purebred dogs should seem no more fancy than Heinz ketchup, and a flea-bitten

Dandie Dinmont terrier no better than Burger King, a queen-sized mattress, a Princess phone, a Countess Mara necktie, Royal Crown Cola, or an After Eight mint—even it comes "By Appointment To Her Majesty the Queen," as did Spratt's miraculous dog biscuits, junk food by today's standards but promoted as the only decent diet for finer dogs and a longtime sponsor of Crufts. Once again, wording was what mattered, and gaining respectability was as easy as calling a low-grade mush of meat by-products with cheap corn and wheat fillers "Pedigree" or "Royal Canin," giving that product a blue ribbon or a crown for a logo, then parading it around the ring at Westminster with dogs said to deserve only the best.

"HIGH CLASS Boston Terriers for Sale," reads an ad in *Dogdom Monthly* in 1920, because selling certificates of fair birth is what kennel clubs do for a living.[43] The Boston terrier was plastered across the cover of the AKC's *Gazette* in 1924 as "An American Gentleman" among other dogs "crowned during the past year," irrefutable proof that "pure" blood could be produced domestically like fine wine.[44] But the rest was business as usual with the same old bowing and scraping before foreigners. Simply being American would never be enough for social climbers at home, and when the fancy wasn't tapping into anti-Anglo paranoia, it was encouraging the opposite, Anglophilia. "What a man Badger would be!" was the title of a 1924 *Gazette* article referring, not to the newly arrived Boston terrier, but to the high-born Airedale (likely a creation of the show ring, a breed that never existed in a part of England called Airedale or anywhere else).[45] "I suppose that pup's purty well bred, eh?" asked another article. "Indeed, yes," it went without saying for pedigree pups, "like all real gentlemen are."[46]

The dog in question was not an American breed but an Irish terrier (billed by the AKC as "one of the oldest terrier breeds" but not a "purebred" with a standard coat, not even in England, until 1881). "Roots of Tradition: America's Great Love of Pure-Bred

Dogs Is Akin to That of Britain's Royal Family" appeared in the *AKC Gazette* in 1946, when a mass consumer culture was about to emerge, reminding the status conscious they could still look abroad for their self-esteem. "Akin" was the operative term to describe the awe-inspiring process by which fair birth was achieved in mass quantities to surpass an Englishman's wildest dreams:

> As NO people on the face of the earth ever produced and registered in their kennel club's stud book so many pure-bred dogs as did the Americans in the past year—nearly 150,000—it might not be amiss to glance at the traditions motivating these *born* dog-lovers. We say "born" advisedly, for there is hardly a fancier who cannot recall the dogs of his or her childhood, the favorite of father and mother, often even those of the grandparents. Average memories stop at the grandparents, but it is safe to assume that this love of good dogs tails right back to the early beginnings of each family, just as the roots of all tradition are buried deep—often springing from lands far distant from the United States.[47]

The AKC's current registration drive pursues the same strategy by urging customers: "Register your dog! Join the fun and tradition!"[48]

With all due respect to the Boston terrier and self-made men, the longer a breed's mythical past, and the more generations that breed was a family tradition, the better it reflected daily on the owners whose choice of pets was a statement about origins. Finally, all men had the right to choose pedigrees equal to their own ambitions. Family pride could be based on faraway forebears rumored to have once had the same exact model of nonmongrel living under their roofs, and new dynasties could be founded on the latest canine crowned at Westminster. It's difficult to imagine a more ulterior motive for having dogs or a thinner stretch of the imagination. Crude methods and blunt instruments were used by the fancy to convince average consumers that good families not only didn't own mutts, but had aristocratic pets.

Once again, the AKC rolled out Freeman Lloyd as proof of authenticity. Lloyd wrote, in an English accent like Robin Leach hosting *Lifestyles of the Rich and Famous*, dozens of articles telling Americans that, so long as they brought "the dogs of our forefathers" on their hunts for fair birth, they could find bits and pieces of tradition and reassemble these fragments at home into a flattering mosaic of self-image.[49] Among *Gazette* titles like "The Majesty of Hounds" and "When Royalty Gives Its Touch," in a series called "Many Dogs in Many Lands: Different Races Favor Divers Breeds," we find Lloyd sitting in a friend's well-appointed mansion off New York's ultra-elite Gramercy Park (where you still need a key to get in). He muses over the lavishly decorated rooms, where it's his privilege to be a chosen guest imagining "long past ancestors" in faraway England. The walls are lined with old hunting books and painted scenes of dogs, horses, guns, and the proper gentlemen who owned them.[50]

This deep-seated belief that nobility can be bought and sold has stood the test of time, if for no other reason than aristocracy has always been up for grabs, in one way or another. The mechanics of the deal aren't always so obvious, but when people are asked to explain their brand-name loyalties to dog breeds, more often than not they refer to royalty with its vast estates and extravagant hobbies. Whenever the AKC mentions "the purebred dog," we can safely assume it still refers to previous owners, real or imagined, listed in the section of the breed standards called "A Look Back." Investing in a purportedly vintage pet is an example of what sociologists call "class imitation," and dog owners typically look up, not down, for their cues. In fact, the pedigree dog cult is so thoroughly saturated with ruling-class references that the ruins of aristocracy absolutely litter the Land of Fancy, and only the most focused snobs can avoid tripping right over them.

Many commercial breeders increase their appeal, for example, with audacious names like Royal Windsor Kennel (a manufacturer of various lapdogs of the fluffy white genus located not in an English castle but in Brazil). The royal list unfurls with Royal Vista Miniature Pinschers (in Virginia), Regal Point Vizslas (in Texas), Royal Court kennel (a Rhode Island breeder sworn to uphold the "essence and integrity" of American Staffordshires)—the list goes on far too long to be inclusive here. The naming of show-ring champions has also been inspired by an age-old fixation on princes and palaces in distant lands. Since these competitions began, accolades have gone to star players with names like Crown Prince, Plantagenet, Princess Wee Wee, and Saucy Queen. Canine bluebloods are linked to their birthplaces with "of," "Von," or "de," turning the dogs into fine wines and the kennels into chateaux. Tyt See of Egham, Amirence King Eider of Davern, Khaos Von Salerno, Gero Von Rinklingen, and Fashion du Bois de la Rayère are among countless examples of aristocratic-sounding titles invented for show ring champs. Entire races receive royal billing. The Chihuahua made its AKC debut as "The Dog of Aztec Royalty."[51] The *Gazette* also celebrated "Queen Victoria and *Our* Collies" (italics mine).[52]

Elitism is built into not just the names but the very bodies of purebreds, showing how very difficult pointless traditions are to shed. Several breeds are born wearing tuxedo jackets like the Boston terrier. Others emerge in regal shades of golden, purple, or even blue, as in Bleu de Gascogne. "The white, or ivory, coat," one book heaps praise upon the limited-edition Kuvasz, "is another tribute to the breed's aristocratic lineage."[53] Feathering on toes has been compared to long nails on the high born who need not work.[54] Dogs have "royal crests," "Roman" noses, "lion" ruffs, and "manes," and the Belvoir strain of foxhound's "black saddle mark" ties it to the equestrian class. "Demi-long dogs have culottes on the rump," reads the AKC standard for the Pyrenean shepherd, referring to the style of trousers nobility wore before the French Revolution. That breed is also said to sport an "uncoiffed" coat and to have a "wind-swept face" (like portraits of Romantic heroes with Royalist leanings?). The hairstyle gives the Pyrenean a "triangular head" but without a Third Estate.[55] "The ridge must be regarded as the escutcheon of the breed," the English Kennel Club standard referred to the heraldic shield carried on backs of Rhodesians until the wording, and little else, was changed under pressure for reform from the BBC after 2008.[56] "The ridge . . . should contain two identical crowns," the AKC standard still refers to that sign of royalty and spinal deformity.[57] According to ancient lore, the infection-prone wrinkles on the faces of pugs and Pekingese once formed the Chinese character for "prince," a legitimate reason for maintaining that disastrous mutation.[58] When human status symbols aren't preserved by inbreeding, they're added cosmetically after birth. A dog groomer in 1890s London monogrammed his clients' animals with family initials he carved right into the fur! A certain Mrs. Beer of Chesterfield Gardens had her family crest, depicting a pelican feeding its young, sculpted onto the back of a poodle.

Still not convinced that grown adults could be naive enough to believe in instant aristocracy through pet ownership? Purveyors of pedigree dog products are likely to buy their advertising space in over-the-top purebred publications like the one called—you can't make this stuff up—*The Blue Book.* Pages are lined with ads for upscale breeders and canine fashion accessories, and advertorial odes to the wisdom of Westminster judges. *The Blue Book* appears in sporadic editions from a creepy clique of New Yorkers who call themselves the Metropolitan Dog Club. Hinting at bygone days of snooty social clubs and racial restrictions, the Metropolitans host meetings, lectures—even benefits for selective breed-rescue efforts that triage animals based on their physical appearance—under the roof of the prestigious National Arts Club on grand old Gramercy Park, a stone's throw from the mansion in which Freeman Lloyd sat pondering the past and communing freely with ancestors romanticized beyond recognition.

CHAPTER EIGHT

SOME HUNTING DOGS

Playing fetch with a ball-obsessed Labrador retriever can be fun, at least to a point. Who would deny a hyperstimulated canine, hopped up on tennis-ball action, its only goal in life? Limited though they were, I had to admire dogs so committed to a simple task and eager to pursue it to the ends of the earth, like Tess the yellow Lab whose habit I was hired to support for one hour each day.

Throw/retrieve, throw/retrieve, throw/retrieve . . . The game never changed, and Tess wouldn't have had it any other way. Her playing field, a narrow strip of asphalt enclosed by a chain-link fence, could have been a miniature tennis court, but in New York, they called it a "dog run." The yellow Lab in my care might have been a tennis-ball-serving machine, but for the contracted time, *she* was the one being served, not me. She returned as fast as she'd been dispatched, laying the subdued green globe ceremoniously at my feet and commanding my full participation once again. An hour was enough for me, though Tess would have run herself to death, if allowed.

"We've always had Labs in the family," Tessie's dad, my paying client, often inserted in the guise of an aside, until his dog's hip dysplasia became too far advanced and my services were no longer required. “Countess Howe preferred blacks, so these were the dogs granddad kept on Long Island,” he said, reminding me of the breed’s illustrious past, which just so happened to overlap with his own family tree. “Most people don’t realize the Duke of Windsor fancied yellows before he abdicated, and only then did he became partial to pugs. Father simply adored them.” This family tradition I was hired to engage in daily reenactments came from a long line of Labrador stock. Tess was sired by a Westminster champ, which didn’t save her from arthritis at a young age, though she could trace her pedigree back to England and Scotland, where her race, called an “English Lab” on this side of the pond, was conceived.

For all his dedication to preserving the past, Tessie’s dad couldn’t seem to find the time even to walk his own dog, which seemed strange because he was always at home when I arrived to pick up the lovely lady. At any moment of the day or night, he answered the door in silk pajamas, a monogrammed smoking jacket of red satin with gold brocade, and matching monogrammed slippers. As befitted a lord of the manor, he condescended to solemnly join the Coach leather leash to Tessie’s collar from the same purveyor. The ritual leashing completed, he sent us on our way to fun and frolic and returned to the sitting room—which could have been any room in that house—to resume his gentlemanly pursuit of watching television.

What program of events was the master overseeing? Mostly soap operas and game shows, but not tonight. I’d come to give Tess an evening romp by the light of street lamps because her dad couldn’t miss the Westminster dog show, which aired at eight from Madison Square Garden, a quick cab ride away, though he’d never taken the trouble to attend. Not just any event merited this man’s attention. More than once he’d told me that only Best in Show was worth watching at the very end because, and I quote: “I don’t want to deal with all the riffraff leading up to it.”

Are retrievers truly happy chasing toys mechanically on the pavement, or is this a poor substitute for what their ancestors *used* to do for a living? Until quite recently, it wasn't automatically assumed that bringing country dogs into cities and making them pets was a wise move. On the contrary, it was considered cruel and self-indulgent to keep Great Danes or border collies locked in tiny one-room apartments, or to leave them to their own devices in New York's crowded, urine-soaked ghettos called "dog runs." Tess was bred to enjoy swimming, and every time I walked this water dog past a filthy, poisonous puddle on the street, she wanted to wallow in chemical sludge. The same goes for golden retrievers. Give one a feces-laced lagoon—which is what most of our dog runs are after a good hard rain—and that dog will plop down to stay. Breeds with oily coats, webbed feet, and a desperate drive to dive are out of their element in cities, suburbs, or anywhere but the country, with a body of water nearby. Lately New York has been growing more hostile to their needs. All dogs have been banned from drinking or frolicking in spring-fed streams and ponds of Central Park, even in the dog days of August. Corporate-backed gardeners and park police say they'd be destroying "the environment" by cooling off, pushing Labs and goldens even farther from their natural niche.

Other dogs are equally out of place on the Isle of Misfit Breeds. A Norwich I knew, whose terrier ancestors chased rodents, raged demonically at air conditioners and ceiling fans in shops along the sidewalk, a real problem when trying to walk her anywhere. Urban greyhounds obviously can't chase hare or deer as their instincts command and are forced to settle for trailing the occasional pigeon from a safe distance on the sidewalk, or window-shopping for squirrels on edges of lawns with signs declaring, "NO DOGS ALLOWED." Jack Russells would probably prefer digging up foxes or badgers on farms, but they're reduced to flying off curbs at passing skateboarders or eying rats that scurry fifty feet below the street grating. To anyone with a flair for observation, high-strung hunters look more frustrated than pleased when reaching the ends of their leashes and nearly snapping their necks. Unemployed animals with traces of ancestral urges are products of a sort of double arrogance. First, we unnaturally bred dogs to be fixated on some narrowly prescribed task. Then we told them, sorry, but you can no longer do the little your genes can remember since you were standardized into show dogs and pets. You'll be forever denied what we made you crave like pooches possessed, and we expect you to pretend it doesn't matter. Everyone makes a fuss over how well Labs adapt to their new surroundings *despite* needing so much more, as though this were a mark of nobility. We praise them for suppressing and abstaining, and while sheer boredom may motivate them to chase tennis balls, they appear jovial, upbeat, and bouncy.

Maybe Labs do have some practical uses in their new urban settings. This sporting breed was invented to be mainly a *man*'s best friend, and for date-baiting purposes, taking Boomer or Bailey for a walk is breaking out the big guns. No other pooch packs more of a punch, for on the street those lady targets are struck from great distances by the sight of an in-charge stalker and his devoted companion ready to retrieve. The Lab wasn't recently renamed a "versatile hunting dog" for nothing. Whether for one-night stands or long-term breeding, a rugged buck in pursuit of a trophy would be hard-pressed to find a friendship with more benefits or a finer tool for bagging babes. The fellow strapped to the yellow Lab is a step ahead of the game, because this particular shape, size, and color of canine has come to embody all that mainstream society wants in a husband and a father. A Lab is thought to have a character as solid as its coat color, with a level of blind loyalty that more spirited dogs would find degrading, and a mechanical predictability that more daring cynophiles find a bit boring—the perfect accessory for budding corporate executives. "I'm a team player and do as I'm told,"

Labs tell the world as they pass. “I'm a good guy and will bring back the ball without fail,” barks the shameless sycophant fetcher. “I come from a good family. I have good genes. I'm a good provider and I'm good with children.” A Lab may not be the brightest bulb on the planet, but as one chronicler of snobbism remarks about its cousin the golden retriever, “I was only barely able to resist examining the chests of these amiable beasts to see if they didn't bear the logo of Ralph Lauren.”[1] The brand hints at wealth, privilege, and private woodland property somewhere in Connecticut. It comes complete with exaggerated ties to nobility that all the duck shoes and hunter-green sweaters in the world can't buy. The Lab's a basic provision for any gentleman worthy of the title, a model of domesticity and gracious living, a faithful protector of town and country and every upscale Main Street leading to a Polo shop. If Norman Rockwell were alive today, he'd surely be painting yellow Labs.

Or maybe he'd be painting Labs yellow. Our familiar friend in that comforting shade has only recently come to represent so many decent and predictable things. As we've already seen, for years *yellow* Labs not only were considered undesirable, but were routinely strangled at birth, culled for color. Off-color specimens were seen as less than Labs and were treated as less than dogs, because yellow, or a slightly deeper shade called “golden” (no longer recognized by the AKC), didn't cut the mustard in the eyes of canine perfectionists. Black Labs were considered better workers, and right into the twentieth century, untold numbers of innocents were sacrificed in the interest of keeping the breed “pure,” which meant black.

In the same boat were dogs born with the misfortune of wearing “liver” coats (a shade similar to today's “chocolates”), because only black was socially acceptable until trendsetters like the Earl of Feversham and Lady Ward of Chiltonfoliat started breeding them. It took three English monarchs keeping the lesser shades at the royal kennels, and assorted nobility unafraid to say they rather fancied the goldens and browns, to convince the common hobbyist that lighter-coated versions were no less fancy than the blacks, that these dogs were honorable and deserved to live. Black remains the sine qua non, nonetheless, on the grounds of HRH Michael of Kent, reigning president of England's Kennel Club, childish though it seems to have favorite colors in dogs or believe a best friend's worthiness is determined by its coat. Queen Elizabeth is known to have a soft spot, and room in her kennels, for the House of Yellow. A separate Yellow Labrador Club has existed in England since 1924, and some American yellow Labbists hope to one day have their own.

Given the range of choices and stunning endorsements, shoppers for the right English gun dogs to keep in their big-city apartments might be interested to know that today's limited selection is a recent invention. Throughout the nineteenth century, "retriever" referred to any dog that had a heightened propensity to fetch fowl once the hunter had discharged, and was not a specific type at first, much less a breed with standard coating. Dogs with a fondness for retrieving—one of several behaviors extracted from the wolf and exaggerated to the point of parody—had been around for at least a thousand years. They varied so much in shape and size, and in the shade, length, and waviness of their coats, that a painting of a two-toned *Labrador Bitch* done by Landseer as late as 1823 looks like a poodle crossed with a border collie to anyone expecting a Lab by today's standard. Not only did these dogs take many forms, they tended to perform more than one single task, at least until advances in firearm technology and a growing need for retrieval of birds killed in larger numbers led to calling certain dogs "retrievers" for the first time, probably in the 1850s. As these hyperspecialized fetchers grew fashionable among gentlemen of means, solid black and solid gold, the epitomes of elegance, became the preferred coatings, and anything less was left for second-class sportsmen.

Golden, for reasons to be revealed, fell into disfavor, and by 1938 the first dog to appear on the cover of *Life* magazine was a black Labrador named Blind of Arden. More recently, anyone in a T-shirt from the Black Dog Tavern is instantly linked to Martha's Vineyard and all it connotes today, and black Labs are bounteous in the Boston area. The original preference for black coats, to the exclusion of all others on this latest accessory of the sporty set, likely comes from the possibility that one of its ancestors was the St. John's water dog. This rough draft of today's most socially acceptable house pet, now extinct, came mainly in black, but with some troublesome markings on the chest and legs that would disqualify him in any reputable show ring today. Like the golden retriever that's spared the street despite those "few white hairs"[2] on its breast (so long as there aren't too many), a small white spot is all that remains on the chest of many a show-quality Lab since the flaw was pardoned and given the noble ring of "medallion."

Birthmarks aside, the resemblance between a Labrador retriever and a semi-mythical sea-dog called the St. John's is uncanny. Seen in the mere handful of old photographs used to prove ancestry, the apparent progenitor looks like an oversized, substandard black Lab, though this humble forebear was never bred for appearance or stylized performances in ritual hunting pageants of the idle rich. Unlike the Lab, with its pedigree whitewashing and penchant for the royal game of tennis, the St. John's is said to have evolved over several centuries by catching hard-to-fetch food for humble masters. A useful companion, this diamond-in-the-ruff took shape on fishing boats traveling to and from the remotest parts of what's now Canada and was only later polished into something of a single-minded dimwit on the estates of English and Scottish nobility, landing comfortably one day on our own living room sofas.

The would-be proto-Lab was not a breed in the modern, commercial sense, but a landrace, or more accurately, a "water-race" since much of a St. John's life was spent at sea, where its worthiness was tested. This strong, devoted, highly skilled, weatherized worker, the product of an undocumented array of who-knew-how-many different no-nonsense dogs of Portuguese, French, and English extraction, played a vital role in the fishing industry off the coast of Newfoundland ("Labrador" referring to the entire region as it was known at the time). Here was a hardy mutt, the result of as many as five hundred years of crossbreeding, a mysterious mix maybe of mastiff, perhaps water spaniels of some sort, or even a French hunting dog called the St. Hubert's hound. No one knew or cared in the icy waters off the North American frontier because fishermen already had their dog and as far as they were concerned he was already perfect. The St. John's dog was said to be able to swim for hours without rest and to embrace his work with tireless enthusiasm, a true Spartan equipped with a water-resistant coat, webbed feet, and a powerful tail that helped with swimming. Remembered for a marvelous ability to dive in and catch live fish beneath the surface, this dog allegedly held fishing nets in his bare teeth while treading water. (Anyone who wants to beef up Lab legends need only visit a lake or puddle where claimers to the throne are known to congregate, or perhaps a fountain in Central Park where they chug like champs carrying sticks the size of tree trunks in their mouths like Olympic torches. The Lab's talents would probably pale by comparison to his said ancestor's abilities, but old habits die slowly and resurface in surprising ways.)

Tracing this pilgrim's progress from fishing boat to public fountain, we see a cult of the Lab forming around various uses over the centuries, not the least of these being to keep high-bred humans entertained. It wasn't the St. John's dog's ruddy fishermen friends but society's born leaders who supposedly sponsored this lowly worker in the late eighteenth century, sending him on his way to fame, fortune, and "purebred" perfection. Whether this was an improvement is a matter of opinion. It's pleasing for Labbists to believe the St. John's social climb began when men of leisure rescued him from the sea and unrefined hands, giving him a fresh start on solid ground linked to the finest family names. Like those ethereal palace Pekes that didn't see the outside world for centuries, memories of a period of sustained rarity in the company of walled-in aristocrats made proto-Labs attractive among all the equally qualified retrievers of the time, which perhaps shared some Newfoundland heritage. The Earl of Malmesbury and the Duke of Buccleuch, credited as the creators of the race—or rather, their hired gamekeepers who did most of the actual work of breeding, training, and caring for the hunting breeds harbored in their highly appointed kennels—tried to keep this dog to themselves for use in private command performances, news of which soon spread across the land. Acting independently, one in England and the other in Scotland, Malmesbury and Buccleuch kept the St. John's "pure," or black, for as long as they could, though crosses with other hunting dogs might explain different coat colors and textures.

Having an address at Heron Court or the Buccleuch estates set the proto-Lab up as a breed apart from the common curs owned by local villagers. Why should a fine and beautiful animal be toiling away his life, wondered these men of fashion, hauling heavy carts to market or holding cod nets for the fish mongers, when he could hold a starring role in the elaborately staged hunting adventures that unfolded against the picturesque estates of the highest nobility? What good was talent unless employed in some noble capacity? The handsome new arrival needed to be taught some manners, it was true. The St. John's had never been a court dog before, though selective breeding and careful training—again, by the hired help—would smooth over his lack of polish and any irregularities in appearance. The pupil became, as ultra-snobbist Freeman Lloyd said of the fully perfected twentieth-century Labrador retriever, "a model of forbearance and discipline" a shining example of "good behavior."[3] Maybe this dog would teach the human help a thing or two. The subservient learned to exercise restraint while his new patrons aimed and shot at birds over bushes and ponds. A few short generations in the controlled environments of enclosed estates, and the made-over mutt had acquired a taste for fetching dead fowl carcasses with as much gusto as he'd ever risen to the challenge of diving into the open sea for live fish, which must have been more exciting and required greater skill. Living in society's upper stratum and learning to share its rarified concerns made this dog more than the mongrel he'd been, or the cross-breed lesser men still said he was, until the Kennel Club, under royal authority, finally intervened in 1903 and knighted him and his descendants with official purebred status.

But ever since the St. John's dog got off the boat, there's been something fishy about the Labrador retriever's family tree. Against a backlog of praise, legend, and a few exceptional deeds, what these new and improved dogs originally *did* for those humans who stooped to scoop them from the sea isn't so impressive. The latest addition to aristocracy's predatory pleasures took part in what was a sort of overdone pageant that seemed no more sporting than any fox hunt with class-coordinated costumes. In fact, the whole operation was as staged and choreographed as any dog show in years to come. According to the Scottish aristocratic style of gun shooting, neither hunters nor dogs made a move before the hired help ran ahead to scare birds into flight for easy killing. More servants trailed closely behind to keep the master's gun loaded, or added to his hunting vigor with a quick gulp of spirits. Among so many actors with specialized tasks to perform, the early version of the Lab, properly attired in his black coat, was restricted by breeding, culling, and often harsh training to retrieve inanimate objects and do virtually nothing else while out of kennel confinement. In other words, as show dogs would one day be bred for stylized appearance, the Lab was bred for a single stylized behavior—maniacal retrieval for a fancy fetch fest—at the expense of other talents and perhaps a more balanced character.

Here was an old dog with a new trick, and how easily we forget that there's a difference between *ritual* hunting, or for pure pleasure, and poaching for survival as the lower classes did with their lowly curs. The question of where function begins and pageantry ends is not as cut-and-dried as assumed, and the AKC's admission that modern-day retriever trials "no longer represent practical hunting situations"[4] is a non sequitur because these games were modeled after previous games designed to mirror the sportsman's self-image and his place in society, not to provide anything vital. "Usefulness came to be shunned as a commoners' trait," writes Donald McCaig, a Virginia farmer and author who, like many, traces the downfall of useful dogs to a preference for fancy show dogs in the nineteenth century.[5] But prior to being remade for the stage, many types had been groomed for dramatic roles in aristocracy's fowling follies and formal hunts where they became playthings for the idle rich.

"Hunting is the amusement and not the business of a gentleman," commented the Duke of Beaufort, making no apology for utter pointlessness in *Hunting*, a nineteenth-century treatise on upper-class diversions.[6] Flash to gentlemanly pursuits of the present day, and an article in *Gun Dog Magazine* gives the Labrador retriever a high likability rating that may not have "anything to do with a dog's skills," a shocking confession, except that sportsmen have long preferred a pooch that's "outgoing, interesting, and just plain fun to be around" to one that isn't. Style often overrides substance as gunmen gladly pass over a more cunning companion for one of the "guys" or "'good ol' boys' ready to belly up to the bar and tell a joke." The Lab is described as "a canine L'il Abner, that splendid comic strip character—kind of gawky and country and always wearing a grin."[7]

Gun dogs like the Labrador retriever would seem to be products of more ease and excess than industry or thrift, and the attraction to sporting breeds is often more about the names of previous owners than usefulness, strictly speaking. By the time of the Lab's arrival on the social scene, upper-class English were the world's leading canine connoisseurs, the inventors of a host of dazzling new breeds, and they wanted to improve any dog that wandered into their kennels. Hired hands did most of the work of breeding, feeding, training, and reloading, while their masters refined luxury hunting to an art form with their educated eyes and an almost instinctive knowledge of which dogs to buy and which to let die, which purveyors carried the latest firearms, and which tailors made the best hunting costumes.[8] The English could lay no claim, it was true, to having first envisioned ritual hunting. The new leaders, who'd read their Greek hunting treatises like they'd studied their French and Italian manuals on court etiquette, self-consciously strove to recreate the legendary pastimes of other ruling classes to whom they believed themselves the rightful heirs. But they extended the idea to extremes. After a few centuries, the English torch bearers had every sport of the turf, chase, ring, and stage neatly covered with animals specialized to perform every minute role imaginable and with apparent ease.

Why anyone even needed Labs is a good question never asked. Continental hunters, for their part, had been content with more versatile dogs. American hunters, before the corrupting influence of *Anglophilia* became deeply rooted in their soil, wanted dogs that did it all. The English were not satisfied with multitaskers. They had dogs allowed only to hunt hare. They had dogs strictly forbidden from chasing anything but birds, and then only certain species of birds, depending on the type of bird dog. They had dogs assigned to birds at wing and dogs confined to birds already grounded. They had dogs for water and dogs for land, then dogs with short legs for some terrains, and dogs with longer legs for others. They had dogs calibrated for tearing the flesh off rats in the fighting pits, dogs designed for tearing the flesh off bulls, dogs for tearing the flesh off bears, dogs for tearing the flesh off badgers, and dogs for tearing the flesh off each other. They had dogs for driving wolves extinct, dogs for tormenting cornered foxes, and dogs for holding larger beasts at bay until their master arrived with his big gun.

To a more demanding degree than their sporting predecessors, the English bred dogs for compulsory setting, chronic flushing, perpetual pointing, and, last but not least, dogs for fanatical retrieving. How much easier did they want to make it on themselves? Listening to modern-day hunters elaborate in hairsplitting detail on why, exactly, they need to send a very specific bird dog with a very specific leg length and a very specific coat color—often to match the local landscape—after a no less specific breed of bird is a constant source of skepticism. Likewise, the argument for buying a single-minded maniac—a dog that will *only* set, point, or retrieve—is that while a more balanced animal might be able to "do it all," he does nothing "perfectly," meaning in the artificially enhanced fashion that betrays luxury, free time, wastefulness, and all those qualities known to come with an item that's been custom made—including a higher price tag.

Aristocratic sportsmen of the old school, and their hangers-on, looked down on the new dog show fanciers at first and wanted nothing to do with the vulgar *arrivistes.* Perhaps their imitators were coming too close for comfort, and they blamed canine beauty pageants, with their concern for form over function, for the degeneration of traditional dogs that only *they* used in fitting and noble ways. The Kennel Club Stud Book, pointer man William Arkwright wrote, was having a "demoralizing influence" and could only be "advantageous to the 'idle' breeds," which so many of the best dogs were on their way to becoming. The new "field trials" were "tainted by the omnipresent spirit of fancy," he claimed, and said little of a dog's real hunting abilities. Arkwright recalled a staged performance in 1901 where a setter actually ran away—"galloped far out of sight of both judges and handler"—and was still awarded first prize! The only purpose of the corrupt new dog business was profit, he claimed, observing: "The modern fancier, unlike the hunter of old, exaggerates useful qualities until they become useless." It would be no less absurd, he added, to "give our servants wages not for their skills, but for their looks!"

Just how useful was ritual hunting with conspicuously handsome gun dogs? Arkwright himself, perhaps the most vocal critic of dog shows in his day, confessed to placing much stock in the role of physical beauty on a hunt. "I know that some sportsmen nowadays affect total indifference about their dogs' appearance," he remarked, as trivial types like Charles Cruft were co-opting the manly world of dogdom, "but if they appreciate the good looks of their wives or their horses, why, in the name of consistency, not their pointers!"[9] Arkwright's question only begs another question: if a wealthy gentleman leisurely hunting quail, partridge, or grouse undisturbed on his vast estate, armed with an absurdly oversized rifle and trailed by an équipage of dogs, drivers, handlers, and reloaders can be considered "sporting," then why not an overweight woman in a pantsuit huffing and puffing around the ring at Westminster or Crufts with an overcombed hairball whose only duties are to heel, look pretty, and not bite the judge?

Bird shooting, fox hunting, and other high-class games are rooted in ritual royal sports no less contrived or stilted than dog shows are today. The gap between form and function widens at the memory of Elizabeth I standing rigidly on an elevated stage in a corset and Elizabethan collar (like those worn by Labs and goldens after their hip surgeries) to take in some deer hunting. Solemnly handed a preloaded crossbow by a young girl dressed as a forest nymph, to musical accompaniment she fired at a chorus of royal bucks, which were hard to miss as they were deliberately herded at the appointed time into a narrow passage by a royal pack of specially trained royal greyhounds.[10]

Only someone impertinent would have dared diminish the regal hunting talents of James I, also an avid arranger of mass slaughters who established himself as a champion sportsman on the world stage. When James wasn't hiring impresarios to stage his bull-baiting events, he was leading a band of hounds, horses, and liveried help, all in the appropriate colors with individual tasks to perform, across a scenic English landscape in search of the royal prey of the day. Like the huntress queen, the outdoorsy king was determined to keep this royal passion in the family. He declared that owning a higher class of dog should be the exclusive legal right of the highest class of people. To sport a greyhound or setter, one first had to demonstrate a minimum income or net worth, or be due to inherit some substantial sum. James himself was king and took whatever he fancied, and royal hunts for deer, hare, or bore were gluttonous, wasteful hobbies as destructive to crops and other personal property as fox hunting would be in later years. England's First Predator was not shy about demanding items that added to his outdoor pleasure. Word was sent out well in advance of a royal hunt. The local gentry and small farmers struggling to live off meager parcels of land borrowed to feed their families were instructed to prepare the stage for His Majesty's latest upcoming adventure and were forbidden from plowing their fields because uneven surfaces were difficult for horses and dogs to cross in style. Fences came down and hedges were trimmed so the mounted monarch could make a graceful passage in one clean and unbroken line. To further enhance the overall effect, subjects were ordered to provide additional dogs and supplies, free of charge, as requisitioned. By the time this parade retreated and the dust began to clear, the royal extravagance had left some resentment in its wake. Locals about to voice their objections were reminded, by the sheer size of these events, that the prey of the day could have easily been them. Legend has it that during one successful hunt, a prized royal hound appeared with a note attached to his royal collar forged from the finest royal silver. The sender implored the figurehead to stop destroying the livelihood of average Englishmen who could not afford to "entertain" His Majesty on such a grand scale. This did not deter the rugged royal hunter from pursuing the sport of kings that was his birthright. "He virtually lived in the saddle," writes Carson Ritchie in *The British Dog*, "partly because on foot he looked supremely ridiculous. He had weak legs which bent under his weight so that he had to lean against someone. . . . James put in all the hunting he could."[11]

A clearer picture emerges of where, exactly, all the pomp and circumstance attending purebred dog ownership got drummed up in the first place. Though the English would one day be considered the original pooch people, many of their hunting rites and the dogs used in these events actually came from froufrou royalty in France, where court and course merged imperceptibly like a high school gym that doubles as a dance floor on prom night. French kings were avid fans of the princely pastimes they pursued with fancy relish. Louis XIII, while still a tender child dauphin, was already using royal lapdogs to chase royal hare in his heavily fortified royal bedroom. Monarchs-to-be were raised with numerous pets, and as adults they sat for fashionable court painters who portrayed them in outdoor settings as rugged but ruffled.[12] Choosing the best animals meant consulting Jacques du Fouilloux's influential fifteenth-century hunting treatise in which quality hounds were ranked by coat color and the caliber of men seen with them.[13]

Though in later years the English could rightly claim to have invented more minutely specialized hunting breeds than anyone else, French aristocrats strove to distinguish themselves as avid sportsmen who knew a "good" dog from a common cur.

By the nineteenth century, being a sportsman meant imitating the English. Fads for pointers and retrievers ignited across the Channel, where Parisian men of fashion imported the latest dogs, guns, and sporting ensembles. Once that unsightly business with Napoleon was settled—with the help of the English race and its thoroughbred horses—Charles X returned from exile to restore respect for monarchy. He could not fail. Inexhaustibly supplied with preloaded guns, servants, and caged animals released on cue as easy targets, he might as well have been playing a video game as hunting wild game. "Charles X was a great hunter," wrote a retired officer from Napoleon's army. "He killed seven or eight hundred animals a day. Having paraded before his eyes an unbroken procession of partridges, rabbits, pheasant and hare, his only problem was in choosing which ones to shoot." Sarcasm gave way to anger and off came the gloves. "This is stupidity," the former officer continued. "Kings do not know the pleasure of hunting because to drink with delight one must first be thirsty. To taste the pleasure of having a full game bag at the end of the day, one must first know what it's like to return with it empty." This royal subject was unimpressed. "Fancy court hunting is a promenade, no different from the shows performed at the Opera."[14]

Monarchy's muckraker was on the mark about sovereign skills, but he missed the point of ritual hunting. The French Revolution gave every man the same hunting rights as a king, but a gentleman's game has never been about putting food on anyone's table—that was for the servants to do.[15] High-brow hunting was for upholding family pride. Prey was to be hunted "beautifully," the Duke of Beaufort prescribed, "handsomely found" and then "handsomely killed."[16] Anything less would have been beneath a gentleman because hunting for "sport" demanded patience, reserve, and the proper stance. It meant holding back before an audience as a person of breeding refrained from digging in at the table—that sort of behavior, again, was for the servants. The goal at the end of the day had less to do with health, athleticism, or fresh air, than looking good to others and reaffirming everyone's proper place in society.

Various methods were employed to keep the tools of the trade out of the wrong hands. For centuries, English commoners' curs capable of competing with aristocratic hounds were permanently disabled, their legs and paws cut to prevent them from playing on a level field. In fact, staying within society's confines and keeping up appearances could be as hard on animals as those formal demands of the show ring. Anyone who believes it should not be a capital crime for a Labrador retriever to be born wearing the wrong coat color might wince at the tradition of punishing animals for acting outside their social stations, against the natural order, or as Caius called such impertinence, with "wantonnes of maners."[17] Bird dogs have been forced to conform to unforgiving standards by devoting their entire lives to exclusive pointing, setting, or retrieving, and no combination of these. Setters and pointers guide the hunter to his target in their own individual styles but must never touch a downed bird, because this is the retriever's territory. Prior to shotguns, when crossbows and arrows were used, in case setters were tempted to do more than stop a few feet short of fowl and throw them up into the net, they had metal pegs jammed into their mouths and fastened around their heads with leather straps.

Dogs have also been punished for not sticking to one species of prey because their masters did not envision them hunting another. The Reverend W. B. Daniel, author of *Rural Sports*, boasted he'd hanged seventy-two of his best spaniels for having mixed hunting genres. These unruly beasts had killed hare without authorization, because as every sportsman knew, only greyhounds were supposed to course hare, while spaniels were made for rustling up birds.[18] Chasing a species without license was a serious affront to the master's breeding abilities, an insult to his flair for commanding the forces of nature. Acting independently was strictly forbidden, and commoners' curs that took it upon themselves to hunt on private deer parks were caught and hanged without trials.

The ultimate aim of ordering nature around has been to keep fellow humans in their proper places. To the present day, English law forbids a tenant from firing upon airborne prey, a privilege reserved for landlords.[19] Neither human nor hound can pursue woodland creatures without woods, another commodity that's been closely guarded. Between the eleventh and the nineteenth centuries, various laws and other forms of discrimination were used by discriminating sportsmen, including the privatization of vast tracts of English land. Long since the dismantling of England's private, enclosed deer parks, where downing a doe was like shooting fish in a barrel, the enclosure movement—the inspiration behind many of today's "useful" English dog breeds—continued to show the rich in a favorable light. Backed by government, large landed interests consolidated their holdings, gradually forcing small farmers to move to crowded cities where they labored in factories if they were lucky.[20] Lush woodlands provided a buffer from the roar of crowds and machinery, and hunting in controlled environments for animals hiding in manmade coverts enhanced the image of the landed classes.

Recent issues of *Gun Dog Magazine* show that even no-frill killers have artistic concerns and strive to find just the right settings for their historical reenactments of aristocratic pursuits. "I have a mind's eye image of a springer spaniel and a woodcock in the soft light of dawn," one sporting journalist confesses.[21] "The huge golden orb of the rising sun was directly behind our dogs—a picture-perfect tableau," another inspired gun toter waxes poetic on the day's carnage.[22] Guns are essential to these exquisite moments. In fact, entire breeds of gun dog owe their existence to a late addition to ritual hunting's stage props, and we have yellow Labs splashing in public fountains and lounging on sofas today because of improvements made to firearms yesterday.

The more convenient guns were made to carry, load, and shoot in the eighteenth century, the more suited they were as tools of a gentleman's trade, though there was an initial period of resistance. The very items Freeman Lloyd described as "elaborate equipment and stately ceremonial" that only the well-off could handle properly, were once thought unfair, unsporting, and ungentlemanly.[23] Much in the way that today's critics of deer hunts and ice fishing roll their eyes at the latest gadgets like sonar tracking devices, closed-circuit underwater cameras, bleeping Game Alerts and Digital Trail Monitors—tools that compensate for a hunter's *lack* of skill and appeal to his boyish sense of space adventure—fowling with heavy artillery was thought to be in bad form. Henri III of France banned guns and setters among nobles and commoners alike in the sixteenth century. James I did the same.[24] Resistance evaporated soon enough, and we can only begin to imagine the exhilarating sense of power and accomplishment that must have come from suddenly being able to down a bird in midflight, a rare event with a crossbow but a distinct possibility with a gun. The sky was the only limit.

The more convenient hunting became, the more convenient shooters wanted it to be. Ritual hunting was further ritualized, and gun shooting increased in status. "They are unused to the science of shooting and of firearms," Lloyd mocked one group of commoners seen in a painting daring to play a gentleman's game. Men of lowly birth were "questionable sportsmen ready and willing to shoot at *anything*." Before long, guns were fully absorbed into the gentleman's repertoire, and the idea of firing in bad form was as offensive to the sensibilities of upper-crust sportsmen as it was frightening to insecure social climbers seeking to emulate their every move by owning all the same accessories, animals included. "Only one of their dogs is other than a mongrel," Lloyd remarked, denigrating those lowly "Cockneys" for pretending to be gentlemen.[25]

Gun dog breeds we know today were created to go with better firearms and then improved to enhance shooting pleasure and provide a bigger buildup to the sportsman's defining moment. This explains the clunky old Clumber spaniel's decline in popularity when guns were made to fire faster, leaving the breed a companion to older gentlemen and to a style of shooting no longer fashionable.[26] Versatile dogs, good enough for generations of nobility on the Continent, were methodically customized by the English as weapons advanced. Setters crouched before bushes and briar patches, as they had in the days of crossbows and nets, but to indicate where the master should aim and shoot. Flushing dogs threw birds like clay pigeons into the air where they were sitting ducks for the well-armed sportsman. Pointers were simply intensified setters. Quirky, erratic beasts, they literally froze into position and pointed like no-brainer laser beams, making absolutely certain the gunman fired in the right direction and made his mark. Meanwhile, dogs with retrieving tendencies waited at heel for the command to reap as many birds as could be hit.

That number increased as guns evolved, and as bird hunting grew more popular, gun dogs were bred to be faster and more focused. At some point, sportsmen realized they didn't really need many of their best dogs anymore because the guns had gotten so much better. Bird hunting was incredibly easy. "At a big modern shoot in England," wrote one gunman in 1903, "or a small one for that matter, the setter or pointer would be of as much use as a fifteenth century cross-bow."[27] Much like the legendary alaunts, said to have gone extinct after firearms were improved for the battlefield, bird dogs had in some ways outlived their purpose and lost the race with technology, further whetting the hunter's appetite for mass shootings. As the game accelerated and canines were often cast aside, sportsmen became overstimulated. They lost that calming influence dogs are famous for furnishing. Killing became industrial and addictive.

By the second half of the nineteenth century, accelerated carnage was becoming costly. Lord de Grey earned the respect of his peers for being one of the premier "big guns" of his day, but he paid a pretty price. On his vast estates and with little help from dogs, in the course of an illustrious firing career, he personally massacred an estimated 250,000 pheasant, 150,000 grouse, and 100,000 partridge, all farm-raised and released on cue by hunting servants who threw these helpless creatures into the air as easy targets. Lord Walsingham's record-breaking 1,070 grouse kills in a single day were counted in his backlog of defining moments, which eventually forced him to sell his vast estates and abscond abroad.[28]

"In retrospect," recalls David Cannadine in *The Decline and Fall of the British Aristocracy*, "it also seems an ominous foretaste of that even greater slaughter which was soon to come, not in the butts of Norfolk or the grouse moors of Scotland, but on the battlefields of Flanders."[29] Ritual hunting's practical defense had long been its ostensible use as a warm-up to the theater of war, "that larger and bloodier field of which it is the image," as the Duke of Beaufort wrote approvingly.[30] Blood sport was believed to increase stamina and to sharpen predatory instincts and leadership skills. But the sportsmanship was questionable. England's First Gentleman, soon to be Edward VII—to whom hunting treatises were dedicated in anticipation of the day His Majesty would point his subjects to their deaths on foreign soil—became an avid annihilator of pigeons, which he shot in princely portions. Not far removed from Elizabeth I hurling arrows from her elevated stage at passing deer to musical accompaniment, England's First Gun fired a rifle from a platform erected at the elite Hurlingham Club in London toward birds time-released in droves from a tower. The monarch sprayed his canon effortlessly into swarms of winged beauties, a pleasure he savored until 1906 when club members voted to ban this sport on humane grounds and told their royal patron, in so many words, to get a grip on himself.[31] Edward was forced to retreat to his vast estate of Sandringham, home of the royal kennels, where his staff reared twenty thousand pheasant from eggs each year for use in gratuitous mass-killing sprees.[32]

Across the pond, the fowl-shooting fad caught on like wildfire among Anglophile men of means who took trains to Long Island for Westminster's hunt club events. "HOW THE YOUNG BLOODS OF NEW YORK SATISFY THEIR TASTE FOR GORE," read one headline in the *Herald*.[33] Like their princely role model—the same man who gave them their tuxedo jackets—Americans continued to use retrievers in their pigeon-shooting rituals, "a fashionable amusement" and "an expensive luxury," according to one of the how-to manuals published at the time.[34] They needed their speedy, four-footed servants, if only to pick up the mountains of bird carcasses when they were finished firing. Timing was essential in these competitions. Faster retrievers earned their owners more silver cups, and an aspiring gentleman could not have too many of those on the mantle. "War was always a better game than hunting," recalled a writer for *Outing*, the American upper-class sports magazine, and all this trigger-happiness left something to be desired.[35] As more crack shots gained admittance to a gentleman's game, high society succumbed to an itching sensation that something dear had been lost in the Age of Improvement. Was this what the Duke of Beaufort had in mind when he wrote that prey should be "beautifully" hunted and "handsomely killed," or had the nobility gone out of ritual hunting?

The nostalgia craze for English pointers could not have arrived at a better moment than the second half of the nineteenth century. This return to a preference for gun dogs exhibiting this one form of obsessive-compulsive behavior—rather than the others—served a luxury niche market of sportsmen who felt, quite frankly, that things needed to be slowed down a bit. Like-minded types with a taste for expensive hobbies and an abiding sense of their breed-apart status decided to turn back the clock with a sort of boutique bird shooting.

Before maniacal retrievers became the darlings of the filthy rich on both sides of the Atlantic, catatonic pointers had been the signs of superior social standing. "In its traditional form," recalls that historian of aristocracy's decline and fall, "shooting had been an integral part of country life. The landowner walked his estate, with a pair of pointers, a muzzle-loaded gun, and a powder of flask, and thought himself lucky if he shot ten birds in a day."[36] In this early version of less is more, pointing dogs were revered not so much for the little they did, but for the direction in which they pointed. It was the odd pause before birds that selective sportsmen found intriguing. Owning a dog with a fine square head, a correct "presentation of the nostrils,"[37] and a costly coat—a specimen that struck a handsome pose with ears tilted and tail raised at precisely the right angles toward a bird with superbly symmetrical plumage—meant having a level of taste, discernment, and patience that most men could not afford. Fast shooting was for the "snap shots" and Cockneys. The gentleman engaged in a slower, contemplative, laid-back style of killing because he knew how to savor the moment and take it all in. Pointers were sometimes even slower than they looked. Like the setter that wasn't there to receive first prize, this "strange-behaving dog," as Ash called the pointer, was notorious for running off and disappearing for hours, sometimes never returning to assume the position.[38]

Considering how erratic and high-strung pointers often were, the gentleman hunter was lucky to shoot any birds at all. From their early use as gun dogs, pointers were so fragile and tightly wound that they'd jump nearly out of their skins at the slightest sound or motion, as at-home pet owners can testify today. Sometimes posing before birds was the only way for them to calm down, so long as they didn't freeze into the opposite extreme not to be moved. Stories abound of dogs needing to be knocked over after indicating where to fire, lying still and statuesque on their sides for an hour or more despite kicks and prods.[39] Sensing a bird nearby and calling attention to it was only part of the answer, and unlike a wolf or any well-rounded dog, the pointer never *acted* on his plan. He just stood there, thinking, or maybe not. Like retrievers that withdrew from the action and fetched after the fact, pointers merely *looked* like they were about to pounce and left the rest of the job of hunting to someone else. This failure to act is known by animal behaviorists as an "abnormal orienting response" and can be compared to staring at television for hours on end. Pointing alone, like exclusive setting and retrieving, is incomplete, juvenile behavior, and breeders encourage immaturity in pointers just as they coax show dogs to come out cute and cuddly with big, wide, cartoon eyes, high baby foreheads, childlike pouting expressions, and soft puppy coats.

Catatonic freezing was exactly what ritual hunters wanted from their overspecialized, overstylized dogs. Those idle and meticulous English drifted so far into what Arkwright himself called "rabid point-worship," that they devised their own way of combining these costly and contemplative canines for use in a sort of weird mechanical ballet.[40] "Backing," or "honoring," involves two or more pointers that are inbred and trained to act in concert and complement each other, only competing up to a point. The English did not invent pointing but can rightly take credit for "backing," and the dance unfolds as follows.[41]

The dogs head out in search of something to point at, and the hunter trails not far behind with his gun ready to go. As soon as one dog senses birds hiding in the undergrowth, he freezes. The duty of the others is to show good manners, not initiative. Rather than rush in and flush the birds away—or take credit for having seen them first by closing in and "stealing" another dog's point—the well-bred losers "honor" the victor for getting in on the ground floor by standing back and pointing respectfully in the same general direction.[42] If the hunter by chance carried surveying equipment on his hunts, he might draw lines from each dog's snout, or triangulate, and find they intersect more or less at the target, making easy killing easier still. Today, "backing" can be experienced virtually by watching videos posted on YouTube. Modern-day ritual hunters are proud to use the latest technology to show off their pointers in this elaborate aristocratic dance.

The custom of preserving pointers on point took hold on both sides of the Atlantic. In fact, a fad for outdoor photography of these dogs in action—or inaction—gripped wealthy men enthralled in point worship. Sportsmen went out armed with guns and cameras, and became so caught up in this craze for stopping time that it's unclear whether a pointer's purpose was to hunt or be *seen* hunting in pictures—or whether shooting referred to the camera or the gun. "Mr. Arkwright recently took a number of photographs of the dogs on the moors," reported Caspar Whitney's ultra-snooty *Outing* magazine, "and in no single case did he lose his shot through the delay contingent on taking the photographs, a fact which demonstrates the keen scenting powers of the dogs, which stood to game at distances that enabled their portraits to be taken without alarming the birds."[43] Pointers helped their owners to kill two birds with one stone, and scenting talents were as crucial for posing as they were for finding prey. "These pictures were not snap shots, but were deliberately taken," wrote another snooty sportsman for *Outing*, using the same term for amateur camera hobbyists lacking artistry as Lloyd might have used for unskilled gunmen.[44]

Pointers were as fashionable on stage as they were on film. In the early years of dog shows, these were about the only types allowed. Decades before yellow Labs hit the social scene, a lemon-yellow pointer named "Sensation" became the logo for the Westminster Kennel Club because, as former AKC president William Stifel recalls, "Westminster was still basically a Pointer club."[45] It might even be said the entire dog fancy, in England and America, began with point worship. Looking back to that early English exhibition at Newcastle upon Tyne, sponsored by a gun maker in 1859, only two classes were featured: pointers and setters. The same was true of many early events to follow, and in America, the first dog shows were also for the most part *pointer* shows.

Dogs were walked out by their handlers, if not into a ring, then onto a rustic scene strewn with bushes, tree branches, and caged birds hidden here and there for them to find. While the pointers froze before suspicious bales of hay, judges took notes on their posture and intensity, and onlookers sat starstruck by these high-tech homing devices of the rich and famous. Pointers were displayed at work on these replica vast estates—like those lapdogs shown curled up in miniature mansions—where they modeled their splendid fringed coats well into the twentieth century. Pointers held their own on stage, just as they posed for outdoor photographs, only with better lighting.

CHAPTER NINE

COMING HOME

What's so offensive about dogs that do it all, but nothing perfectly? It seems the more tasks an animal can perform, the closer it comes to being a mongrel. Before returning to the Lab's North American comeback as a "purebred" with letters patent under its collar, it might be instructive to consider how sportsmen on either side of the Atlantic were persuaded they needed England's eugenically improved dogs in the first place.

The gap between society's "useful" sporting dogs and its throw-pillow pets narrows further when we reflect that, throughout virtually all of English history, mutts were dealt disadvantages. Commoners' curs were mutilated and disabled by law, and along with their owners could be hanged for poaching on a rich man's estate or deer park, and yet the poor with their pariahs managed somehow to survive and flourish. Men dressed in any old clothes, accompanied by dogs with asymmetrical markings, did not hunt beautifully or handsomely, but they found their sustenance in tasteless ways. Conditions for performing without an audience were harsher than anything men of quality with their picture-perfect animals ever had to endure in the spotlight. Unrefined breadwinners and their half-breed greyhounds called "lurchers," for example, were infamous for getting around laws, and fences, and taking what they needed. There was no uniformed staff to pave their way with flowers and music, and color-coding would have gone unnoticed because they tracked their families' food at night illicitly. Pausing to inhale the fresh air or point out an amusing rock formation would have been difficult to enjoy under such stress. Surely, these were the more skillful hunters and hounds, not the rich and their fancy companions who seemed to need inner road maps, GPS systems, and *catalogues raisonnés* to find the prize. Perhaps educated folk hated the rough-hewn types because it was their strength, stamina, and cunning, not an eye for scenery or class camaraderie, that got these meaner types home in one piece. Society's underdogs obviously overcame centuries of prohibitive pricing, unfair game laws, mandatory mutilation, and a host of obstacles placed in their path, the proof being that so many commoners and mutts are still alive and with us today!

For hunting unostentatiously for food and not fun, ill-bred men and their lowly curs have shouldered much abuse and suffered more grief than they've deserved for thinking they might do what their social betters did best. Yet despite the valiant efforts of the upper classes to keep the tools of the trade out of the wrong hands, some hunters have sworn that mutts rule over their fancy cousins in both brains and balls. Gordon Stables aimed to nip this rumor in the bud. "'I'll produce a dog,' I've heard a man say," he wrote, "'that, as far as points and appearance go, you wouldn't give two pence for, who shall retrieve and set against any fashionable dog you can show me.'" Rubbish! "A mongrel may often, in the eyes of a novice, look as well as—if not better than—an animal of the highest breeding and pedigree; but, believe me, a mongrel is never so good, either for sporting purposes or on guard, as a thorough blood."[1] Aspiring sportsmen simply had to take the expert at his word and employ in their fledgling safaris only recognized breeds able to produce the proper papers. Never having given mutts so much as a fighting chance to prove themselves, how would they have known better? Card-carrying members of the upper classes and their hordes of imitators were no more willing to see through the outlandish claims of haughty sportsmen than they wished to expose the transparent lies of eugenics, because doing either wasn't in their own best interests.

What sources should consumers consult before patronizing a "reputable" breeder of high-bred hunting hounds or deciding which English gun dogs are best for their New York apartments? "These may be found in the sporting print shops," Lloyd advised in "Pure Breeds and their Ancestors," a lengthy series of articles he wrote for the AKC's *Gazette*. "The sporting artists of old enjoyed the delight of placing the man, his gun, and his spaniel together. That, indeed, represented the *tout ensemble* of the sportsman's surroundings in those far-off days."[2] The thought of hunting in bad form was as offensive to the sensibilities of upper-crust sportsmen as it was threatening to insecure social climbers eager to emulate their every move by owning all the same gear. Over the ages, surprisingly few dissidents have dared to raise their voices and contradict reigning notions on what distinguishes high-class hunting dogs from unremarkable mongrels. On those rare occasions when they do, however, their impertinence is impressive.

"The author had a retriever," one Englishman had the audacity to call a nondescript mutt, "as perfect in its business as, perhaps, one of its kind ever was." And what *kind*, exactly, was that? The beast on whose behalf the author of *The Young Sportsman's Manual* spoke in 1849, ten years prior to supposedly the first dog show, was "bred between the bull-dog and smooth terrier." This hybrid mess, admittedly, looked nothing like any of the retrievers soon to be recognized as "breeds" by royalty's Kennel Club. Yet, the author insisted, "this rare creature was as complete in all the duties of a land-retriever as in those of a water-spaniel." A randomly bred monstrosity that could do it all, and with no family tree to support him? Impossible. The rogue sportsman's earnest testimonial must have been treated as heresy at the time, since so few people have heard it since. Refusing to back down, he sang his dog's praises. "In sagacity and courage, if she ever had a parallel, she never had a superior."[3]

Sixty years later, in 1909, when registries were well on their way to being the only way to go for canine consumers, whether to hunt, show, or show off on sidewalks, the same Virginia medical doctor who advised treating a good dog "like a white man" partially redeemed himself by exposing a flaw in the breedist's dogma. The doctor drove a convincing wedge. "Having had considerable experience afield with bird dogs of varied accomplishments, pedigrees, training records, and other supposedly necessary qualifications to make them good hunters," he said as he presented his credentials,

> I have naturally made some comparisons now and then between these favored canines and the common run of "pick ups" found here and there at the farmhouses all over our state, and who are of uncertain lineage and utterly unknown to fame. I have so frequently been astounded at the good work done by these unkempt dogs that I sometimes wonder if many good dogs are not overtrained, and maybe overbred! It is a fact well known that many of our best men in all walks of life are self made men, and certainly some of the very best dogs I have known have been essentially self broken and self developed.

Intelligent, skillful, reliable dogs with no breeding or training? The physician illustrated his claim with the story of one plain but high-performance "plug of a dog" he'd had the privilege of knowing and loving. "The animal was certainly of a very unprepossessing appearance. He was a kind of sorrel setter, with a decided suspicion of bull dog cross about his face. He looked sheepish and guilty, and had a woebegone eye. . . . I never saw a more unpromising dog, nor have I ever hunted with a better one."[4]

This was before the Labrador retriever arrived to dispel all doubts on the superiority of purebreds. While American consumers were still wavering between having Bostons or collies as family pets, the Lab's victorious return to its ancestral home was being given quite a buildup. "The Lab's success in America is a tribute to the dog himself rather than to his importer," claimed Richard Wolters in his definitive book on the breed, skirting around the fact that the Labrador arrived on American soil under the snootiest of circumstances.[5] After a long residency with the Malmesburys, the Buccleuchs, and families of their ilk, the erstwhile mutt was back to claim his throne in a young nation already fixated on wealth and social standing.

Wolters continued, commenting on the refashioned Saint John's water dog:

> The Lab's return to North America was actually part of a fad, a whim of the times. During the Roaring Twenties—the jazz era, the flapper society, the time of the Charleston, F. Scott Fitzgerald, and good Scotch whiskey—wealthy Americans were fascinated by the royalty of Europe. American wealth could buy anything except an official social order such as in England and Scotland. The "in" thing of the times was to have British aristocracy amongst one's friends. Nothing could be more elegant than an invitation to shoot down grouse on the Scottish moors.[6]

A contemporary of this fad concurred on the Lab's heyday of the twenties and thirties: "In the very early days there were a number of wealthy Americans who patterned themselves after the

British gentry."[7] The same class of people who'd scoured foreign nations for palace artifacts and stud-in-laws were importing the whole Labrador experience lock, stock, and barrel. Money was no object when recreating a noble pastime. As with collie and pointer fads, entire kennels and kennel men familiar with the breed were brought over on steamships. The Blooming Grove Hunting & Fishing Club in Pennsylvania, the Wyandanch Club on Long Island, Westminster's gun club, and like-minded venues across the country catered to their limited membership's every hunting whim. "The clubs had regular recruiters who brought in young Scottish gamekeepers," Wolters also had to admit, "and many wealthy families turned their estates into Scottish shooting preserves."[8] Spendthrift American sportsmen, eager to surround themselves with all the trappings and then insert themselves like crown jewels, bought up as much land as they could and had the latest artillery delivered from the finest London houses. New York's Abercrombie & Fitch became official purveyor of sporting outfits and accessories, also selling guns and publishing books on dogs.[9] Properly clad, handsomely armed, and primed with manuals on hunting etiquette, rich Americans needed something to shoot. So they reared their own birds as English and Scottish lords had done for generations. An estimated one hundred thousand were raised and brought down each year by a small number of well-to-do who, when they weren't catering to foreign nobility, were keeping mostly to themselves.

Retriever mania had been brewing for years, and the only surprise was how long it took for Americans to catch on. The first Labs were logged into the AKC's Stud Book in 1917—golden retrievers had to wait until 1925 for their moment in the sun—but their popularity seemed written by royal decree. Back in England, George V had shown his family's inimitable examples at Crufts, as though to tease the public with something it could never have. He kept a promise made to his mother, Queen Alexandra, never to release their genes into the general population. Breeders were inconsolable, but the royal reluctance was a heads-up to potential buyers that there was something very special about these dogs.[10]

George VI, like his father before him, wasn't shy about showing off his Labs and then keeping them out of circulation. Who let the dogs out? Malmesburys and Buccleuchs passed on their family recipes to members of their circle, and slowly but surely specimens began arriving in New York Harbor wrapped in every credential but a royal seal. The stellar cast of previous owners sent this dog's reputation in advance. It was an established fact that Lord Knutsford was the first president of the Labrador Retriever Club of Great Britain (currently steered by the Duke of Wellington). A better recommendation would have been hard to find. Lorna Countess Howe, in an uncommon move away from lapdogs for a woman, was elected the club's second commander. Lady Hill-Wood was entrusted with the third presidency, adding a ring of authenticity that only a true Buccleuch by birth could bestow. Across the pond, Labs were entrenched among the old elite, and America's new elite was eager to dig itself in.

Wolters finally came out with it: "There would develop a certain snob appeal in importing and running Labradors."[11] Maybe the Lab's appeal had at least as much to do with people as it did with dogs, because the list of early owners was a veritable *Who's Who* of American plutocracy. Among the first to have dibs on dogs off the boat were Mrs. A. Butler Duncan, the famous Phipps family, the Guests, and the Harry Peters. J. P. Morgan showed himself true to form by nabbing an original. The Livingstons, as always, occupied center stage in dogdom. Jay F. Carlisle started one of the first important domestic kennels, and W. Averell Harriman was another big breeder. Samuel Milbank, Marshall Field (whose imported

English wife was the American Lab's first club president), August Belmont, John Olin, Dorothy Howe (a Scottish importation like the dog)—pretty much everyone who was anyone either owned, bred, or imported Labs with aristocratic-sounding names like King Buck, Duke of Kirkmahoe-Tare of Whitmore, Boli of Blake, Orchardton Doris of Wingan, Earlsmoor Moor of Arden, Caumsett Don of Kenjokaty-Kateren, Sab of Tulliallan-Peconic, and Dandy of Adderley-Chatford. Now the only problem was figuring out what to do with these legendary dogs trailed by such lengthy titles.

Included on the list of Lab-owning luminaries was real estate mogul Robert Goelet, on whose vast Orange County estate the breed's miraculous powers of retrieval were first showcased in 1931.The name Glenmere Court drove home the comparison to Scottish nobility, in case someone had missed the many other references. Freeman Lloyd, the dog fancy's English ambassador and official interpreter, was on hand to make sure the right message was conveyed. "On the 8,000 acre Glenmere Court Estate of Robert Goelet," wrote Lloyd, opening his dispatch in *Popular Dogs* by giving the raw acreage so readers knew precisely the caliber of people concerned, "took place this country's initial field trials for retrievers."[12] The rest read like a guest roster for a fancy cotillion with the same illustrious names that crowded the society columns. In another article done for the *AKC Gazette* two months later, Lloyd would use his English standing to overreach by actually calling Glenmere "the *seat* of Robert Goelet" (italics mine) as though the real estate mogul were landed gentry. Guests summoned to Goelet's domain were dignitaries from near and far. The Duke and Duchess of Windsor were frequently called to court, though they'd left Labs along with the crown and moved on to pugs, which traveled better. Americans were inheriting a sort of hand-me-down dog, really, needed nonetheless for this "new diversion connected with countryside sports." Reproducing an aristocratic pastime required accuracy in every detail, and the full effect had to be dashing. Lloyd described the Glenmere event as nothing less than a "renaissance of the Labrador in the United States."[13]

The first Lab performance staged in America was as stilted as any royal shooting spree in foreign lands. The new recreation was aimed at mimicking "Scottish shooting style" an ocean away from Scotland where these games had been pure theater all along. Field trials involved too many people, too many dogs, too many guns, too many birds, and too many rules. As in traditional shoots on that distant turf, ritual hunters walked richly dressed in an orderly line across a field where farm-raised pheasants were strategically planted in their path. Individual trials consisted of three shooters, each with his own personal gun attendant, and two handlers with Labs waiting patiently at heel. The troupe forged ahead until several trained "bird boys," placed at left, right and center, chased their foregone conclusions out of the brush, where they'd placed them for easy shooting. Pheasants couldn't fly much higher than chickens, and bagging them was no great feat. Water fowl were birds of a different feather. Ducks were also mass-produced for defining moments but had to be trained to fly from point A to point B, which just so happened to be right across the gunmen's own established route. Men, staff, and dogs advanced repeatedly, shooters stopping and firing, then pausing to shoot again, across a scene that was supposed to be the Scottish moors but looked more like New York State. "Behind them strode the gallery," Lloyd reported starstruck, "among whom were many women of much social distinction and affluence."[14]

Where did the dogs come in? Easy as it was to lose Labs in the crowd, if "the gallery" looked closely enough they could be seen performing basically the same task on land and water. Sportsmen discharged their guns in a firing frenzy to impress the wives, and the dogs' task was to dash ahead at the handler's command, find as many birds as they could, and deliver them unscathed. Labs weren't much more than glorified garbage collectors and might have been replaced by any of the retrieving dogs that still found work at pigeon-shooting events. But in the judges' eyes, this breed was different. Upper-class bird shooting was about style, and Labs put on happy faces and showed a new kind of briskness and enthusiasm. Maybe some of their excitement rubbed off on the sportsmen, who seemed to care only about making their own roles easier. The Duke of Beaufort had said that hunting should be "the amusement and not the business of the gentlemen," and wealthy Americans were determined to act the part. In fact, the first field trial for Labs was deliberately scheduled on a Monday so that anyone too attached to a desk could not attend! At least one mogul, unable to leave his office back in Manhattan, sent his regrets along with his Labs, after the example of foreign dignitaries who dispatched their canine ambassadors to Westminster from afar.

Those who attended had a grand time, less with the dogs than with each other, at this meet and affairs to follow. Between sumptuous luncheons, formal dinners, and drunken parties where Scotch flowed freely and Scottish dog handlers were kept awake all night by the revelry, ideas surfaced on how to make the next function less strenuous than the last. "Walk ups" were soon replaced by stationary shoots. Players stepping down from chauffeur-driven town cars needed no longer trouble themselves with walking because birds were kept in spring-loaded boxes and catapulted into the air. Without batting a wing, targets found themselves suspended at the wrong end of a rear-loaded shotgun without knowing how. Having shooters stand in position awaiting their turns also spared the gallery from exerting itself. Seated with wide bottoms hanging over folding lawn chairs and armed to the teeth with knitting needles were "them fancy ladies all dressed up in their Abercrombie and Fitch field clothes," recalled Jack "Bad Jack" Cassidy, a fireman from Brooklyn and one of the first nonsociety types to compete in Lab trials.[15] "Tower shoots" were another favorite of pampered guests at Glenmere, though these games had been declared unsporting at London's Hurlingham Club. Thirty or so shooters stood around an elevated cage and fired into hundreds of birds released at the appointed time. Retrievers fetched in high numbers, proving themselves worthy of the company they kept. The gallery knitted away.

It was in these controlled environments, and under recherché circumstances, that America's own tried-and-true working dog, the no-nonsense Chesapeake Bay retriever, was bumped by his fancier cousin as favorite hunting companion. What made the newcomer seem so special, apart from the list of previous owners? Besides the happy-go-lucky attitude, the Labrador was blessed with "common-sense and strategy," according to Lloyd, who sang his praises to an American audience. The breed possessed "a fine intellect begotten of large and educated brains," he hailed, unclear as usual on whether he was talking about the dog or the owner.[16] Rumors of the little prince's superior skills soon spread from coast to coast, though how this happened remains a mystery. High society's field trial results were seldom made public—perhaps for fear that champions might look good enough to steal—so how did outsiders learn of the Lab's stupendous powers? The simple fact of these momentous events at vast estates and private clubs was enough to stimulate "the ordinary dog owner," as Lloyd called the duly impressed commoner by whom "the field accomplishments of any retriever may be read, marked and inwardly digested."[17]

Largely due to favorable press in these early years, "Lab" is a household name today, and most Americans have never heard of their own American retriever, the "Chessie." Proud Lab owners can be found on blogs tracing their dogs' pedigrees back to kennels that no longer exist and previous owners who've been dead for generations. Little do imitators know that early importers wanted as little to do with newcomers as they did with these animals or the subalterns they'd hired to soil their hands handling them. The sporting dog situation on posh parts of Long Island, for example, was not much different from the show ring events held in nearby Mineola, or in Madison Square, where status symbols often weren't even shown by their rightful owners. "Owners and trainers did not socialize with each other," according to the author of *Legends in Labradors*, who confirms how strict the caste system was. "And in the beginning, owners rarely ran their own dogs."[18] As for dealing with the dogs for which they'd paid thousands per eugenically perfected head, apart from the occasional visit to their highly appointed kennels adjoining many-winged manors on vast estates—in the tradition of English royalty taking tours of menageries at Windsor and Sandringham—America's sporting set couldn't be bothered. This hands-off relationship brings to mind my years spent walking and training dogs for New York's most opulent households. In the most affluent families, not even children are expected to walk their own pets, and the hired walker, groomer, acupuncturist, aroma therapist, and celebrity behaviorist are escorted in through the delivery entrance to instruct the servants on how to handle high-priced specimens of *Canis* that are *familiaris* to everyone but their owners.

Lab loftiness continued well into the century, though the transition from elite shooting accessory to middle-class coach potato would not be smooth. Upper-class sponsors had too much of their identities invested in these foreign affectations, and seeing them fall into the wrong hands was as difficult as any process of letting go. As with early dog shows and so many breeds that had since fallen out of fashion, the original intent was to use their social positions to draw attention to yet another expensive importation, then to tease the public with items it didn't deserve to have. But the mob was demanding equal rights to be unequal, and gluttons for punishment seeking approval from higher-ups were given a run for their money. Presuming to enter field competitions on an equal footing, for example, was like poaching on a lord's estate. Clamorers for acceptance were snubbed for actually raising, training, and handling their own dogs, because in the minds of seasoned sportsmen who imported handlers with their hounds, this simply wasn't done. Showing up at Long Island field trials with homespun dogs, wearing clothes with the wrong labels, and toting guns purveyed by unknowns were surefire invitations to ridicule. Outsiders were often made to feel outclassed the moment they arrived by an old guard withholding that "wholesome feeling of being at home among friends" the Duke of Beaufort had described.[19]

"Mixing a Wisconsin milkman and a Wall Street banker who belonged to a fine shooting club and had his own professional trainer was bound to have its effects," Wolters recalled of the latter-day Long Island game milieu. "Just because they both had good dogs did not mean they had equal social status."[20] Rather than welcome strangers and let them break bread at the same table as the entrenched, after-trial dinners were eventually discontinued to avoid the awkwardness. Field trial fever spread across the country like a marathon, but nowhere, according to witnesses whose feelings had been hurt and social climbs thwarted, was there more resistance to change than on uptight Long Island where, as late as the 1960s, retriever competitions were notoriously snooty affairs. "By the time my wife and I reached Butte, Montana with our dogs," recalled one of the rubes slighted in passing, "we felt that we really belonged. After their trial we were invited to the club's annual dinner as their guests. But we'd started our campaign trialing across the country in Long Island where we couldn't get as much as a 'Good morning' while airing our dogs in the designated area."

Unpleasant memories from back East bring to mind the uneasy melting pot of dog owners competing in the film *Best in Show.* Private parties, tiaras, and poodle ice sculptures didn't rule in the end, but impartial judges couldn't stop the flow of bad blood among Lab owners, and "one had the feeling on the Island that the pedigree of the owner was more important than that of the dog."[21]

CONCLUSION

FRANKENSTEIN'S LAB

or

The Price They Pay for Living in the Castle

Prominent New York socialite James L. Kernochan thought he was minding his own business early one morning in 1896 when he took the usual train from his opulent Manhattan townhouse to his vast Long Island estate. Dressed in the finest fabrics and joined by fellow members of the elite Meadowbrook Hunt Club, this gentleman of wealth, leisure, and conspicuous waste was headed back to Hempstead to be depicted by society columnists as reigning Master of the Beagles in upcoming events, news of which would return to Manhattan faster than he'd left.

A leading sportsman of the highest caliber ever to ride against an English hunting scene, Kernochan had been mentioned on many occasions, along with his wife, for pursuing the sport of kings on horseback and sharing body parts of slaughtered prey as trophies of their noble pursuit. The companion riding by his side on the train that morning was not his wife, but a fashionable French bulldog bitch that had won him second prize in the "Non-Sporting" class at Madison Square Garden the day before.

If Kernochan was just sitting there, trying to mind his own business, this was a strange way to go about it—or was showing the rest of the world what it could not afford, and didn't deserve to own, his own business after all? The sordid events that followed might serve as a cautionary tale of calamities befalling the uppity pet owner unwise enough to advertise who he is, where he comes from, and where he's headed.

"J. L. KERNOCHAN BEATEN," read the headline in the *Times* later that day. "Attacked by Firemen Who Objected to His Prize French Bulldog." Why would anyone take exception to a harmless, inbred monstrosity that could barely breathe or walk without medical attention? Not all passengers seemed to appreciate this perfect pooch or the message she was meant to convey in loudspeaker fashion. While Kernochan sat proudly with his breed apart from common curs of the villages they passed, gathering a few rows behind was a mob of burly working-class onlookers, "most of whom had been drinking" and whose attention had been roused. While their social superior accepted a silver cup and kudos on his exquisite taste in four-legged luxury items the day before, these ill-bred, low-paid public servants were attending the popular Washington's Birthday parade and celebrating in taverns.

By the next morning when they boarded the train in the same direction for a very different destination from the fancy pet owner's, the firemen, "some of whom were ugly," were full of alcohol and needed only a spark to set them aflame. "Some of the firemen did not like French bulldogs," the *Times* explained politely, and in a combined effort to express their personal preferences, they "began to make uncomplimentary remarks about the appearance of the animal." Kernochan was annoyed but tried to show his good breeding by telling one ruffian to "mind his own business" as he himself was trying to do. The fireman "forced himself into Kernochan's seat, and knocked the dog from the seat to the floor." This poor inbred monstrosity had become "the innocent cause" of an impromptu class conflict aboard a crowded smoking car.

Within moments, some twenty reinforcements of "drunken firemen" joined the rough-cut assailant to do further violence to the offensive Frenchie and her master. Kernochan's grooms, always within shouting distance, intervened and "a lively fight" ensued for "a run of about ten minutes" during which train doors were held firmly shut by proletarians so "the fight might be more strictly a private affair." The controversial canine was kept shielded in a corner by the body of a groom, but Kernochan received "a terrific blow over the eye," another on the mouth, and kicks to the back, chest, and ribs, followed by further punches to the face. Society's gentleman and his gentleman's gentlemen were greatly outnumbered and severely plummeted by their inferiors. The coachman was knocked to the floor and kicked mercilessly. The foreman was thrown through a window. Warrants were sworn later that day, with "public sympathy" and "much indignation" arising over "the brutal conduct of the Far Rockaway firemen" who had begged to differ with the ruling of a Westminster judge.[1]

Luckily for the squeamish, this harrowing tale doesn't end in tragedy. A harmless nonhuman bred to be a poseur, not a fighter—in fact, the only party minding her own business that day because she was physically incapable of doing much more than sit and snort—wasn't sacrificed for a disagreement over coat color or ear shape. "Margot" didn't suffer too dearly for being seen with the Right People in between the wrong places. But at the end of a day of bitter class conflict, who's to blame if pooches are, indeed, hurt for standing or sitting in the crossfire? Onlookers feel slighted and want to knock flashy high hats down a few notches, even if they must plow through their canine accessories first.

"He who meanly admires mean things" was Thackeray's definition of a snob in "The Snobs of England, by One of Themselves."[2]

In other words, anyone who buys into the snobbish way of thought by taking the outward signs of pride and prejudice too seriously and then getting nasty is just as bad as the next person and every bit as snooty. The firemen trying to take out their class consciousness on a house pet were no nobler than the owner who taunted them with his wealth and social standing. Likewise, the author of the present irreverent volume might even be tortured into a confession of reverse snobbery, but we can agree: dogs are always innocent, even if people are not. And no dog, no matter how inbred, sickly, freakishly deformed, or mentally feeble, deserves to die for being an unwitting status symbol.

Yet however shocking and appalling these tales of retaliation, it should come as no surprise that by carefully twisting and pulling elastic beasts into things they were never meant to be, we have carelessly placed them in harm's way. There's simply no denying that coddled canines have been forged for centuries into unnatural shapes, sizes, and coat colors—forced into stylized behaviors extracted from the wolf and exaggerated to the point of parody. As we've seen, dogs have been inbred to wear royal crests, lion manes, ermine robes, and tuxedo jackets. They've been made to trot like royal horses, walk with regal bearing, hobble on Queen Anne legs, clown like court jesters, retrieve like black pages, and point at what they can't be bothered getting themselves. Bogus breeds have been whipped up like artists' conceptions based on aristocratic ancestors that are but distant relations, no relation at all, or never existed—like the so-called "Cavalier King Charles spaniel,"[3] "Queen Elizabeth Pocket Beagle,"[4] "Pharaoh hound," "Chinese crested," and, another counterfeit, the "golden retriever."

It should be obvious by now that fancy dogs were deliberately designed as insignias of class, ancestry, racial purity, national identity, and any other false claim to privilege purveyors could concoct. This was the original intent and appeal of "purebreds" from the first shows of the nineteenth century. To claim that dogs weren't painstakingly repackaged to carry on elitist traditions or that pet preferences are neutral and innocuous expressions of personal taste is to be in denial. Status has always been the main attraction, and most recognized breeds paraded around show rings give people more ways to win blue ribbons and silver cups, to stand with distinction in the public square, or extend their own stumpy family trees.

Tragically for the dogs themselves, the envy of onlookers sometimes gives way to anger. What's surprising is how rarely mean-spirited snootiness provokes the socially insecure into lowering themselves to taking action. The assault on Kernochan and his ostentatious quadruped isn't the only time a pet was asked to pay a price for its social ties. This unkind altercation was polite compared to the civil strife, economic crises, revolutions, and wars that have been tougher on canine Mini-Me's than breedists want to be reminded. While Kernochan was provoking a group of earthy laborers with an item beyond the reach of mere mortals and about to begin tearing up farms by fox hunting on Long Island, an ardent dispute over land ownership was placing hounds in harm's way back on the British Isles. Angered to see their livelihoods threatened by the kingly sport, English farmers decided to protect their crops with hostile barbed-wire fencing, spoiling a day's pleasure and hurting any hunters, hounds, and horses that passed. Neighboring Irish were no less irate over the constant reminder of oppression from afar this "truly British pastime" of fox hunting truly was. Saboteurs fudged defining moments of Anglophile sportsmen by poisoning entire packs of their finest pedigreed foxhounds.

"There was never a time when dogs were responsible for more class hatred than at the start of the nineteenth century,"[5] writes canine historian Carson Ritchie, referring to the tightening of game laws in England where hunting rights continue to reflect a certain classism.[6] In the years leading up to canine beauty pageants, "even possession of a sporting-dog by a poor Irishman might lead to a conviction for poaching, while in England, laws were equally severe."[7] Foxhounds were friendly compared to the bullmastiffs designed to look and act intimidating while guarding vast estates and deer parks of the landed class from trespassers. The breed came to symbolize class distinction and privilege.[8] Hoity-toity hench hounds, bred and trained to detain by an arm or a leg, got a bad rap from hungry locals, and along with the master's gamekeepers, these ungentle giants were shot by organized gangs who believed every man had a natural right to hunt and feed his family. By forbidding generations of commoners from owning certain types, and taking dogs by force so they alone could find protein, upperclassmen drew unflattering attention and acquired a backlog of resentment.

Beyond the British Isles, dogs have been no less harshly abused because their masters misused them. There were roundups and burnings of pets during the French Revolution, and in Italy, Bernabò Visconti, born to one of Europe's oldest families, set a bad precedent by making his poor subjects pay for the upkeep of his five thousand royal greyhounds.[9] Spain was another fertile ground for cyno-snobbery and spite. One forgotten hobby of the Inquisition, Mark Derr reminds us, was its careful approach to breeding. "Spain at the time was fixated on the concept of blood purity, *limpieza de sangre*, which its soldiers and priests applied to humans as well as animals."[10] Antique hound historian René Merlen attributes anti-canine sentiment in the Hebrew tradition to some lingering anger against former Egyptian masters who deified their pets but didn't value the lives of ordinary people.[11] More recently, "bloodhounds" got their name, not from the trail of Southern slave blood they followed, but from the "pure" substance said to be flowing in their veins.

Members of any canine class can suffer when classes take up arms against one another. "It was not a good idea, apparently, with tempers still running high, to walk a dog that was the symbol of a fallen cause," said Roger Caras, referring to Holland's early attempt at nationalism in the eighteenth century. The Keeshond was named after revolutionary dog owner, Kees de Gyselear. After a failed coup in 1787, the breed was marked by its previous owner and shunned by the reigning House of Orange, which preferred pugs.[12] During Russia's revolution, borzois, aristocratic hounds in near-identical pairs with matching coats, used to hunt wolves, were singled out by Bolsheviks and systematically snuffed along with their easily spotted masters. The borzoi was driven to near extinction—if that's the proper term for discontinuing a product of artificial selection—for its ties to the ruling class, which had exclusive right of ownership.

As for Chinese payback, no one can say exactly what became of those "sleeve dogs" not siphoned off to pay an empress's dry-cleaning bills for ensembles they were bred to match. All but a few in the imperial kennels are said to have been destroyed in 1912,[13] but lacking evidence of an all-out Pekingese pogrom, legends of using palace pooches to humiliate subjects at court, even executing dog-nappers, didn't inspire much puppy love. Considering China's track record on inhumane behavior, it seems likely that at least a few Pekes and members of other doggy dynasties were used in venting rage against reminders of the old regime. A tax on useless pet dogs—versus the eating kind—was levied in 1947. The Communist Party considered them a "symbol of decadence and a criminal extravagance" and banned luxury dogs from entire cities.[14] "Those who are against Chairman Mao will have their dog skulls smashed into pieces" is popularly remembered as a rallying cry of the Cultural Revolution. Though pet ownership is quickly catching on among a new breed of capitalist—like that Chinese developer who recently bought the world's most expensive dog—tokens of the bourgeoisie don't fare well when impromptu rabies scares send mobs into streets clubbing them to death by the hundreds of thousands.

In the same vein, much of the appeal of Cuba's famous Havanese dogs is the claim that untold numbers were put down when upper-class patrons took flight for Miami, saving their necks and leaving best friends to fend for themselves—and making these dogs more rare and enticing. These fragile, fluffy inheritors of the past have only recently had their thrones restored by counterrevolutionary snobs in the United States and Europe, where they're becoming more desirable by the day. Romania's extermination of Transylvanian hounds and Hungarian greyhounds, pooch purges in Estonia, Poland, Czechoslovakia—upper-class canines often share the same fate as those Cuban canines left behind.[15]

By the early twentieth century, English anger against anything Teutonic had been simmering, and World War I was a good excuse for settling an old score. At least one defenseless dachshund was destroyed, stoned to death in the English town of Berkhamsted, for being born with the wrong papers.[16] Dachsies were officially dropped by Crufts in 1915 as a public show of patriotism, and were shunned across the kingdom in the interwar years.[17] They were renamed "liberty hounds" in the United States, where sauerkraut became "liberty cabbage"[18] (a forerunner to "freedom fries" in post-9/11 America, where a fad for French bulldogs has developed despite the recent rise in anti-French feelings).

The English had a tick against another German breed, the German shepherd, a point of pride for its homeland and Hitler's last friend. The breed was appropriated in 1911 and redubbed "Alsatian" after the disputed territory. The name was not returned to its original owners, in either English or Continental dog shows, until the 1970s. A similar makeover was given to the British crown in

1917, when, to avoid any unbecoming resemblance to the barbaric tribe, the House of Sachsen-Coburg und Gotha was christened House of Windsor, currently better known for its ties to corgis and pugs.

After the dachshund's brief nosedive in wartime America, the slow acceptance of another Axis breed, the Akita, provides another interesting tale of doggy borders. Said to have first set paws on American soil as a Seeing Eye dog to Helen Keller in 1937, the breed was followed by reinforcements in 1956, when occupational forces returned with Japanese loot on leashes. Still, the Akita was not recognized as a breed by the AKC until 1972.

On no occasions do dogs feel more pressure to bear human enmities or pick up the tab for fickle friends than during hard economic times, when keeping them as pets can no longer be justified. Forged into useless household items, the vast majority of purebreds stand out as shameful signs of excess and waste when thriftiness is in style. Wartime food rationing has pushed many breeds to the brink of extinction. "Crufts closed its doors during the years 1917–21," writes Katharine MacDonogh in *Reigning Cats and Dogs*, "when food shortages made the very idea of exhibiting toy dogs tasteless." Even royalty risked public wrath for not complying with short-lived disapprovals of showiness, and "British monarchs kept a progressively lower profile and rarely exhibited. They also began to eschew 'foreign' breeds, electing to keep such 'British' breeds as Clumbers and Labradors—neither of which was of British origin—and cairns and corgis, both quintessentially national breeds."[19] Commoners' companions haven't fared as well as royal favorites, and during World War II hundreds of thousands of British dogs, and pets of all kinds, were put down by their owners due to food rationing.[20]

Peacetime economic woes are often as hard on hounds because disposable luxury items are the first to go when times are tough. Fair-weather friends decide they can no longer afford kibble or perhaps have lost their homes, as seen in the recent spike in abandonment rates and the wholesale euthanasia carried out in overcrowded shelters across the United States.[21] How could over-the-top admirers find so much of their identities in pets one moment, then casually discard them as "just dogs" the next? "Why the schizophrenic gap?" asks Elizabeth Marshall Thomas.[22] Contradictions can be traced, in large part, to having dogs for the wrong reasons. Half-baked notions of nobility, purity, trainability, and beauty don't stand up to scrutiny or stress and are easily shed in times of crisis. Sales pitches fall short of promises, and buyers fall out of love.

More recently—but backward enough to make us wonder if these people are kidding or what—a vast array of ancillary products have splintered from this quaint notion of upholding pedigrees. In the age of DNA, cotton-swab sampling, Ralph Lauren, and Ancestry.com, the many goods and services aimed at encouraging delusions of grandeur in humans have their closely related canine clones. An astounding assortment of props, trinkets, cheap tricks, and sealed certificates are placebos for the socially insecure, and as long as the prices are kept sufficiently high to make the advertising claims sound believable, they continue to find buyers. How much do you love your dog? The website ilovedogs.com offers a $3.2 million jeweled dog collar called the "Amour, Amour." Among other items priced at seven figures and more, this was dubbed "the Bugatti of dog collars" by *Forbes*. "The 52-carat Amour, Amour is the 'World's Most Expensive' dog collar." That will show the world how much a dog is loved. For less-favored pups, Louis XV–style dog beds from Paw Printz Pet Boutique sell for a mere $24,000, and custom-made doggy mansions start at $10,500. Descending the love ladder, there's the Royal Dog Poncho, the Royal Stewart Tartan Dog Coat, the Royal Dog Gate, the Windsor Castle Royal luxury dog bed (also available in Scottish Inn and Gramercy Park styles), and the Pet Royal King Costume for Small Dogs (complete with red cape, scepter, and ermine-trimmed crown). The upscale Pacific Urns company provides "Unique Jewelry Cremation Designs for People and Pets" determined to live on after they're gone, and the Hammacher Schlemmer catalog offers a do-it-yourself "Canine Genealogy Kit" to help you narrow your dog's ancestry to a few noble breeds (not included are red arrows marking the inherited health problems that plague each of the noble canine families). "Wear your bragging rights!" urges an ad from Perpetua Life Jewels for custom pendant vials displaying strands of "your special Dog's unique DNA."

Oddly enough, the DNA revolution of recent years and the marvelous advances made possible by science seem to be frightening people in the opposite direction. Much in the way that agricultural progress in the nineteenth century inspired a counterrevolutionary fad for breeding farm animals to be beautiful—leading to dog shows as we know them—new knowledge is encouraging an old retreat to more comforting thoughts of blood purity, racial superiority, and class distinction, ideas with a powerful draw that many people don't want to abandon.

Studies on canine health don't consider the human, or cultural, factor—the subject of this book—that's kept us from improving dogs as much as we might. Heads buried in family closets and digging for old bones, stalwart breedists showed heroic determination in the eighties, nineties, and naughties by escorting their royal corgis and Labs along the sidewalk runway. Sights set high, they ignored some pretty gruesome musculoskeletal defects gathering along the way. They were not thwarted by new studies showing soaring cancer rates or hip dysplasia as high as 73 percent in golden retrievers, which didn't discourage sales of that breed from skyrocketing during those very same years.[23] Rin Tin Tin retains a place in the AKC's top-ten pantheon despite famously failing health.[24] Diehards haven't been daunted by the swelling body of evidence that something is terribly wrong with many brands of choice, or the chance that maybe dog owners play a role in nurturing a health crisis by buying into it. The daily appearance of the neighborhood bulldog, dachshund, or Lab on wheels has only strengthened their mission to support their favorite types at any cost.

The fact that breedism can be traced to eugenics may be too close for comfort among champions of pedigree dogs. But like it or not, past and present merge to show that even, or especially, the most educated and advantaged people ignore the big picture when self-image is in the balance. This ongoing tradition of linking random appearance and contrived ancestry to accidents of birth is codified and preserved in the very standards "the best of the best" are held up against at Westminster and Crufts to represent *us* in the best light. Those intricate demands on coat color, skull shape, nose length, ear tilt, tail curvature—or hit-or-miss behavioral ticks people find "predictable" because they make dogs seem less dangerous and dirty—are what make brands appear distinct from others and superior to no-name generics anybody on the street could walk but no one would recognize. Remove breed standards and the royal house of cards comes crashing down.

"The first culling, of course, should be made at birth," advises the author of *The Joy of Breeding Your Own Show Dog*, reprinted as recently as 2004, on what to do when pups don't come out as predicted. "The responsible breeder will raise only those puppies that are correct in color and normal in conformation. Any malformed or mismarked puppies or weaklings should be put to sleep"[25]—because, after all, who's going to want to buy a dog that doesn't meet its breed standard? One of the more arresting points made by the BBC documentary *Pedigree Dogs Exposed* was that in "cosmetic culling" breeders are selecting for traits that are, in many cases, neither correct nor normal but in fact deformities with serious health consequences. Healthier but substandard littermates are sacrificed for mutants, which as in ancient times are revered as sacred. Symmetrical ridges on Rhodesians, equidistant spots on Dalmatians—the practice of culling for looks presumably goes on less now than in the past, though no one was ever fond of discussing this dirty business in public, and even the Humane Society has no statistics on the subject.

Question their time-honored customs and the experts get real upset. But according to one outside agitator, even show dogs can't seem to win. If not eliminated from the running for substandard coat color or jaw shape, they die slower deaths for actually meeting their standards and carrying the messages they were designed to convey. A British study, "Inherited Defects in Pedigree Dogs. Part I: Disorders Related to Breed Standards," won the prestigious George Fleming Prize from the *Veterinary Journal* in 2009. Focusing on the top fifty of the UK's recognized doggy dynasties, researchers at the Royal Veterinary College of the University of London identified 322 inherited disorders characteristic of individual breeds. Among these breed-specific defects, 84 were found to be caused, directly or indirectly, by conforming to the very breed standards used to hand out prizes in show rings—and to decide which dogs are worthy of places in our hearts and homes. The number of disorders was observed to be rising each year, and many of these are linked to "extreme morphologies," like the bulldog's face that breeders don't want to lengthen, or the dachshund's back they refuse to shorten. Among the 238 health problems said to be unrelated to standards, we can safely assume that many are genetic mishaps piled up over years of inbreeding for looks and lineage while giving second-class status to other concerns. Not only have standards not been improving an affected breed, they've been "predisposing it to a heritable defect."[26]

The *Pedigree Health Report*, another radical intrusion published with a noble imprimatur that's actually starting to mean something by the Royal Society for the Prevention of Cruelty to Animals, also tries to undo damages done in the name of good breeding.[27] Readers brave enough to peruse those grim pages will note the high price our best friends have been paying for high birth, and anyone with a stomach for the bad news behind all that cuteness will have difficulty dodging the conclusion that Best in Show winners and their vast progeny are bred to be too "good" for their own wellness. The rising costs of canine nobility and "appearance-driven breed standards" are crippling disability, blindness, deafness, cancer, epilepsy, hemophilia, chronic discomfort and pain, surgery, more discomfort, and more pain. Enforcing standards by keeping populations "pure" hasn't been inducing order in the animal kingdom but wreaking havoc by distracting from health, performance, and longevity; bending the dog's mortal frame to fit Procrustean market demands for increasingly "exaggerated anatomical features that reduce quality of life"; and driving gene pools to "extinction" levels, as per *Pedigree Dogs Exposed*. Dogs have been affected on both sides of the pond, where the Humane Society suggests health problems are on the rise.[28] While individual breeds suffer differently in the United States and United Kingdom, it doesn't take a population geneticist to suspect that the stellar rate of cancer mortality achieved in the American golden retriever might be due to its having one of the poorest percentages of breeding sires. The fetish for rarity and distinction has undiversified the breed genetically, a death sentence for any breed or species, and snobbery threatens to make goldens as rare as Saint John's water dogs.

More sad tidings for American dogs were delivered by the University of California, Davis, in 2013.[29] The inescapable conclusion of a large study conducted over fifteen years was that breeds finish first against so-called "mixed breeds," if only in their higher number of health problems. Breeds took ten out of twenty-four classes of disease, confirming what popular wisdom and pet insurance companies had been saying all along.[30] Mutts did rival breeds in thirteen disorders, where they more or less tied with their "improved" cousins, but then fell short of breeds in all but one defect, and a minor one at that. Rather than acknowledge the glass of good health to be more than half-full for randomly bred dogs, for some strange reason—AKC funding, perhaps?—UC Davis' official news release opened with an undignified I-told-you-so: "Purebred Dogs Not Always at Higher Risk for Genetic Disorders," read the headline and "mixed breeds," we were told, don't "necessarily" have certain health advantages.

No one ever said that any single randomly bred organism was guaranteed to turn out perfect, just that mutts were more likely to be healthy overall, which still turns out to be abundantly true. The slanted interpretation that UC Davis made of its own findings didn't mention the fact that several of the top-ten breeds the AKC declares socially acceptable each year on the eve of Westminster—with disclaimers on quality in the products it promotes,[31] whether prize-winning sires and their vast progeny, or dogs from puppy mills and "reputable" breeders alike—are top-heavy with a number of congenital health problems.[32] Once again, the human factor had the intended effect, and the thrust of the UC Davis news release was paraphrased identically in headlines across the country: "Mutts not always healthier, genetically, than purebred dogs."[33] Consumers were misled down the same path, encouraged to go on betting their next purchase would be better than the last. If only scientists would be given a little more time, they were told, a way would be found to salvage their shallow concerns about appearance and make good on those promises of exclusivity that some people need to feel special. A little more fidgeting with DNA in closed registries, and juggling priorities by picking and choosing which illnesses to tolerate in each genetically compromised type, and hobbyists could have their cake and eat it too.

It shouldn't take scientists to tell us that animals don't need to breed "true to type" to be individuals with their own merits, "personalities," idiosyncrasies, and endearing quirks.[34] Any open-minded novice should notice that the way dogs have been bred by experts since the nineteenth century represents a radical break from the past. You don't have to be an animal rights extremist to see that a fine flush face hinders breathing; prominent eyes can't be shielded; luxuriant skin and pendulous ears are prone to infection; an opulent coat makes walking a heroic act; a stalwart chest made Marley die from a twisted stomach; a back as long as a family tree supports euthanasia in corgis, dachsies, and silkies—or that fair birth by Cesarean approaching 100 percent probably *should* lead to the extinction of many breeds with noble brows.[35] Not only health and longevity are compromised by esthetics and clubbiness, but again, so is quality of life, which is much harder to measure. "The person who sets the standards has to realize that the way a dog looks will affect the whole of its life," Chris Laurence, Dog Advisory Council member and former chief veterinary officer for the Royal Society for the Prevention of Cruelty to Animals, tells *Dog World* magazine. "Some dogs can't breathe or walk freely because of the way they look. They have to realize that and modify the standards accordingly."[36]

Why not lighten up and give those pups a break by rewriting standards that ask too much and asking judges to reset their priorities? What harm could there be in giving bulldogs an extra millimeter or two of breathing room to the face? How about letting breeds wed outside their social stations? Because they would no longer be commercial breeds as we know them, and scientists who don't take into account the cultural or human factor fall short of giving the big picture of what, exactly, dogs are up against.

Attempts to change breed standards have led to class action lawsuits.[37] Expecting the fancy to loosen them is "like asking them to rob a granny," says professor of animal behavior Paul McGreevy of half-assed efforts to breed hip dysplasia from troubled breeds like the Labrador retriever.[38] If only Labs no longer had to *look* sort of like their ideals lodged at the royal family's Sandringham kennels, they might be improved to more than a mere 18 percent of one study group—funded by AKC grants—with "excellent" hip configuration. Discontinuing the bulldog might upset fans who put the breed on skateboards because it can barely walk, but would probably push its rate of dysplasia below a shocking 72 percent, or 67 percent for the pug, which ranked number two.[39] Conformation, which gets the lion's share of attention, has magical powers of distraction to customers using dogs to improve their own image, and telling them to change their identities at this late date is like asking a "pit bull" to loosen its grip.

Not even those controversial designer dogs of recent years are free from the health problems faced by purebreds. Forged from unsanctioned intermarriages between different doggy dynasties to the disapproval of purists like the AKC, established breeders, and owners of more conservative blends who say they prefer the old favorites that can't breathe, hybrids offered a short-lived hope for a healthier, more democratic form of dog breeding. Done properly, these unions make anatomical extremes like flat faces less extreme, and the benefits of genetic diversity need not be argued. But screening parents is uncommon, and offspring often inherit the worst traits from both breeds instead of the best. The window for improvement is being missed, and though the *Wall Street Journal* calls them "high-end mutts"[40] and the *New York Times* mentions "the rise of the mutt as commodities,"[41] these designer dogs don't need the AKC's recognition to be, for practical purposes, the equivalents of purebreds. Flashy *nouveaux* with preposterous names like Morkies, Chorkies, Puggles, Boggles, Doodleman Pinschers, and Shihtzapoos are born with the same basic credentials for snootiness as their parents from "old" families. Like them, they're bred from bitches forced to produce dozens of litters, often by Cesarean. They fetch prices in the thousands, come with pedigrees, carry meaningless papers, and are listed in their own social register called the American Canine Hybrid Club. Like purebreds proper, pretenders are sold in mass quantities with little regard for the health or temperament of individual dogs. They, too, arrive in homes sick and distressed, because they were born with all the same disadvantages. Sometimes they even manage to outclass their social betters. Based on a small number of animals included in a study by the Orthopedic Foundation for Animals, the Labradoodle would seem to suffer from a higher rate of hip dysplasia than either the Labrador or the poodle, and a potential benefit of crossbreeding can be offset by economics and carelessness.[42]

"It is a myth," writes the AKC, "that purebreds are more prone to hereditary disorders than mixed breeds."[43] While hybrid vigor is a theory that still has a few stodgy critics and offers no ironclad guarantees, it's less a transparent myth than purebred superiority in any sense other than social or commercial, and to deny this is to be silly. No-nonsense statistics from the pet insurance industry, sliding premium scales,[44] hard-knocks experience of broken-hearted dog owners, and research behind an article from Jemima Harrison, creator of *Pedigree Dogs Exposed*, agree on this. "Hybrids have a far lower chance of exhibiting the disorders that are common with the parental breeds," one study concludes.[45] "Their genetic health will be substantially higher." Another finds: "Mongrels were consistently in the low risk category" for fatal illnesses. "Mongrel dogs are less prone to many diseases than the average purebred dog," adds another. "Crossbreeds lived longer than average," concludes a study on cardiovascular disease. "In both dogs and cats, purebreds had an almost two-fold higher incidence of malignant tumours than mixed breeds," are the results of a study on cancer. "Mongrels low-risk for locomotor problems and heart disease," says another study. "The median age at death was 8.5 years for all mixed breed dogs and 6.7 years for all pure breed dogs," says yet another. "For each weight group, the age at death of pure breed dogs was significantly less than for mixed breed dogs." Still another: "Higher average longevity of mixed breed dogs. Age at death when split into three age bands: mixed breeds 8, 11, 13, purebreds 6, 10, 12." Inbreeding to meet standards seems to be the enemy of good health.

Many breeds are becoming so special they risk having diseases named after them. "Shar-pei fever," "Pug Dog Encephalitis" (PDE), "Leonberger polyneuropathy"—puppies with AKC papers are farmed by the thousands at puppy mills, then their illnesses are harvested and studied for the improvement of a small elite by "Breeders of Merit" (unbound by law or oversight to comply with AKC recommendations). At this very late date, a cornucopia of defects accumulated over years of misdirected purpose breeding are also the focus of studies aimed at helping humans suffering from the same problems in smaller percentages. As a kind of throwback to the courtly custom of keeping lapdogs because, it was believed, they somehow absorbed illness from their human holders,[46] widespread hemophilia in German shepherds, epilepsy in dachshunds and boxers, enlarged hearts in Newfoundlands,[47] degenerative retinal disease in schnauzers and poodles, narcolepsy and obsessive-compulsive disorder in Dobermans, sleep-related breathing disorders in bulldogs,[48] excessive skin on Shar-peis[49]—a growing list of abnormalities offers even less incentive to improve dogs when they continue serving mankind in the most unexpected ways.

The media's portrayal of this veritable goldmine for research, including a 2012 *National Geographic* article apparently timed to coincide with that year's Westminster show, makes no reference to how this data came about.[50] A kind of long-term, institutionalized cruelty that makes vivisection look humane is used to make "good" dogs look heroic for keeping up the good work, and those responsible for the preventable buildup of diseases self-congratulatory for having been so irresponsible all these years to give scientists something to study. "I'm not enthusiastic about line breeding to maintain pure-breed characteristics in dogs—it is the principal cause of many painful disorders that afflict them," writes Ewen Kirkness, a scientist at the J. Craig Venter Institute who has worked on the dog genome, in a recent e-mail. "But if the practice exists, and it doesn't look like it'll go away anytime soon, we might as well learn as much as we can from those dogs that are being bred as pets."[51]

"It is thought that white boxers are deaf or blind," says one breeder, defending his brand against critics by explaining that the rate of "only 20 percent" is actually "very low."[52] The sad truth is that you can give a devoted breedist all the facts and figures in the world and he'll still find ways to dismiss or rationalize the most appalling health problems. Once again, that human factor rears its ugly head. For lack of any other conceivable answer, one possible explanation, not an excuse for this denial could be some residual belief that disability and suffering are simply the price of nobility. Noblesse oblige isn't cheap, and has been around a lot longer than modern science or DNA studies. The same strange reasoning behind breed-specific rescue, where paupers are restored their rightful thrones because . . . well, because they're princes born deserving special treatment, says dogs must uphold their undershot jaws and bear their heavy armor as worthy ladies and gentlemen must also perform the duties of their social class. In fact, many health problems only recently acknowledged by the mainstream media aren't as newsworthy as they seem, but have endured over the years perhaps to motivate people to continue buying breeds.

From the founding of the first breed club in England, it must have been difficult not to notice that bulldogs, currently among the most expensive breeds for veterinary care *and* the most fashionable to have in New York City (based on AKC registrations),[53] were designed less for health, longevity, or mobility—or the purses of prize winners, breeders, registries, veterinarians, and pharmaceutical companies—than to uphold a certain social code. "And yet, with all this dandy dogs die like their humbler brethren—probably sooner," the *Strand Magazine* concluded as early as the 1890s[54] when Thorstein Veblen mentioned the many "monstrosities" being prepped for luxurious lifestyles in finer homes.[55] As the century drew to a close and dog shows were drawing crowds, human and canine elites were paying dearly for their fair birth, and a dog's suffering may have been seen as a mirror image of a half-mythical human condition known as neurasthenia. The symptoms were quite similar to the effects of inbreeding in dogs. Said to afflict refined and fragile specimens of the old ruling class unable to adjust to the vulgarity of modern life, and "social climbers" as well, this mysterious illness was no cause for shame but worn as a badge of pride.[56] Over a century later, poor health in many dog dynasties is poorer than ever, and yet critics continue to be ignored when calling for more sensible standards and less inbreeding—or an end to breeding altogether.[57] They're up against compelling new evidence showing breeds with more inherited disorders and behavior problems are, in fact, *more* popular, not less.[58] Add to today's invisible health crisis the fact that purebreds represent as many as 30 percent of dogs dumped in US shelters and you have a pretty good argument against pet production, period.[59]

The assumption of this book has been that the preventable suffering of a single animal is too high a price to pay for flattering the socially insecure, supporting the illusion of the perfect pet, or helping humans. We need to look at our dogs and ask: Do I really need all this formal fuss-budgeting and excess baggage on class and race to love you? If the answer is yes, then maybe we shouldn't have dogs, and responsible legislation with real enforcement might one day force us to live up to the claim that we're a dog-loving culture. More terrifying to purists than having no dogs at all is the thought of a mongrel melting pot, so we might also ask ourselves this time: If we're going to impose human values and beliefs on nonhumans, shouldn't we at least use the ones we profess to have? Maybe mixing the races won't solve all canine health problems, but an occasional indiscretion with an outsider is the healthy choice for many a family tree, and an elopement with a chorus girl or groom can be a genome's best friend.

Grim and grueling—and avoidable—as the present-day predicament for dogs could be seen at the end of the day, there are some signs of intelligent life. People are learning to shed their prejudices when it comes to canines by breaking inbred habits and renewing this observer's faith in humanity, just a little. Many will stay snobs about their own race, class, or both, but fewer want to force their companion species into molds even humans have trouble fitting. Evidence of a profound change in public opinion: in recent months, I've been astounded on city sidewalks to meet a new breed of dog owner, a type almost overeager to apologize, unsolicited and to every passing stranger, for having a breed by saying it's "a rescue"—in case anyone should get the wrong idea. More and more, dog lovers are casting aside those "how to find the perfect pet" manuals and bogus breed books, and simply saving the lives of homeless creatures and learning to love them. As an ad for J. Crew that challenges us to stop wearing animals as sweaters observes: "You prefer pedigreed fabrics and shelter dogs. We know you're out there."

ACKNOWLEDGMENTS

Thanks to Catherine Laur White for her input, support, and eternal friendship; Penn Whaling at the Ann Rittenberg Literary Agency and my editors Gayatri Patnaik and Rachael Marks for believing in this book; my many sources for daring to speak the truth; M. J. Kane and members of the Ladies of the Bleeding Heart book group for helping with the title; and all my faithful friends for their encouragement.

Special thanks to a world of dogs for being who you are regardless of breed, creed, or coat color.

NOTES

INTRODUCTION

1. Melinda Beck, "When Cancer Comes with a Pedigree," *Wall Street Journal*, May 4, 2010, http://online.wsj.com/news/articles/SB10001424052748704342604575222062208235690; Purdue University School of Veterinary Medicine et al., *Golden Retriever Club of America National Health Survey, 1998–1999* (GRCA, 1998), http://www.grca.org; and *Pedigree Dogs Exposed*, directed by Jemima Harrison, BBC One, August 19, 2008.
2. Mark Derr, "The Politics of Dogs," *Atlantic Monthly*, March 1990, http://www.stirlingcollies.com/id133.html.
3. Mark Derr, *Dog's Best Friend: Annals of the Dog-Human Relationship* (Chicago: University of Chicago Press, 2004); Stephen Budiansky, "The Truth About Dogs," Part III: "The Problem With Breeding," *Atlantic Monthly*, July 1999, http://www.theatlantic.com/past/docs/issues/99jul/9907dogs3.htm; Michael Lemonick, "A Terrible Beauty," *Time*, June 24, 2001, http://content.time.com/time/magazine/article/0,9171,163404,00.html; Jonah Goldberg, "Westminster Eugenics Show," *National Review*, February 13, 2002, http://www.nationalreview.com/articles/205141/westminster-eugenics-show/jonah-goldberg; J. L. Fuller and S. P. Scott, *Genetics and the Social Behavior of the Dog* (Chicago: University of Chicago, 1965); Advocates for Animals, *The Price of a Pedigree: Dog Breed Standards and Breed-Related Illness* (Edinburgh: Advocates for Animals, 2006), http://www.onekind.org/uploads/publications/price-of-a-pedigree.pdf.
4. Patrick Burns, "AKC Speeds to Collapse," *Terrierman's Daily Dose*, February 14, 2013, http://terriermandotcom.blogspot.com.
5. "Dog Breeds: The Long and the Short and the Tall," *Economist*, February 19, 2009, http://www.economist.com/node/13139635.

6. Fuller and Scott, *Genetics and the Social Behavior of the Dog*, 405; Patrick Burns, "Inbred Thinking," *Terrierman's Daily Dose*, May 26, 2006, http://terriermandotcom.blogspot.com; Christopher Landauer, "'Health Testing' in Dogs Is Limited," *Border-Wars*, May 18, 2013, http://www.border-wars.com; Christopher Landauer, "How Linebreeding Causes Disease Expression," *Border-Wars*, February 24, 2014, http://www.border-wars.com; Jemima Harrison, "Breeding—Not Bitching—for the Future," *Pedigree Dogs Exposed—The Blog*, May 15, 2014, http://pedigreedogsexposed.blogspot.com/2014/05/breeding-not-bitching-for-future.html.
7. Jasper Copping, "Ban 'Unhealthy' Dog Breeds, Say Vets," *Telegraph* (UK), December 10, 2013, http://www.telegraph.co.uk/health/petshealth/10508781/Ban-unhealthy-dog-breeds-say-vets.html.
8. Edward Ash, *This Doggie Business* (London: Hutchinson & Co., 1934), 205.
9. W. G. Stables, *The Practical Kennel Guide* (London: Cassell Petter and Galpin, 1875), 19.
10. Gordon Stables, "Breeding and Rearing for Pleasure, Prizes, and Profit," *The Dog Owner's Annual for 1896* (London: Dean and Son, 1896).
11. Louis Hobson, "Guest Shots," *Canoe.ca*, October 10, 2000, http://jam.Canoe.ca.
12. Stables, *The Practical Kennel Guide*, 115.

CHAPTER 1

1. "Handsome Dan" and his successors have a history crowded with health problems. The first dog to hold this office—a creature that looked like a cross between an alligator and a bullfrog—did manage to live to the ripe old age of eleven, quite a feat for the breed. Dan I was stuffed and displayed in a glass case at Yale University's Payne Whitney Gymnasium where he can be viewed today. Heirs to the throne haven't fared so well, nor have bulldogs serving as mascots to teams across the country who have imitated Yale's bad example. Even descendants of multiple prize-winners are prone to heart attacks and retire or expire at a very young age due to hip dysplasia, arthritis, kidney disease, emotional instability, and so on.
2. H. S. Cooper and F. B. Fowler, *Bulldogs and All About Them* (London: Jarrolds, 1925), 29.
3. R. G. Thorne, *The History of Parliament: The House of Commons, 1790–1820*, 5 vols. (London: Secker & Warburg, 1986), 622.

4. John Caius, *Of Englishe Dogges* (Charleston, SC: Nabu Press, 2012; orig. pub. 1576), 25.
5. Cooper and Fowler, *Bulldogs and All About Them*, 28.
6. William Taplin, *The Sportsman's Cabinet; or, a Correct Delineation of the Various Dogs Used in the Sports of the Field . . .* (London: J. Cundee, 1803), 86.
7. Cooper and Fowler, *Bulldogs and All About Them*, 18–20.
8. Taplin, *The Sportsman's Cabinet*, 86.
9. "10 Dogs with the Priciest Vet Bills," *Main St.*, July 10, 2011, http://www.mainstreet.com/slideshow/smart-spending/10-dogs-priciest-vet-bills.
10. "AKC Names 10 Most Popular Dog Breeds for 2013," *Examiner.com*, February 1, 2013, http://www.examiner.com/article/akc-names-10-most-popular-dog-breeds-for-2013.
11. James Watson, *The Dog Book* (New York: Doubleday, Page, 1906), 397–98.
12. Cooper and Fowler, *Bulldogs and All About Them*, 25.
13. Jane Lucille Brackman, "A Study in the Application of Semiotic Principles and Assumptions of Systems of Division, Classification and Naming," PhD diss., Claremont Graduate University, 1999.
14. Watson, *The Dog Book*, 398.
15. Cooper and Fowler, *Bulldogs and All About Them*, 48.
16. Ibid., 28.
17. Ibid., 57.
18. Edward Ash, *This Doggie Business* (London: Hutchinson & Co., 1934), 113.
19. Gordon Stables, "Breeding and Rearing for Pleasure, Prizes, and Profit," *The Dog Owner's Annual for 1896* (London: Dean and Son, 1896), 42, 72.
20. Freeman Lloyd, "Many Dogs in Many Lands," *AKC Gazette*, February 1924. For this and other citations from the *AKC Gazette*, I relied upon bound volumes located in the American Kennel Club archive, in New York City.
21. Cooper and Fowler, *Bulldogs and All About Them*, 29.
22. Ibid., 36.
23. Watson, *The Dog Book*, 398.
24. Johan and Edith Gallant, *SOS Dog: The Purebred Dog Hobby Re-Examined* (Las Vegas: Alpine, 2008), 86–92.
25. Rawdon Lee, *A History and Description of the Modern Dogs of Great Britain and Ireland (Non-Sporting Division)* (London: Horace Cox, 1894), 208–10.
26. Cooper and Fowler, *Bulldogs and All About Them*, 37.

27. "Underdog" originally referred to the loser in the fighting pit, a tragic figure pitied in a poem by David Barker, who wrote in the 1870s: "If they say I am wrong or am right/I shall always go in for the weaker dog/For the under dog in the fight." David Barker, "The Under Dog in the Fight," *Poems by David Barker*, with historical sketch by J. E. Godfrey (Bangor, ME: Samuel S. Smith and Son, 1876), 103.
28. *L.B.A.: Leavitt Bulldog Association*, http://www.leavittbulldogassociation.com.
29. Bob the baby bulldog never made it to his first birthday. The vet wasn't sure which of his many ailments finally did him in. Bob's two daddies were mad with grief, and against every law of educated consumer behavior and common sense, they went out and bought two more of the same.

CHAPTER TWO

1. John Mandeville et al., "Focusing on Breed Standards," *AKC Gazette*, February 1984.
2. "Pembroke Welsh Corgi: Breed Standard," American Kennel Club, http://www.akc.org.
3. Mandeville et al., "Focusing on Breed Standards."
4. Richard Wolters, *The Labrador Retriever: The History—the People* (Los Angeles: Petersen Prints, 1981), 154.
5. "Labrador Retriever: Breed Standard," American Kennel Club, http://www.akc.org.
6. Ibid.
7. "Pedigree Dogs Exposed," directed by Jemima Harrison, BBC One, August 19, 2008.
8. *Treasures of the Kennel Club: Paintings, Personalities, Pedigrees and Pets* (London: Kennel Club, 2000).
9. O. F. Vedder, "The War of the Bat and the Rose Ear," *AKC Gazette*, November 30, 1924.
10. Ibid.
11. "French Bulldog Club," *New York Times*, April 7, 1897.
12. Vedder, "The War of the Bat and the Rose Ear."
13. "Dogs of High Renown," *New York Times*, June 5, 1898.
14. James Watson, *The Dog Book* (New York: Doubleday, Page, 1906), 707.
15. "Dogs of High Renown."
16. Vedder, "The War of the Bat and the Rose Ear."
17. A.-K. Sundqvist et al., "Unequal Contribution of Sexes in the Origin of Dog Breeds," *Genetics* 172, no. 2 (February 2006): 1121–28, http://www.ncbi.nlm.nih.gov/pmc/articles/PMC1456210/.

18. Mark Derr, "Collie or Pug? Study Finds the Genetic Code," *New York Times*, May 21, 2004, http://www.nytimes.com/2004/05/21/us/collie-or-pug-study-finds-the-genetic-code.html.
19. Edward Ash, *This Doggie Business* (London: Hutchinson & Co., 1934), 43.
20. Mark Derr, "The Politics of Dogs," *Atlantic Monthly*, March 1990, http://www.stirlingcollies.com/id133.html.
21. "A Dog's Life," *Dateline* (NBC), April 26, 2000, http://www.caps-web.org/.
22. Mary Pilon and Susanne Craig, "Safety Concerns Stoke Criticism of Kennel Club," *New York Times*, February 9, 2013, http://www.nytimes.com/2013/02/10/sports/many-animal-lovers-now-see-american-kennel-club-as-an-outlier.html?pagewanted=all&_r=0.
23. John Caius, *Of Englishe Dogges* (Charleston, SC: Nabu Press, 2012; orig. pub. 1576), 34.
24. Mark Derr, *How the Dog Became the Dog* (New York: Overlook, 2011), 157–58.
25. Robert K. Wayne, "Molecular Evolution of the Dog Family," *Trends in Genetics* 9, no. 6 (June 1993): 218–24, doi: http://dx.doi.org/10.1016/0168-9525(93)90122-X.
26. One study ranked dogs by their degree of "cuteness" or lack of resemblance to wolves and then tested them for any correlation to wolflike behavior. Surprisingly, the puppylike golden retriever, with its wide, imploring eyes, domed infantile forehead, fluffy juvenile coat, and "soft" mouth, showed more wolf traits for conflict-related behavior than the German shepherd dog, deliberately designed to resemble a wolf. Deborah Goodwin et al., "Paedomorphosis Affects Agonistic Visual Signals of Domestic Dogs," *Animal Behavior* 53 (1997): 297–304, http://members.home.nl/mfcjanssen/AnimBehav1997.pdf.
27. Annie Coath Dixey, *The Lion Dog of Peking* (New York: Dutton, 1931), 245.
28. "Get to Know the Golden Retriever," American Kennel Club, http://www.akc.org.
29. Gordon Stables, "Breeding and Rearing for Pleasure, Prizes, and Profit," in *The Dog Owner's Annual for 1896* (London: Dean and Son, 1896), 14.
30. Alan Beck and Aaron Katchner, *Between Pets and People* (West Lafayette, IN: Purdue University Press, 1996), 168–70; Stephen Jay Gould, "Mickey Mouse Meets Konrad Lorenz," *Natural History* 88, no. 5 (May 1979): 30–36.
31. Jason Goldman, "Man's New Best Friend? A Forgotten Russian Experiment in Fox Domestication," *Scientific American* blog, September 6, 2010, http://blogs.scientificamerican.com/guest-blog/.

32. D. Phillip Sponenberg, "Livestock Guard Dogs: What Is a Breed, and Why Does It Matter?," *Akbash Sentinel* (1998): 44, http://www.akbashdogsinternational.com.
33. Roger Caras, *A Celebration of Dogs* (New York: Times Books, 1982), 190.
34. William Burrows, "Queen Victoria and Our Collies," *AKC Gazette*, July 31, 1924.
35. Derr, "Collie or Pug?"
36. Watson, *The Dog Book*, 612.
37. Jesse Gelders, "Science Remakes the Dog," *Popular Science Monthly*, November 1936.

CHAPTER THREE

1. Oscar Wilde, *The Importance of Being Earnest* (London: Leonard Smithers, 1899), 132.
2. W. M. Thackeray, *The Book of Snobs* (New York: D. Appleton, 1853), 54.
3. David Cannadine, *The Decline and Fall of the British Aristocracy* (New York: Anchor, 1990), 300.
4. Ibid.
5. Carol Midgley, "The Order of the Elitist Anachronism," *Sunday Times* (London), July 14, 2004, http://www.thetimes.co.uk/tto/opinion/article2037158.ece.
6. Robert Noel, College of Arms, interviews by author, June 22, 2009, and March 21, 2011.
7. Ibid.
8. Katie Thomas, "A Country Dog Charms the Big Show in the City," *New York Times*, February 15, 2011, http://www.nytimes.com/2011/02/16/sports/16best.html.
9. Noel, interviews.
10. Ibid.
11. Ibid.
12. "The Arms and Crest of Frederick Gavin Hardy," http://www.college-of-arms.gov.uk.
13. Alan Beck and Aaron Katchner, *Between Pets and People* (West Lafayette, IN: Purdue University Press, 1996), 171.
14. Patrick Burns, "Pet Insurance Data Shows Mutts ARE Healthier!," *Terrierman's Daily Dose*, April 4, 2009, http://terriermandotcom.blogspot.com.
15. Louis Fallon, "American Dog Show History Began June 4, 1874," *Dog Press*, http://www.thedogpress.com/ClubNews/History-of-Dog-Shows_Fallon-076.asp.
16. William Stifel, "Harbingers of Westminster," *AKC Gazette*, February 2002.

17. David Hancock, dog historian, e-mail to author, May 4, 2012.
18. Michael Clayton, foxhound historian, e-mail to author, May 14, 2012.
19. John Marvin, "Great Dog Men of the Past," *AKC Gazette*, March 1975.
20. René Merlen, *De Canibus: Dog and Hound in Antiquity* (London: Allen, 1971), 122.
21. Mark Derr, *A Dog's History of America* (New York: North Point, 2004), 164, 336.
22. Michael Clayton, e-mail to author, May 15, 2012; John Marvin, "How the Earliest Show Standards Came About," *AKC Gazette*, May 1967.
23. Gordon Stables, "Breeding and Rearing for Pleasure, Prizes, and Profit," *The Dog Owner's Annual for 1896* (London: Dean and Son, 1896), 114.
24. Carson Ritchie, *The British Dog* (London: Robert Hale, 1981), 110.
25. Frank Jackson, *Crufts: The Official History* (London: Pelham, 1990), 14.
26. H. W. Lacy, "Whence Came That Dog of Boston," *AKC Gazette*, January 1924.
27. Charles Henry Lane, *Dog Shows and Doggy People* (London: Hutchinson and Co., 1902), 264.
28. Harriet Ritvo, *The Animal Estate: The English and Other Creatures in the Victorian Age* (Cambridge, MA: Harvard University Press, 1989), 54–55.
29. William Tegetmeier, *Poultry for the Table and Market versus Fancy Fowls* (London: Horace Cox, 1892), 27, 89, 15, 7.
30. *Country Life in America*, May–October 1915.
31. Arthur Jones, "New Frenchies Are Coming Back," *AKC Gazette*, March 1, 1939.
32. Margaret Derry, *Bred for Perfection: Shorthorn Cattle, Collies, and Arabian Horses Since 1800* (Baltimore: Johns Hopkins University Press, 2003), 16.
33. Ritvo, *The Animal Estate*, 74–75.
34. Tegetmeier, *Poultry for the Table and Market versus Fancy Fowls*, 16, 3, 6.
35. Edward Ash, *This Doggie Business* (London: Hutchinson & Co., 1934), 113.
36. Tegetmeier, *Poultry for the Table and Market versus Fancy Fowls*, 2.
37. Lane, *Dog Shows and Doggy People*, 270–410.

CHAPTER FOUR

1. "Forced Sterilization," *Anderson Cooper 360°*, CNN, May 31, 2012, http://www.allthingsandersoncooper.com/2012/05/anderson-cooper-anderson-how-i-cheated.html; https://www.youtube.com/watch?v=bB95dA3gKTI.
2. Freeman Lloyd, "Many Dogs in Many Lands," *AKC Gazette*, July 31, 1924.

3. "Welsh Springer Spaniel," *Dog Breed Health*, http://www.dogbreedhealth.com/welsh-springer-spaniel/.
4. Gordon Stables, "Breeding and Rearing for Pleasure, Prizes, and Profit," *The Dog Owner's Annual for 1896* (London: Dean and Son, 1896), 13.
5. Charles Davenport, *The Trait Book*, Eugenics Record Office, Bulletin No. 6 (Cold Spring Harbor, NY, 1912).
6. Ian MacInnes, "Mastiffs and Spaniels: Gender and Nation in the English Dog," *Textual Practice* 17, no. 1 (2003): 21–40, doi: 10.1080/0950236032000050726.
7. "Exhibit on the Sense of Elegance in Fur Feeling," Cold Spring Harbor Laboratory, *Image Archive on the American Eugenics Movement*, http://www.eugenicsarchive.org.
8. Stephen Jay Gould, *The Mismeasure of Man* (New York: W. W. Norton, 1981).
9. Noah Webster, *An American Dictionary of the English Language* (New York: S. Converse, 1828).
10. "Shetland Sheepdog: Breed Standard," American Kennel Club, http://www.akc.org.
11. Patrick Burns, "True Terriers," *Terrierman's Daily Dose*, November 25, 2011, http://terriermandotcom.blogspot.com.
12. David Hancock, *The Heritage of the Dog* (Boston: Nimrod, 1990), 253.
13. Kevin Stafford, *The Welfare of Dogs* (Netherlands: Springer, 2006), 64.
14. Hancock, *The Heritage of the Dog*, 185.
15. Freeman Lloyd, "What Is 'Correct' Conformation?," *AKC Gazette*, July 1943.
16. Stuart Brown, "What Is a Breed Standard?," *AKC Gazette*, November 1947.
17. C. A. Bryce, *The Gentleman's Dog, His Rearing, Training and Treating* (Richmond, VA: Southern Clinic Print, 1909), iv.
18. Lloyd, "Many Dogs in Many Lands." The expression "nigger in the woodpile" originated in the Deep South and referred to fugitive slaves in hiding.
19. Jane Brackman, "Downton Abbey Dog: Right Breed, Wrong Color," *Bark*, April 5, 2012, http://thebark.com/content/downton-abbey-dog-right-breed-wrong-color.
20. Durham University, "Modern Dog Breeds Genetically Disconnected from Ancient Ancestors," news release, *Science Daily*, May 21, 2012, http://www.sciencedaily.com/releases/2012/05/120521163845.htm.
21. Raymond Coppinger and Richard Schneider, "Evolution of Working Dogs," in *The Domestic Dog: Its Evolution, Behaviour, and Interactions with People*, ed. James Serpell (Cambridge, UK: Cambridge University Press, 1995), chap. 3.

22. Per Arvelius, e-mail to author, June 21, 2012.
23. Erik Wilsson, e-mail to author, June 15, 2012.
24. Patrick Burns, "Rosettes to Ruin: Making & Breaking Dogs in the Show Ring," *Terrierman's Daily Dose*, n.d., http://terriermandotcom.blogspot.com.
25. J. Jeffrey Bragg, "Purebred Dog Breeds into the Twenty-First Century: Achieving Genetic Health for Our Dogs," *Seppala Kennels*, 1996, http://www.seppalakennels.com.
26. Russell Hess, e-mail to author, June 25, 2013.
27. Hancock, *The Heritage of the Dog*, 142.
28. Janis Bradley, "The Relevance of Breed in Selecting a Companion Animal," National Canine Research Council, 2011, http://nationalcanineresearchcouncil.com/.
29. Raymond and Lorna Coppinger, *Dogs: A Startling New Understanding of Canine Origin, Behavior & Evolution* (New York: Scribner, 2001), 246.
30. Stephen Budiansky, "The Truth About Dogs," Part III: "The Problem With Breeding," *Atlantic Monthly*, July 1999, http://www.theatlantic.com/past/docs/issues/99jul/9907dogs2.htm.
31. Kenth Svartberg, "Breed-Typical Behaviour in Dogs—Historical Remnants or Recent Constructs?," *Applied Animal Behaviour Science* 96, no. 3 (February 2006): 293–313, doi: http://dx.doi.org/10.1016/j.applanim.2005.06.014.
32. David Cyranoski, "Genetics: Pet Project," *Nature* 466 (August 26, 2010): 1036–38, doi: 10.1038/4661036a.
33. Stafford, *The Welfare of Dogs*.
34. Roger Caras, *A Celebration of Dogs* (New York: Times Books, 1982), 190.
35. M. B. Willis, "Genetic Aspects of Dog Behavior with Particular Reference to Working Ability," in *The Domestic Dog*, ed. Serpell, chap. 4.
36. United States Border Collie Club, http://www.bordercollie.org.
37. Willis, "Genetic Aspects of Dog Behavior," 62.
38. "Changes to the Show Border Collie Herding Test," Kennel Club website, June 8, 2011, http://www.thekennelclub.org.uk.
39. Patrick Burns, "Maybe They Need to Train the Sheep?," *Terrierman's Daily Dose*, October 1, 2011, http://www.terriermandotcom.blogspot.com.
40. Cyranoski, "Genetics: Pet Project."
41. Charles Krauthammer, "AKC Should Keep Its Snout Away From Border Collies," *Washington Post*, July 18, 1994, http://community.seattletimes.nwsource.com/archive/?date=19940718&slug=1920894.
42. Lucy Cockcroft, "Pedigree Dogs Are Becoming Stupid as We Breed Them for Looks, Not Brains," *Telegraph* (UK), January 18, 2009, http://www

.telegraph.co.uk/news/newstopics/howaboutthat/4283328/Pedigree-dogs-are-becoming-stupid-as-we-breed-them-for-looks-not-brains.html.

43. Fiona Macrae, "Why a Mongrel Will Always Trump the Pedigree Chump," *Daily Mail* (UK), January 27, 2008, http://www.dailymail.co.uk/sciencetech/article-510703/Why-mongrel-trump-pedigree-chump.html.
44. Jenny Barlos, e-mails to author, November 20–December 2, 2010.
45. Kim Wolf et al., Animal Farm Foundation, interview by author, October 4, 2011.
46. Kelly Gould, e-mail to author, October 2, 2011.
47. Kelly Gould, interview by author, September 28, 2011.
48. Susan Orlean, "Why German Shepherds Have Had Their Day," *New York Times*, October 8, 2011, http://mobile.nytimes.com/2011/10/09/opinion/sunday/one-dog-that-has-had-its-day.html.
49. Macrae, "Why a Mongrel Will Always Trump the Pedigree Chump."
50. *Guide Dogs*, https://www.guidedogs.org.uk.
51. Chuck Jordan, e-mail to author, March 29, 2012.
52. Joe Flood, "The Expendables: Inside America's Elite Search and Rescue Dog Training Center," *BuzzFeed*, April 26, 2013, http://www. buzzfeed.com/joeflood/the-expendables-inside-americas-elite-search-and-rescue-dog.

CHAPTER FIVE

1. "Map of the Week: Where the Dogs Are," *Toronto Star*, October 23, 2008.
2. William Arkwright, "The Fancier versus the Collie," *Kennel Gazette*, August 1888.
3. James Watson, *The Dog Book* (New York: Doubleday, Page, 1906), 344.
4. William Burrows, "Queen Victoria and Our Collies," *AKC Gazette*, July 31, 1924.
5. Arkwright, "The Fancier versus the Collie."
6. Ibid.
7. Patrick Burns, "Westminster & the Death of the Fox Terrier," *Terrierman's Daily Dose*, July 17, 2004, http://www.terriermandotcom.blogspot.com.
8. Patrick Burns, e-mail to author, March 1, 2012.
9. Annie Coath Dixey, *The Lion Dog of Peking* (New York: Dutton, 1931), 243.
10. Edward Topsell, *Topsell's History of Beasts*, ed. Malcolm South (London: Robert Hale, 1981), 183.
11. "Heraldry, Stourton, 1790," *Ancestry Images*, http://www.ancestryimages.com/proddetail.php?prod=e5937&cat=120.
12. Topsell, *Topsell's History of Beasts*, 66.

13. Ibid., 65.
14. John Caius, *Of Englishe Dogges* (Charleston, SC: Nabu Press, 2012; orig. pub. 1576), 25.
15. Freeman Lloyd, "Working with Hounds and Gun Dogs," *AKC Gazette*, September 30, 1925.
16. Topsell, *Topsell's History of Beasts*, 65.
17. William Taplin, *The Sportsman's Cabinet; or, a Correct Delineation of the Various Dogs Used in the Sports of the Field . . .* (London: J. Cundee, 1803), 81.
18. Robert Hubrecht, "The Welfare of Dogs in Human Care," *The Domestic Dog: Its Evolution, Behaviour, and Interactions with People*, ed. James Serpell (Cambridge, UK: Cambridge University Press, 1995), chap. 13.
19. Thomas Bewick, *A General History of Quadrupeds: The Figures Engraved on Wood* (Newcastle upon Tyne, England, 1790), 339.
20. Lloyd, "Working with Hounds and Gun Dogs."
21. Topsell, *Topsell's History of Beasts*, 181.
22. René Merlen, *De Canibus: Dog and Hound in Antiquity* (London: Allen, 1971), 96.
23. H. S. Cooper and F. B. Fowler, *Bulldogs and All About Them* (London: Jarrolds, 1925), 206.
24. Edward Ash, *This Doggie Business* (London: Hutchinson & Co., 1934), 150.
25. Bruce Fogle, *The Encyclopedia of the Dog* (London: DK Publishing, 2000).
26. Roger Caras, *A Celebration of Dogs* (New York: Times Books, 1982), 63.
27. Anonymous.
28. Senan Molony, "Sun Yat Sen—Will Eat Again," *Encyclopedia Titanica*, http://www.encyclopedia-titanica.org.
29. "AKC Meet the Breeds: Chow Chow," American Kennel Club, http://www.akc.org.
30. Greg Craven, "Breeder Buzz: The Dog for Cat People," *Exceptional Canine*, http://www.exceptionalcanine.com.
31. "American Eskimo Dog: Breed Standard," American Kennel Club, http://www.akc.org.
32. Edward Laverack, *The Setter: With Notices of the Most Eminent Breeds Now Extant . . .* (London: Longmans, Green, 1872), 8, http://books.google.com/books.
33. *Tsavo Leonbergers*, tsavoleonbergers.com/theleonberger.asp.
34. "Heraldry, King, 1790," *Ancestry Images*, http://www.ancestryimages.com.

35. Tracy Miller, "World's Most Expensive Dog? Tibetan Mastiff Puppy Sells for $2 Million in China," *New York Daily News*, March 19, 2014, http://www.nydailynews.com/life-style/world-expensive-dog-tibetan-mastiff-sells-2-million-article-1.1726647.
36. "Lyin' Kings? Chinese Zoo Keeps Dog in Lion Enclosure," *Toronto Star*, August 16, 2013, http://www.thestar.com/news/world/2013/08/16/lyin_kings_chinese_zoo_accused_of_trying_to_pass_off_dog_as_african_lion.html.
37. Topsell, *Topsell's History of Beasts*, 127.
38. Unless otherwise specified, terminology for dogs is taken from Gerald and Loretta Hausman, *The Mythology of Dogs* (New York: St. Martin's, 1997); AKC "Breed Standards" and *AKC Gazette*; and oral tradition.

CHAPTER SIX

1. Freeman Lloyd, "Greyhounds in History," *AKC Gazette*, March 31, 1926.
2. Alva Rosenberg, "You Can't Keep a Good Dog Down: Although of Humble Origin, the Boston Terrier Has Instincts of a Gentleman," *AKC Gazette*, October 31, 1924.
3. Michael Fox, *Behaviour of Wolves, Dogs and Related Canids* (New York: Harper & Row, 1971), 205.
4. Temple Grandin and Mark J. Deesing, "Genetics and Animal Welfare," in *Genetics and the Behavior of Domestic Animals*, Temple Grandin, ed. (San Diego: Academic Press, 1998; revised 1999), 319–41, http://www.grandin.com.
5. Katharine MacDonogh, *Reigning Cats and Dogs: A History of Pets at Court Since the Renaissance* (New York: St. Martin's, 1999), 135.
6. "Boston Terrier Deafness," *Boston Terrier Club of America*, http://www.bostonterrierclubofamerica.org.
7. David Cannadine, *The Decline and Fall of the British Aristocracy* (New York: Anchor, 1990), 113.
8. Lynn Kipps, "The Great Guisachan Gathering," *Golden Retriever Club of Scotland*, http://www.goldenretrieverclubofscotland.com.
9. Carson Ritchie, *The British Dog* (London: Robert Hale, 1981), 161–62.
10. Judith Lytton, *Toy Dogs and Their Ancestors* (London: Duckworth, 1911), 53.
11. Westminster Kennel Club, *Act of Incorporation, Rules and List of Members* (New York: W. F. Weeks, 1885).
12. Cleveland Amory, "The Great Club Revolution," *American Heritage*, December 1954.

13. "Membership" and online brochure, *Goodwood*, http://www.goodwood.co.uk/kennels/membership/membership.asp.
14. Amory, "The Great Club Revolution."
15. Milton Rugoff, *America's Gilded Age* (New York: Holt, 1989), 80.
16. "The Dogs of Celebrities," *Strand Magazine*, July–December 1894.
17. Lytton, *Toy Dogs and Their Ancestors*, 6, 279, 302.
18. "Society at the Dog Show," *New York Times*, October 23, 1902.
19. "The Coming Bench Show," *New York Times*, May 2, 1880.
20. "Society at the Dog Show."
21. "Dogs Worthy of Respect," *New York Times*, February 24, 1892.
22. "High-Priced Dogs," *New York Times*, April, 29, 1883.
23. "Ladies' Dog Show This Week," *New York Times*, November 1, 1903.
24. Ibid.
25. "Ladies Will Show Dogs," *New York Times*, October 25, 1903.
26. "High-Priced Dogs."
27. "Dogs of Noble Parentage," *New York Times*, February 12, 1892.
28. "Fashions in Dog Flesh," *New York Times*, February 27, 1891.
29. "Dogs Worthy of Respect."
30. Ibid.
31. "Fashions in Dog Flesh."
32. "Pets of the Household: Judging the Points of Aristocratic Dogs," *New York Times*, October 24, 1884.
33. "The Next Great Dog Show," *New York Times*, March 27, 1878.
34. "The Coming Dog Show," *New York Times*, May 12, 1878.
35. "Blue-Blooded Animals," *New York Times*, March 30, 1879.
36. "The Dog Show," *New York Times*, April 27, 1880.
37. "New-York Dog Show," *New York Times*, April 22, 1883.
38. "High-Priced Dogs."
39. MacDonogh, *Reigning Cats and Dogs*, 106.
40. "Blue-Blooded Animals."
41. "Ladies Will Show Dogs."
42. "Dogs of Noble Parentage."
43. Frank Jackson, *Crufts: The Official History* (London: Pelham, 1990); William F. Stifel, *The Dog Show: 125 Years of Westminster* (New York: Westminster Kennel Club, 2001).
44. Gordon Stables, "Breeding and Rearing for Pleasure, Prizes, and Profit," *The Dog Owner's Annual for 1896* (London: Dean and Son, 1896), 143.
45. "Crufts Winner Accused of Having Facelift," *BBC Newsround*, March 31, 2003, http://news.bbc.co.uk/cbbcnews/hi/animals/newsid_2902000/2902169.stm.

46. Lytton, *Toy Dogs and Their Ancestors*, 281.
47. "Dogs Hold High Carnival . . . Society Visits Aristocratic Canines in the Garden," *New York Times*, February 25, 1892.
48. "The Coming Dog Show."
49. "Looking at the Dogs," *New York Times*, May 9, 1883.
50. Jackson, *Crufts: The Official History.*
51. "The Coming Dog Show."
52. "Looking at the Dogs."
53. "Dogs Worthy of Respect."
54. "Interest in Toy Dogs. Pets in Glass Houses Attract the Crowd on Closing Day," *New York Times*, November 7, 1903.
55. "Society Views the Dogs . . . Colored Maid for Toy Dogs," *New York Times*, December 19, 1901.
56. Stifel, *The Dog Show*, 98.
57. "Dogs Hold High Carnival."
58. "Dogs of Noble Parentage."

CHAPTER SEVEN

1. Edward Axtell, *The Boston Terrier and All About It* (Battle Creek, MI: Dogdom, 1910), 146.
2. Alva Rosenberg, "You Can't Keep a Good Dog Down: Although of Humble Origin, the Boston Terrier Has Instincts of a Gentleman," *AKC Gazette*, October 31, 1924.
3. J. Varnum Mott, MD, *The Boston Terrier: Its History, Points, Breeding, Rearing, Training and Care . . .* (New York: Field and Fancy Publishing, 1906), 42. "If you go outside that number," ultra-snob Ward McAllister had warned, "you strike people who are either not *at ease* in the ballroom or else make other people not at ease." Erich Homberger, *Mrs. Astor's New York* (New Haven, CT: Yale University Press, 2002), 212.
4. Rosenberg, "You Can't Keep a Good Dog Down."
5. Ibid.
6. H. W. Lacy, "Whence Came That Dog of Boston," *AKC Gazette*, January 1924.
7. James Watson, *The Dog Book* (New York: Doubleday, Page, 1906), 523.
8. Joseph Graham, "American Variations of the Sporting Dog," *Outing* (1904): 737.
9. Charles Henry Lane, *Dog Shows and Doggy People* (London: Hutchinson and Co., 1902), 272.
10. "The Next Bench Show. Proposing to Surpass the Great Alexandra Palace Exhibition," *New York Times*, February 27, 1881.

11. William F. Stifel, *The Dog Show: 125 Years of Westminster* (New York: Westminster Kennel Club, 2001), 22.
12. "Fine Dogs to Be Shown," *New York Times*, October 12, 1902.
13. "English Judges Stir Dog Fanciers," *New York Times*, June 5, 1915.
14. Lacy, "Whence Came That Dog of Boston."
15. Ibid.
16. Axtell, *The Boston Terrier and All About It*, 13, 41–43.
17. Stories about "founding fathers" of dog dynasties, while convenient for narrative purposes, should be taken with a grain of rock salt. These tales are tall and require the same suspension of disbelief as the claim one breeder made to me (at the AKC's "Meet the Breeds" event in New York City) that George Washington himself was responsible for singlehandedly creating the American version of the foxhound. As per standard myth-making procedure, breeders, breed clubs, and the AKC trace the arrival of the proto-Boston terrier to Anglophile Robert C. Hooper, who supposedly imported the first dog from England in the 1860s and started this noble race on a path to perfection. Hooper was a wealthy landowner in the Boston area, but though the *Times* obituary credits him as being "prominent in the horse circles and club life of the city" and "one of the original promoters of the revival of steeplechases in the United States," there's no mention of him being the first man to own any sort of dog. Nor will we ever know the precise social background of all Pekingese dogs in the world, which, according to the *Times*, were descended from Queen Victoria's own personal pet (never known to have mated), or be certain of the imperial origins of Lady Algernon's famous "Goodwood line" (dogs whose apparent ancestors were recently shown to have never mated). England's Corgi Club had high hopes that a recent archeological find in a Welsh bog would link, once and for all, the pets free-ranging in Buckingham Palace to the queen's ancestral home. An old bone was unearthed, but that bone was dropped for mysterious reasons and no DNA tests were run. Likewise, so-called "Chinese crested" dogs probably never got closer to an Asian palace than a royal Wee-Wee Pad in Chinatown, and I would go so far as to venture that self-evident facts about retriever bloodlines traceable to Malmesburys, Buccleuchs, and Tweedmouths are in the same category of myth or half-truth. Robert Hooper obituary, *New York Times*, August 14, 1908; "Famous Dog-Mother," *New York Times*, February 25, 1912; David Feller, "Imperial Legacy," *AKC Gazette*, October 2008; "Ninth Century Bones May Be of First Royal Corgi," Associated Press, April 21, 2004, http://www.nbcnews.com/id/4798993/#.U_ZCFvldV1Y; Jacqui Mulville, Cardiff University, Wales,

e-mail to author, January 16, 2012; Patrick Burns, "Mutant Dog Confused for Mutant Pig," *Terrierman's Daily Dose*, June 9, 2012, http:www.terriermandotcom.blogspot.com.

18. Lacy, "Whence Came That Dog of Boston."
19. Angela G. Ray and Harold E. Gulley, "The Place of the Dog: AKC Breeds in American Culture," *Journal of Cultural Geography* 16, no. 1 (Fall–Winter 1996): 89–106, DOI: 10.1080/08873639609478348.
20. Watson, *The Dog Book*, 521.
21. Axtell, *The Boston Terrier and All About It*, 146.
22. Feller, "Imperial Legacy."
23. James Watson, "The Origins of the French Bulldog," *Country Life in America*, June 1915.
24. Watson, *The Dog Book*, 528.
25. Lacy, "Whence Came That Dog of Boston."
26. Mott, *The Boston Terrier*, 50.
27. Freeman Lloyd, "Working with Hounds and Gun Dogs," *AKC Gazette*, September 30, 1925.
28. Gordon Stables, "Breeding and Rearing for Pleasure, Prizes, and Profit," *The Dog Owner's Annual for 1896* (London: Dean and Son, 1896), 177.
29. Lacy, "Whence Came That Dog of Boston."
30. Roger Caras, *A Celebration of Dogs* (New York: Times Books, 1982), 121.
31. "Looking at the Dogs," *New York Times*, May 9, 1883.
32. Ibid.
33. Ibid.
34. Axtell, *The Boston Terrier and All About It*, 10.
35. Rosenberg, "You Can't Keep a Good Dog Down."
36. Stables, "Breeding and Rearing for Pleasure, Prizes, and Profit," 177.
37. Lacy, "Whence Came That Dog of Boston."
38. Axtell, *The Boston Terrier and All About It*, 4.
39. Lacy, "Whence Came That Dog of Boston."
40. Rosenberg, "You Can't Keep a Good Dog Down."
41. Lacy, "Whence Came That Dog of Boston."
42. David Hancock, *The Heritage of the Dog* (Boston: Nimrod, 1990), 312.
43. Advertisement for R. F. Helmer, Syracuse, NY, *Dogdom Monthly*, April 1920, 85.
44. *AKC Gazette*, January 31, 1924.
45. Fred Kelly, "What a Man Badger Would Be!," *AKC Gazette*, September 30, 1924.
46. Sutherland Cuddy, "Herman and His Dog," *AKC Gazette*, August 31, 1926.
47. E. Yarham, "Roots of Tradition," *AKC Gazette*, March 1946.

48. "Benefits of Registration," American Kennel Club, http://www.akc.org.
49. Freeman Lloyd, "With the Dogs of Our Forefathers," *AKC Gazette*, March 31, 1925.
50. Freeman Lloyd, "Many Dogs in Many Lands," *AKC Gazette*, September 30, 1924.
51. Ida Garrett, "The Dog of Aztec Royalty," *AKC Gazette*, December 31, 1925.
52. William Burrows, "Queen Victoria and Our Collies," *AKC Gazette*, July 31, 1924.
53. Gerald and Loretta Hausman, *The Mythology of Dogs* (New York: St. Martin's, 1997), 170.
54. Annie Coath Dixey, *The Lion Dog of Peking* (New York: Dutton, 1931), 244.
55. "Pyrenean Shepherd: Breed Standard," American Kennel Club, http://www.akc.org.
56. "Breed Information Centre: Rhodesian Ridgeback," Kennel Club, http://www.thekennelclub.org.uk/.
57. "Rhodesian Ridgeback: Breed Standard," American Kennel Club, http://www.akc.org.
58. V. W. F. Collier, *Dogs of China & Japan in Nature and Art* (New York: Frederick A. Stokes Company, 1921), 170.

CHAPTER EIGHT

1. Joseph Epstein, *Snobbery: The American Version* (New York: Mariner, 2003), 114.
2. "Golden Retriever: Breed Standard," American Kennel Club, http://www.akc.org.
3. Freeman Lloyd, "Among the Retriever Dogs," *AKC Gazette*, March 1, 1932.
4. "Retriever Field Trials: History of the Sport," American Kennel Club, http://www.akc.org.
5. Donald McCaig, "Give This Dog a Job," *New York Times*, July 5, 1992.
6. Mowbray Walter Morris, *Hunting* (London: Longmans, Green, 1885), 189–90.
7. Joe Arnette, "Likable 'Guys,'" *Gun Dog Magazine*, September 23, 2010, http://www.gundogmag.com.
8. "It doesn't cost any more to feed 'pretty' dogs," a famous breeder of yellow hunting Labs with perfect skulls and traditional "otter" tails tells *Gun Dog Magazine.* Does this mean she only feeds dogs if they're "pretty"? James Spencer, "Braemar Labradors: Good Looking Shooting Dogs," *Gun Dog Magazine*, September 23, 2010, http://www.gundogmag.com.

9. William Arkwright, *The Pointer and His Predecessors: An Illustrated History of the Pointing Dog from the Earliest Times* (London: Arthur L. Humphreys, 1902), 72, 81, 85, 83, 80, 89.
10. Carson Ritchie, *The British Dog* (London: Robert Hale, 1981), 91.
11. Ibid., 105.
12. Katharine MacDonogh, *Reigning Cats and Dogs: A History of Pets at Court Since the Renaissance* (New York: St. Martin's, 1999), chap. 1.
13. Jacques du Fouilloux, *La vénerie de Jacques du Fouilloux, Gentil-homme...* (Paris: A. Poitiers, de Marnefz, et Bouchetz, freres, 1561).
14. Elzéar Blaze, *Le chasseur au chien d'arrêt* (Paris, 1846), 255–58.
15. James Robinson, *Readings in European History* (New York: Ginn, 1906), 435.
16. Morris, *Hunting*, 317, 190.
17. John Caius, *Of Englishe Dogges* (Charleston, SC: Nabu Press, 2012; orig. pub. 1576), 27.
18. Ritchie, *The British Dog*, 162.
19. Emma Griffin, *Blood Sport: Hunting in Britain Since 1066* (New Haven, CT: Yale University Press, 2009), 159.
20. Patrick Burns, "The Glory of British Dogs," *Dogs Today*, August 2010, www.dogstodaymagazine.co.uk.
21. Joe Arnette, "A Close To Perfect Union," *Gun Dog Magazine*, September 23, 2010.
22. Richard Hirneisen, "In The Company of Dogs," *Gun Dog Magazine*, September 23, 2010.
23. Freeman Lloyd, "Many Dogs in Many Lands," *AKC Gazette*, September 30, 1924.
24. Arkwright, *The Pointer and His Predecessors*, 45, 53–54.
25. Freeman Lloyd, "Pure Breeds and Their Ancestors," *AKC Gazette*, July 31, 1927.
26. David Hancock, *The Heritage of the Dog* (Boston: Nimrod, 1990), 233.
27. E. Cumming, "Modern English Gun Dogs," *Outing* (December 1903).
28. David Cannadine, *The Decline and Fall of the British Aristocracy* (New York: Anchor, 1990), 364.
29. Ibid.
30. Morris, *Hunting*, 191.
31. Cathy Bryant, the Hurlingham Club, e-mail to author, August 6, 2010, with selections on pigeon shooting. London's Hurlingham Club still exists. A pigeon remains the insignia of the elite establishment, though birds, and the gun dogs used as "concentrators" to hurl them upward for easy shooting, have long been banned from the premises. Pigeon

shooting was ended for humane reasons, though dogs were employed only until they got in the way in 1872 and bit a coachman! Sitting in place of those hard-wired flushing spaniels is a cute little wide-eyed Cavalier seen in a photo from a recent club picnic. He sits on the lawn staring up at a silver tray of crudités.

32. Cannadine, *The Decline and Fall of the British Aristocracy*, 364.
33. William F. Stifel, *The Dog Show: 125 Years of Westminster* (New York: Westminster Kennel Club, 2001), 35.
34. Capt. Albert Money, *Pigeon Shooting: With Instructions for Beginners . . .*, A. C. Gould, ed. (New York: Shooting and Fishing Publishing, 1896), 9.
35. P. D. Q. Zabriskie, "Fox-Hunting about Rome," *Outing* (December 1903): 327.
36. Cannadine, *The Decline and Fall of the British Aristocracy*, 364.
37. Arkwright, *The Pointer and His Predecessors*, viii.
38. Edward Ash, *This Doggie Business* (London: Hutchinson & Co., 1934), 148.
39. John Walsh, *The Dog in Health and Disease* (London: Longmans, Green, 1859), 188. Similar accounts were made of greyhounds so intensely overbred for speed and enthusiasm that they couldn't be *stopped* from playing the royal game of hare chasing. Racing on enhanced levels of stimulation, they often ran to the point of collapse. They collided with each other, breaking those thin, aristocratic necks. Greyhound packs were known to shoot themselves right off cliffs (Ritchie, *The British Dog*, 126).
40. Arkwright, *The Pointer and His Predecessors*, 84.
41. Ibid., 56.
42. Rick Van Etten, editor, *Gun Dog Magazine*, e-mail to author, September 9, 2010.
43. Cumming, "Modern English Gun Dogs."
44. Edward Donnaly, "Photographing Field Dogs In Action," *Outing* (1904): 592.
45. Stifel, *The Dog Show*, 34.

CHAPTER NINE

1. Gordon Stables, "Breeding and Rearing for Pleasure, Prizes and Profit," *The Dog Owner's Annual for 1896* (London: Dean and Son, 1896), 115.
2. Freeman Lloyd, "Many Dogs in Many Lands," *AKC Gazette*, July 31, 1924.
3. Craven (pseud. for John William Carleton), *The Young Sportsman's Manual; or, Recreations in Shooting* (London: Bell & Daldy, 1867), 103.
4. C. A. Bryce, *The Gentleman's Dog, His Rearing, Training and Treating* (Richmond, VA: Southern Clinic Print, 1909), 113–14.

5. Richard A. Wolters, *The Labrador Retriever: The History—the People* (Los Angeles: Petersen Prints, 1981), 73.
6. Ibid., 72.
7. Lord George Scott and Sir John Middleton, *The Labrador Dog: Its Home and History* (London: H. F. and G. Witherby Ltd., 1936), 121.
8. Wolters, *The Labrador Retriever*, 72.
9. Ralph Lauren has since assumed the role of making Americans look British, while A&F has turned its attention to tight abs and collegiate crotches.
10. *Royal Dogs* (London: The Kennel Club, 2006).
11. Wolters, *The Labrador Retriever*, 73.
12. Ibid., 78.
13. Freeman Lloyd, "Among the Retriever Dogs," *AKC Gazette*, March 1, 1932.
14. Wolters, *The Labrador Retriever*, 78.
15. Ibid., 112.
16. Lloyd, "Among the Retriever Dogs."
17. Wolters, *The Labrador Retriever*, 78.
18. Nancy Martin, *Legends in Labradors* (Spring House, PA: Self, 1980), 123.
19. Mowbray Walter Morris, *Hunting* (London: Longmans, Green, 1885), 268.
20. Wolters, *The Labrador Retriever*, 108.
21. Ibid., 109. Hunting on Long Island has a solid tradition of snootiness. One of the first texts on gun hunting published in America (Anonymous, *Heath-Hen Shooting on Long Island*, 1783) describes the "so very Majestical an amusement" that was "provided with a brace of the best Pointers." The author's dogs were "made in England," and a typical hunt ran as follows: "Suppose my party to consist of two Gentlemen. I would provide a single horse-chair . . . a Servant in the second chair, to carry the Dogs, (of which there should be two brace at least), provisions, liquors, tea, sugar, etc.," and last but not least "powder and shot." John Phillips and Lewis Hill, eds., *Classics of the American Shooting Field* (Boston: Houghton Mifflin, 1930), 1–3.

CONCLUSION

1. "J. L. Kernochan Beaten," *New York Times*, February 24, 1896.
2. W. M. Thackeray, *The Book of Snobs* (New York: D. Appleton, 1853), 21.
3. Contrary to popular lore, and some respected dog writers, the so-called "Cavalier" is not an old breed but, like so many others, an invention of the show ring. Breeders competed at Crufts in the 1920s to produce a historical replica based on court paintings from the time of Charles II.

Not only is the bogus breed plagued with health problems, but the resemblance to its would-be ancestor is slight at best.

4. The "Queen Elizabeth Pocket Beagle" was created, like the "Cavalier," based on old paintings by a woman from Indiana in 2002.
5. Carson Ritchie, *The British Dog* (London: Robert Hale, 1981), 157.
6. Emma Griffin, *Blood Sport: Hunting in Britain Since 1066* (New Haven, CT: Yale University Press, 2009), 159. The Ground Game Act of 1880, still in effect today, allows tenants to hunt hares and rabbits but gives landlords the exclusive right to kill winged prey.
7. Ritchie, *The British Dog*, 157.
8. Roger Caras, *A Celebration of Dogs* (New York: Times Books, 1982), 96–97.
9. Katharine MacDonogh, *Reigning Cats and Dogs: A History of Pets at Court Since the Renaissance* (New York: St. Martin's, 1999), 73.
10. Mark Derr, *A Dog's History of America* (New York: North Point, 2004), 24.
11. René Merlen, *De Canibus: Dog and Hound in Antiquity* (London: Allen, 1971), 20.
12. Caras, *A Celebration of Dogs*, 143.
13. MacDonogh, *Reigning Cats and Dogs*, 225.
14. "Dogs in China," *Facts and Details*, http://factsanddetails.com/china/cat12/sub81/item266.html.
15. MacDonogh, *Reigning Cats and Dogs*, 226.
16. Graham Greene, *A Sort of Life* (New York: Penguin, 1971), 64.
17. "World War I Impact on America," *Facts on File*, http://springfieldus2.wikispaces.com/file/view/WW+I.pdf.
18. "War & Peace: Liberty Cabbage," *Time*, January 27, 1941, http://content.time.com/time/magazine/article/0,9171,801203,00.html.
19. MacDonogh, *Reigning Cats and Dogs*, 120–21.
20. Clare Campbell, "Panic That Drove Britain to Slaughter 750,000 Family Pets in One Week," *Daily Mail* (UK), October 14, 2013, http://www.dailymail.co.uk/news/article-2460094/Panic-drove-Britain-slaughter-750-000-family-pets-week.html.
21. Jackie Damico, "Mortgage Meltdown Results in Pets Going to the Pound," CNN.com, November 21, 2008, http://www.cnn.com/2008/US/11/21/pets.foreclosure/index.html?eref.
22. Alan Beck and Aaron Katchner, *Between Pets and People*, preface by E. Marshall Thomas (West Lafayette, IN: Purdue University Press, 1996), x.
23. E. R. Paster et al., "Estimates of Prevalence of Hip Dysplasia in Golden Retrievers and Rottweilers and the Influence of Bias on Published Prevalence Figures," *JAVMA* (*Journal of the American Veterinary*

Medical Association) 225, no. 3 (February 1, 2005): 387–92, doi: 10.2460/javma.2005.226.387.

24. J. M. Fleming et al., "Mortality in North American Dogs from 1984 to 2004: An Investigation into Age-, Size-, and Breed-Related Causes of Death," *Journal of Veterinary Internal Medicine* 25, no. 2 (March–April 2011): 187–98, doi: 10.1111/j.1939-1676.2011.0695.x.
25. Ann Seranne, *The Joy of Breeding Your Own Show Dog* (Hoboken, NJ: Howell, 1980), 202.
26. Lucy Asher et al., "Inherited Defects in Pedigree Dogs: Disorders Related to Breed Standards," *Veterinary Journal* 182, no. 3 (August 2009): 402–11, doi: 10.1016/j.tvjl.2009.08.033.
27. Nicola Rooney and David Sargan, *Pedigree Dog Breeding in the UK: A Major Welfare Concern?* (London: RSPCA, 2008).
28. Carrie Allan, "The Purebred Paradox: Is the Quest for the 'Perfect' Dog Driving a Genetic Health Crisis?," *All Animals* (May–June 2010): 17–23, http://www.humanesociety.org.
29. "Purebred Dogs Not Always at Higher Risk for Genetic Disorders, Study Finds," news release, *UC Davis News and Information*, May 28, 2013, http://www.news.ucdavis.edu/search/news_detail.lasso?id=10613.
30. Patrick Burns, "Pet Insurance Data Shows Mutts ARE Healthier!," *Terrierman's Daily Dose*, April 4, 2009, http://www.terriermandotcom.blogspot.com.
31. "About Registration," American Kennel Club, http://www.akc.org/reg/about.cfm.
32. Fleming et al., "Mortality in North American Dogs."
33. "Purebred Dogs Not Always at Higher Risk"; "Mutts Not Always Healthier, Genetically, Than Purebred Dogs," *Chicago Tribune*, May 30, 2013; Eryn Brown, "Mutts Not Always Healthier, Genetically, Than Purebred Dogs," *Los Angeles Times*, May 30, 2013, http://articles.latimes.com/2013/may/30/science/la-sci-sn-genetic-disorders-dogs-20130530.
34. Natalie Angier, "Even Among Animals: Leaders, Followers and Schmoozers," *New York Times*, April 5, 2010, http://www.nytimes.com/2010/04/06/science/06angi.html?ref=science.
35. Katy M. Evans and Vicki I. Adams, "Proportion of Litters of Purebred Dogs by Caesarean Section," *Journal of Small Animal Practice* 51, no. 2 (February 2010): 113–18, doi: 10.1111/j.1748-5827.2009.00902.x.
36. "Breeding Debate," *Dog World*, December 7, 2011.
37. Jane Brackman, "Body Language: Breeders, Judges and Historians Talk about Breed Standards—Why They Work and When They Don't," *Bark*, Fall 2013, http://thebark.com/category/author/jane-brackman.

38. Lissa Christopher, "Hip Pain a Bone of Contention for Pedigree Pooches," *Sydney Morning Herald*, December 25, 2009, http://www.smh.com.au/national/hip-pain-a-bone-of-contention-for-pedigree-pooches-20091223-lder.html.
39. Orthopedic Foundation for Animals, "Hip Dysplasia Statistics: Hip Dysplasia by Breed," http://www.offa.org/stats_hip.html.
40. Ellen Gamerman, "High-End Mutts Sit Up and Beg for a Little Respect," *Wall Street Journal*, December 24, 2005, http://online.wsj.com/news/articles/SB113538296120430945.
41. Jon Mooallem, "The Modern Kennel Conundrum," *New York Times*, February 4, 2007, http://www.nytimes.com/2007/02/04/magazine/04dogs.t.html?_r=1&oref=slogin.
42. Orthopedic Foundation for Animals, "Hip Dysplasia Statistics."
43. "AKC Facts and Stats: Why Purebred?," American Kennel Club, http://www.akc.org/press_center/facts_stats.cfm?page=why_purebred.
44. Burns, "Pet Insurance Data Shows Mutts ARE Healthier!" http://terriermandotcom.blogspot.ca/
45. Jemima Harrison, "Are Mongrels Healthier Than Pedigrees?" *Dogs Today*, October 2010, http://www.facebook.com/note.php?note_id=481860411368.
46. Royal courts once used lapdogs, not only to attract fleas from their holders but to act as "comforter dogs," which, it was believed, literally absorbed human illnesses from proper ladies and gentlemen. "And though some suppose that such dogges are fyt for no seruice," wrote dog historian and Queen Elizabeth's personal physician, John Caius, in 1570, "borne in the bosom of the diseased and weake person" it was observed that "the disease and sicknesse, chaungeth his place and entreth (though it be not precisely marcked) into the dogge, which to be no vntruth, experience can testify, for these kinde of dogges sometimes fall sicke, and sometime die, without any harm, outwardly inforced." Here was proof of "the virtue which remaineth in the Spaniell gentle." John Caius, *Of Englishe Dogges* (Charleston, SC: Nabu Press, 2012; orig. pub. 1576), 21–22.
47. "Gentle Giants Could Help Cure Human Heart Problem," *BBC News*, October 28, 1998, http://news.bbc.co.uk/2/hi/health/203435.stm.
48. James Serpell, "Anthropomorphism and Anthropomorphic Selection—Beyond the 'Cute Response,'" *Society & Animals* 11, no. 1 (January 2003): 83–100, http://research.vet.upenn.edu/portals/36/media/serpell_anthropomorphic.pdf.
49. Jonathan Amos, "Shar-pei Wrinkles Explained by Dog Geneticists," *BBC News*, January 12, 2010, http://news.bbc.co.uk/1/hi/sci/tech/8453794.stm.

50. Evan Ratliff, "How to Build a Dog," *National Geographic*, February 2012, http://ngm.nationalgeographic.com/2012/02/build-a-dog/ratliff-text.
51. Ewen Kirkness, e-mail to author, February 23, 2012. "Boxer Genome Is Best in Show," says the *Genome News Network* about the breed's outstandingly poor health, which made it the ideal candidate for studying disease. "Unlike a dog show—in which grooming, obedience, and gait are prized—this contest was about genetic variation. The Genome Institute wanted the dog with the least genetic variation in its genome, because this should make the assembly of the genome sequence easier." Obama's choice of First Dog was also wise if the intention was to study congenital illness. The chronically inbred Portuguese water dog had been named the world's rarest breed by Guinness in 1981. Kate Dalke, "Boxer Genome Is Best in Show," *Genome News Network*, http://genomenewsnetwork.org/articles/05_03/best_show.shtml; Michael Wall, "Obama's Pick for First Dog Solidly Scientific," *Wired*, February 25, 2009, http://www.wired.com/2009/02/obamadog.
52. "The Truth About White Boxers!," *Big Sky Boxers*, n.d., http://www.bigskyboxers.com/white_boxers.php.
53. "10 Dogs with the Priciest Vet Bills," *Main St.*, October 10, 2011, http://www.mainstreet.com; "Top Breeds in Major U.S. Cities," American Kennel Club, http://www.akc.org.
54. William Fitzgerald, "Dandy Dogs," *Strand Magazine* (January–June 1896): 549.
55. Thorstein Veblen, *The Theory of the Leisure Class* (Auckland, NZ: Floating Press, 2009; orig. pub. 1899), 168.
56. "Neurasthenia," *Science Museum*, n.d., http://www.sciencemuseum.org.uk/broughttolife/techniques/neurasthenia.aspx; "Neurasthenia," *WebMD*, February 25, 2014, http://www.webmd.com/mental-health/neurasthenia.
57. Scott and Fuller's landmark study in behavioral genetics already concluded back in the 1960s that, while "a pure breed is far from being a homogeneous group," the "purebreds usually contain genes which produce physical defects" and "current dog breeding practices can be described as an ideal system for the spread and preservation of injurious recessive genes." Not only are standardized "types" not as behaviorally unique as their sales pitches claim, short of the most superficial traits, breeds often fall short of uniformity—unless, of course, "predictable" means more likely to be sick and short-lived. J. L. Fuller and S. P. Scott, *Genetics and the Social Behavior of the Dog* (Chicago: University of Chicago Press, 1965), 295, 389, 405. More recently, in 2013, a forum of scientists and

writers warned, once again, about bad breeding practices and elicited only a handful of comments from *New York Times* readers. "The Ethics of Raising Purebred Dogs," Opinion Pages: Room for Debate, *New York Times*, February 12, 2013, http://www.nytimes.com/roomfordebate/2013/02/12/the-ethics-of-raising-purebred-dogs.

58. S. Ghirlanda et al., "Fashion vs. Function in Cultural Evolution: The Case of Dog Breed Popularity," *PLOS One* 8, no. 9 (September 11, 2013): e74770; doi:10.1371/journal.pone.0074770, http://www.plosone.org.
59. "Animal Overpopulation: United States Facts & Figures," Oxford-Lafayette Humane Society, http://www.oxfordpets.com/.

INDEX

Abercrombie & Fitch, 205, 209–10
Academy for Dog Trainers, 93
Afghan hounds, 115, 139
Airedale terriers, 105, 159, 167
Akitas, 222
alaunts, 58, 59, 60, 194. *See also* heraldry
Albert, Prince Consort, 68
Alexander the Great, 112
Alexandra (queen), 206
Algernon Lennox, Lady, 140, 251
Allyen, Edward, 67
American Canine Hybrid Club, 231
American Eskimo dogs, 122
American Indian Dogs, 52
American Kennel Club (AKC), 5, 6, 26, 48, 50, 104, 105, 205, 222, 225; and border collies, 95, 96; and Boston terriers, 127, 128–29, 152–53, 154, 156–57, 158–60, 164, 165, 251; Breeders of Merit program, 232; breed misclassification by, 52; and breed standards, 25, 33–34, 38–39, 43, 83–84, 87–88, 102, 120, 121, 122, 158, 159, 165, 169, 225, 230; and bulldogs, 22, 25, 234; and class, 40, 129, 132–33, 134, 135, 139, 156, 158–59, 161, 166, 167–69, 170, 202, 207; and English standards, 133; and eugenics, 77, 84, 87–88, 102; and fraudulent pedigrees, 46; and French bulldogs, 35; health study funding by, 228, 230; on hybrid vigor, 231; incorporation of, 38–39, 156; and Kennel Club (UK), 135; and Labrador standard, 35, 177; and Meet the Breeds, 251; and mongrels, 74, 166, 230; origins of, 38–39, 157, 199; and outcrossing, 91; and puppy mills, 46, 228, 232; *vs.* purpose breeding, 92, 98; and Pyrenean standard, 171; on retriever trials, 183; and Rhodesian standard, 171; and social clubs, 137, 156. *See also* DNA testing for disease
American Museum of Natural History, 80
American Society for the Prevention of Cruelty to Animals (ASPCA), 51, 74, 94, 102
American Staffordshire terriers, 59, 111, 159, 170
America's Gilded Age (Rugoff), 138
Ancestry.com, 223

Animal Farm Foundation, 98
Arkwright, William, 106, 107, 185–86, 197, 198
Arvelius, Per, 91
Ash, Edward, 8, 24, 45, 71, 196
ASPCA. *See* American Society for the Prevention of Cruelty to Animals
assistance dogs, 83, 98; Animal Farm Foundation, 98; Assistance Dogs of America, 98; crossbreeding of, 100–101, 102; golden Labrador retrievers as, 100–101, 102; Guide Dogs of America, 101; Guide Dogs (UK), 101; Labrador–German shepherds as, 101; pit bulls as, 98. *See also* crossbreeding
Assistance Dogs of America, 98
Australian cattle dogs, 119
Axtell, Edward, 152, 157–58, 164, 165

Baker, Robert, 46
Barlos, Jenny, 98
basenjis, 15, 33
basset hounds, 2, 60, 71; and Hush Puppies, 166
beagles, 33, 59, 60, 128, 143, 214
Beaufort, Mowbray Walter Morris, Duke of, 183, 189, 194, 195, 209, 212
Belgian Malinois, 100
Belmont, August, 135, 207
Best in Show (film), 3, 8, 213
Bewick, Thomas, 116
bichon frises, 66, 71, 123
Bird, May, 141
Bismarck, Otto von, 140
Bleus de Gascogne, 170
bloodhounds, 59, 109. *See also* blood purity
blood purity, 51, 90, 224; American belief in, 30, 87, 132, 136–39, 141–42, 158, 167; and bloodhounds, 219; blue blood, 80; "The Bluebloods," 132; as breeding priority, 5, 101–2; and breed standards, 44, 84; Caius on, 46–47; and class, 134–36; and coat style, 131, 177, 181; in dogs *vs.* wolves, 47, 51–52; *vs.* health, 5, 6–7, 77, 79, 136, 227; *limpieza de sangre*, 219; *vs.* purpose breeding, 90, 100, 102; reexamined, 44–46; and stud books, 45, 91, 135. *See also* eugenics; inbreeding; pedigrees
blood sport, 18, 67; animal baiting, 16–21, 22, 23, 25, 28, 44, 59, 66, 67, 68, 70, 108, 112, 117, 162, 185, 187; and class, 67–68, 161, 200–12, 218–19; crossbows, 187, 190, 192, 193; deer parks, 191, 200, 219; dog fighting, 160, 161, 185; fox hunting, 52, 59, 64, 68, 78, 87, 183, 185, 186, 187, 218; and game laws, 65, 118, 201, 218; guns and dogs, 63, 169, 179, 182, 183–84, 185, 186, 189, 190, 191–99, 202, 205, 208–10, 212, 256; ritual *vs.* practical hunting, 91, 179, 181–92, 200–204, 208–10; royal hunting pageants, x, 59, 65, 86, 186–90, 255; and terriers, 90, 108, 117, 126, 161, 175; and war, 194, 195. *See also* dog shows; retrievers
Blooming Grove Hunting & Fishing Club (Pennsylvania), 205

The Blue Book (dog magazine), 171
Boggles, 231
The Book of Snobs (Thackeray), 55, 216
border collies, 3, 92, 94–96, 104, 109, 159, 175, 178; in mental illness research, 96; US Border Collie Club, 95. *See also* American Kennel Club
borzois (Russian wolfhounds), 33, 107, 115, 135, 140, 141; Bolshevik extermination of, 220
The Boston Terrier and All About It (Axtell), 152
Boston Terrier Club of America, 154, 156, 165
Boston terriers, x, 125–29, 130, 131, 132, 149, 151–54, 168, 204; *The Boston Terrier and All About It*, 152; Boston Terrier Club of America, 154, 156, 165; and bulldogs, 128, 153, 161–65; and Buster Brown shoes, 166; and Camel cigarettes, 166; deafness in, 128, 131; ear cropping of, 116; and English white terriers, 128; and fighting dogs, 116, 159–64; and French bulldogs, 128, 153, 155, 162; and lion dogs, 121; promotion of, 127, 160–61, 164, 166–67; standardization of, 129, 130, 131, 152, 154–59, 165, 166; and Studebakers, 166. *See also* American Kennel Club; extreme anatomies; founding father myths
boxers, 52, 59, 114; blindness in, 233; deafness in, 233; in disease research, 260; health problems in, 4, 232; in sequencing dog genome, 260
Bradbury, William, 143
Bradley, Janis, 93
breed standards: arbitrary nature of, x, 33–35, 42–43, 44–45, 72–73, 83–85, 86, 158, 225; English origins of, 38, 46, 154–55; form *vs.* function in, 27, 89–96, 99–100, 101–2, 107–9, 130, 260; *vs.* health, 4, 6, 41–42, 43, 72, 86, 118, 171, 225–27, 229, 232, 233; and other species, 108, 113–15, 120–24, 129–30; recent origins of, 43–44, 49; reform of, 229–30, 234; standardization of dogs, 21, 24, 33–35, 37, 42–43, 60, 66, 165, 166. *See also* American Kennel Club; blood purity; eugenics; extreme anatomies; reproductive uniformity
The British Dog (Ritchie), 188
Brussels griffons, 41
Bryce, C. A., 88
Buccleuch, Walter Francis Montagu Douglas Scott, 5th Duke of, 34, 181, 204, 206, 251
Budiansky, Stephen, 93
The Bulldog Club Incorporated (UK), 24
Bulldog Club of America, 114, 162, 165
bulldogs, x, 10–13, 28–30 104, 114, 155; and agricultural fairs, 70–71; and alaunts, 59; artificial insemination of, 11; and Boston terriers, 128, 153, 161–65; Bulldog Club of America, 114, 162, 165; Bulldog Club Incorporated (UK), 24; and Bulldog Gin, 28; Cesarean birth of, 11, 26; in disease research, 232; and early dog shows, 73; forced matings

of, 26; and French bulldogs, 15, 35, 36–37, 40, 128; and Mitchell Gold, 166; health problems in, ix, 4, 25, 41, 162, 225, 226, 229, 230, 232, 234, 238; history of, 16–18, 19–28, 67, 68, 108; and JOCKO (underwear), 28; Leavitt bulldogs, 28; and lion dogs, 111, 112, 113; origins of, 16–21; standardization of, 23–26, 27; as team mascots, 16. *See also* blood sport; Boston terriers; extreme anatomies; French bulldogs
bullmastiffs, 219
bull terriers, 20, 73, 159, 163, 165; aggression in, 27
Burke's Landed Gentry (social register), 134
Burke's Peerage (social register), 134
Burns, Patrick, 92, 109

Caius, John, 17, 46, 111, 190, 259
cancer, 4; in breeds *vs.* nonbreeds, 231–32; in golden retrievers, 4, 5, 224, 227; in Scottish deerhounds, 4, 59
Cannadine, David, 194, 196
Canning, George, 17
Caras, Roger, 51, 94, 120, 163, 220
Cardigan Welsh corgis, 159. *See also* extreme anatomies; founding father myths
cardiovascular disease: in breeds *vs.* nonbreeds, 231, 232; in Brussels griffons, 41; in bulldogs, 41, 162, 238; in French bulldogs, 41; in Newfoundlands, 232; in pugs, 41
Carlisle, Jay F., 206
Cassidy, Jack, 210
Catahoula Leopard Dogs, 113
Cavalier King Charles spaniels, 3, 7, 105, 119, 121, 217, 255; and court paintings, 256, 257. *See also* founding father myths
Central Park (New York City), 3, 52, 180; dog restrictions in, 175
Charles II, 256
Charles X, 190
Chesapeake Bay retrievers, 119, 210
Chihuahuas, 3, 60, 121, 170
Chiltonfoliat, Lady Ward of, 177
Chinese cresteds, 71, 217, 251. *See also* founding father myths
Chorkies, 231
chow chows, 100, 113, 115, 119, 121
Clayton, Michael, 243
Clumber spaniels, 193, 222. *See also* blood sport
cocker spaniels, 33, 60, 114, 115, 128; health problems in, 118; in mental illness research, 93–94; rage syndrome in, 94
collies, 113, 114, 133, 143, 164, 204, 205; Lassie, 107, 109; working *vs.* show, 51–52, 107–8
comforter dogs, 259
coonhounds, 121
Cooper, Anderson, 76, 77, 89
Coppinger, Raymond, 93
Coton de Tuléars, 119
Country Life in America (magazine), 70
"Craven" (pseud. for John William Carleton), 202
crossbreeding: of bulldogs, 162; of designer dogs, 45, 231; and golden Labrador retrievers, 100–101; of greyhounds, 59; health benefits of, 86, 231–32; and Labrador–German shepherds, 101. *See also* assistance

dogs; blood purity; designer dogs, hybrid vigor
Cruft, Charles, 67, 140, 146–47, 186
Crufts (dog show), 34, 53, 62, 64, 65, 68, 186, 205, 225; BBC boycott of, 5, 95; and blood sport, 66–68, 186; and Cavaliers, 256–57; cheating at, 145; and eugenics, 87, 95, 102; expansion of, 146–47; *vs.* health, 145; Spratt sponsorship of, 146, 167; in wartime, 221, 222; and Westminster, 5, 87, 132. *See also* dog shows
curs. *See* mongrels
Czechoslovakia: dog extermination in, 221

dachshunds, 33, 140, 108, 139; in disease research, 232; health problems in, 225, 226, 229, 232; wartime treatment of, 221, 222. *See also* extreme anatomies
Dalmatians, 3, 130–31, 145, 153; health problems in, 131, 226
Dandie Dinmont terriers, 71, 167
Daniel, W. B., 190
Darwin, Charles, 62, 81
Dateline (TV program), 46
The Decline and Fall of the British Aristocracy (Cannadine), 194
Derby, Edward Henry Stanley, 15th Earl of, 135
Derr, Mark, 6, 47, 219
designer dogs, x, 45; American Canine Hybrid Club, 231; Cesarean birth of, 231; health of, 230–31. *See also* crossbreeding
Dickert, J. E., 148
DNA testing for disease, 6, 224, 228–29
Doberman pinschers, 2; in disease research, 232; ear cropping of, 116; health problems in, 232
Dog Advisory Council (UK), 229
dog fancy, defined, 6
dog shows, xi, 48, 87, 133, 155, 202, 218, 221, 234; and aggression in dogs, 93–94; and agricultural fairs, 63, 68–71, 224; and blood sport, 17, 18, 63, 66–68, 144, 163, 182–83, 185–87, 211; and breed standards, 43; and bulldogs, 21, 23; *vs.* "canine Olympics," 53; Centennial Exposition of 1876, 63; cheating in, 144–45, 149; early New York shows, 140–44, 147–49, 163–64; expansion of, 144, 145–47, 149–50; Great American Mutt Show, 74; and honorifics, 56, 60; International Dog Show, 63; Ladies' Kennel Association of America show, 148–49; Mineola Dog Show, 211; Newcastle upon Tyne, 63, 68, 94, 199; New York Poultry Society, 63; origins of, 38, 46, 49, 62–73; Peterborough Royal Foxhound Show, 64; and pointers, 63, 199; P. T. Barnum's Great National Dog Show, 63; and retired champions, 99; and social Darwinism, 87–88; and "Talbots," 59; and working dogs, 27, 106–9. *See also* Crufts; Westminster Kennel Club Dog Show
Dogues de Bordeaux, 35, 121
Doodleman Pinschers, 231
Downton Abbey (BBC series), 89
Duncan, Mrs. A. Butler, 206

ear cropping, 116–17, 123
Edward VII (Edward Albert, Prince of Wales), 132, 135, 194–95
Elizabeth I, 67, 186–87, 195, 259
Elizabeth II, 5, 114, 178. *See also* Kennel Club (UK)
The Encyclopedia of the Dog (Fogle), 119
English white terriers, 128. *See also* Boston terriers
Estonia: dog extermination in, 221
eugenics, 76–77, 137, 157, 166, 200, 202, 211, 225; breeds and races in, 77, 79, 82–84, 87–88, 134, 225; and breed standards, 83–86, 87, 88, 91; errors of, 79; history of, 78–82; mongrelization in, 78, 84, 88; *vs.* traditional breeding, 89–93; and working dogs, 83, 85, 89–102. *See also* American Kennel Club; blood purity
extreme anatomies, x, 5, 35, 106, 108–9, 127, 162, ; and agricultural fairs, 69–71; and behavior, 90, 94; and bulldog "expression," 23–26; and Cesarean birth, 11, 42; defined, 4; *vs.* health, 25, 27, 41–42, 71–72, 108–9, 118, 119, 171, 226, 227, 229, 230, 232. *See also* breed standards; inbreeding

Federal Emergency Management Agency (FEMA), 101
Feversham, Charles William Duncombe, 2nd Earl of, 177
Field, Marshall, 206
Fogle, Bruce, 119
Fouilloux, Jacques du, 188
founding father myths, 46, 51–52, 160, 217, 251
foxhounds, 59, 60, 64, 66, 86, 115, 171, 218, 219, 251. *See also* founding father myths
fox terriers, 86, 108, 115, 137, 145
Frasier (TV show), 15
French Bull Dog Club of America, 36, 39, 42
French bulldogs, 31–33, 43, 44, 115, 118–19, 141, 214, 215, 216; and Boston terriers, 128, 153, 155, 162; and bulldogs, 15, 35, 36–37, 40, 128; French Bull Dog Club of America, 36, 39, 42; health problems in, 4, 41–42; and lion dogs, 122; recent comeback of, 221; standardization of, 35–41, 45. *See also* extreme anatomies
French Revolution, 54, 133, 171; and animal massacres, 219; and hunting rights, 189

Gallant, Johan and Edith, 26
Galton, Francis, 81
gastric dilatation-volvulus (GDV). *See* twisted stomach
genetic diversity, 227, 230; and sequencing dog genome, 260; *vs.* superficial diversity, 86. *See also* crossbreeding; hybrid vigor; inbreeding
The Gentleman's Dog (Bryce), 88, 203–4
gentrification: of Boston terriers, 163; and breed popularity, 105; of landraces, 51
George III, 56
George V, 205
George VI, 206
German shepherds, 52, 77, 92, 100, 102, 104, 109, 128, 241;

crossbreeding of, 101; in disease research, 232; health problems in, 4, 100, 108–9, 221, 224–25, 232; renamed Alsatians, 221; Rin Tin Tin, 108–9. *See also* extreme anatomies
Goelet, Robert, 207
Goldendoodles, 98
golden Labrador retrievers, 100–101, 102. *See also* assistance dogs; crossbreeding
golden retrievers, xi, 2, 7, 13, 75, 85, 86, 89, 94, 97, 98, 100, 106–7, 177, 179, 217; aggression in, 48, 83, 93–94, 160–61, 241; and agricultural fairs, 71; and AKC art collection, 50, 77; AKC recognizes, 205; in cities, 175; crossbreeding of, 98, 100–101, 102; and fraudulent pedigrees, 46; and gentrification, 105; Guisachan gathering of, 134; health problems in, 4, 5, 118, 186–87, 224, 227; and lion dogs, 121, 122; in mental illness research, 93–94; Tweedmouth barons and, 134; and wolves, 48. *See also* blood sport
Good Morning America (TV show), 74
Goodwood Estate, 137
Gordon setters, 52, 114
Gould, Kelly, 99, 100
Gould, Stephen Jay, 82
Great American Mutt Show, 74
Great Danes (Danish boarhounds, German mastiffs), 119, 122, 140, 141, 175
Grey, Frederick Oliver Robinson, 4th Earl de, 194
greyhounds, 60, 114, 117, 175, 191, 255; and class, 59, 66, 86, 115, 129, 187, 201, 219. *See also* blood sport; heraldry; lurchers
Grogan, John, 229
Guest, Christopher, 8
Guide Dogs of America, 101
Guide Dogs (UK), 101
Guinness, Mrs. Benjamin, 141
Gun Dog Magazine, 183, 191
Gyselear, Kees de, 220

Hammacher Schlemmer, 224
Hancock, David, 85, 87, 92, 166
Harriman, William Averell, 82, 206
Harrison, Jemima, 231
Harrison, Mrs. R. T., 148
Havaneses, 221
hemophilia, 79, 136, 227; in German shepherds, 232
Henri III, 192
heraldry, 57–62, 72, 111, 115, 171, 194; alaunts in, 58, 59, 60; "Arms of Dr. F. G. Hardy," 61–62; in dog grooming, 171; greyhounds in, 59, 60; Heralds' College (College of Arms), 57, 61; modern breeds in, 60–62; Shrewsbury (earls of), 59; Stourton crest, 111; Talbot hounds in, 59, 60; wolves in, 58
Hess, Russell, 92
Hill-Wood, Lady, 206
The History of Four-Footed Beasts (Topsell), 110
honorifics, 56; and dog breeds, 57–62. *See also* heraldry
Hooper, Robert, 251
horses, 82, 111, 29, 120, 186, 187, 189; and canine form, 114, 115, 171, 217; and class, 59, 66, 115,

129, 153, 164, 169, 171, 218; and zebra hybrids, 113. *See also* breed standards
Howe, Dorothy, 207
Howe, Lorna Countess, 206
Humane Society of the United States, 46, 226, 227
Hungarian greyhounds: Romanian extermination of, 221
Hunting (Beaufort), 183
Hurlingham Club, 195, 210, 254
hybrid vigor, 138, 230; evidence of, 231–32. *See also* American Kennel Club; crossbreeding; genetic diversity

Ibizan hounds, 52
inbreeding, 5, 88, 115, 122, 126, 129, 152, 165, 171, 217; and aristocracy, 136, 138; calls to reduce, 234; coefficients of, 77; for disease research, 260; in dogs and wolves, 47; for extreme anatomies, 11, 26, 94; of farm animals, 70; *vs.* health, 46, 70, 79, 94, 131, 136, 215, 227, 234, 260; and intelligence, 97; for sequencing dog genome, 260; for stylized behavior, 197–98; *vs.* traditional breeding, 90, 92, 94. *See also* blood purity; extreme anatomies; genetic diversity
Institute of Veterinary Animal and Biomedical Sciences (Massey University, New Zealand), 86
Irish setters, 85
Irish terriers, 167
Irish water spaniels, 145
Irish wolfhounds, 52
Italian greyhounds, 115

J. Craig Venter Institute, 233
J. Crew, 119, 235
Jack Russell terriers, 15, 92, 104, 175. *See also* Parson Russell terriers
James I, 67, 187–88, 192
Japanese Chins, 121
Japanese spaniels, 148, 155
Josslyn, Lizzie Adele, 141
The Joy of Breeding Your Own Show Dog (Seranne), 225

Karl of Prussia, 141
Karma Dogs, 99–100
Keeshonds, 220
Keller, Helen, 222
Kennel Club (UK), 5, 6, 25, 43, 87, 91, 95, 106, 159, 171, 182, 185, 202; aristocratic origins of, 132, 135; president of, 135, 178. *See also* American Kennel Club
Kernochan, James L., 214–16, 218
Kerry Blue terriers, 119
The King's Speech (film), 54
Kirkness, Ewen, 233
Knickerbocker Club, 137
Knutsford, A. Holland Hibbert, 3rd Viscount, 206
Kuvaszes, 170

Labradoodles, 98; health problems in, 231
Labrador–German shepherds, 101. *See also* assistance dogs; crossbreeding
The Labrador Retriever (Wolters), 34
The Labrador Retriever Club (US), 207
Labrador Retriever Club of Great Britain, 206

Labrador retrievers, 2, 75, 77, 97, 100, 114, 118, 120, 173–74, 176–77, 192, 199, 200; in AKC's "top ten," 128; American debut of, 204–7; and Black Dog Tavern (Massachusetts), 179; Blind of Arden, 179; in cities, 175, 176; color preferences in, 34–35, 82, 86, 89, 114, 120, 177–79, 182, 190; crossbreeding of, 98, 100–101, 102; culling of, 34, 177, 190; and *Downton Abbey*, 89; early field trials of, 207–13; and eugenics, 82, 86, 88; fraudulent pedigrees for, 46; and gentrification, 105; health problems in, ix, 4, 86, 173, 174, 186–87, 224, 225, 229, 230, 231; in heraldry, 61–62; *The Labrador Retriever*, 34; Labrador Retriever Club (US), 207; Labrador Retriever Club of Great Britain, 206; *Legends in Labradors*, 221; "Marley" of *Marley & Me*, 229; and Michael of Kent, 135; and Saint John's water dog, 34, 179–82; and stylized behavior, 182–85; in wartime, 222; Yellow Labrador Club (UK), 178. *See also* blood sport; extreme anatomies; Saint John's water dogs

Lady and the Tramp (film), 84

Lakeland terriers, 159

landraces, 50–51, 58, 131, 179; gentrification of, 51

Landseer, Edwin Henry, 116, 178

Larson, Greger, 90

Lauren, Ralph, 137, 177, 223, 256

Laurence, Christopher, 229

The Leash (social club), 137

Leavitt, David, 28. *See also* Olde English Bulldogges

Legends in Labradors (Martin), 211

Leonbergers, 122; in disease research, 232; health problems in, 232

Lhasa apsos, 121, 122

line breeding: *vs.* health, 233. *See also* inbreeding

lion dogs, 115, 130, 149, 217; Foo dogs, 121; and modern breeds, 19, 30, 31–32, 105, 110, 111, 113, 114, 121–23, 160, 171; origins of, 120–21; Shishi dogs, 121; tiger-dogs, 111–12, 113; Topsell on, 111. *See also* breed standards

Little Britain (BBC series), 72

Lloyd, Freeman: on ancestry, 169, 172; on blood sport, 161; and bulldogs, 25; on dog shows, 64–65; and eugenics, 87, 88, 89; on greyhounds, 129; on Labradors, 181–82, 207–8, 210; on springer spaniels, 77; on Staffordshires, 111; on upper-class hunting, 192, 193, 199, 202

longevity, 4, 227, 229, 234; in breeds *vs.* nonbreeds, 63, 231, 232, 234, 260

Louis XIII (king), 188

Löwchens, 121, 122, 123

lurchers, 200. *See also* greyhounds; mongrels

Lytton, Judith Neville (Lady Wentworth), 139, 145

MacDonogh, Katharine, 222

Malmesbury, James Edward Harris, 2nd Earl of, 34, 181, 204, 206, 251

Malteses, 121–22, 143
Martin, Nancy, 211
mastiffs, 141; and alaunts, 58, 59; and animal fighting, 19, 20, 116–17; and bulldogs, 16, 19, 20; and German shepherds, 52; as lion dogs, 111, 113, 121, 122, 123; and Saint John's water dogs, 180; as tiger-dogs, 112, 113
McAllister, Ward, 136
McCaig, Donald, 183
McGreevy, Paul, 230
Meadowbrook Hunt Club, 214
Merlen, René, 219
Metropolitan Club, 137
Metropolitan Dog Club, 172
Michael of Kent, 135, 178. *See also* Kennel Club (UK)
Milbank, Samuel, 206
mixed-breed dogs. *See* mongrels
mongrels, xi, 8, 9, 74, 104, 156, 235; and Boston terriers, 131; and bulldogs, 25; and class, 47–48, 65, 66, 87, 110, 129, 132, 168, 193, 200–202; in creating breeds, 45–46; as "curs," 8, 83, 97, 103, 191; "curs" and class, 47, 66, 164, 181, 183, 189, 190, 200, 215; health/longevity in breeds *vs.*, 63, 227–28, 231–32, 234, 260; and humane movement, 67; intelligence in breeds *vs.*, 97; and Labradors, 182; as "mixed breeds," 48, 101, 103; as "mutts," xi, 1, 3, 4, 8, 44, 47, 48, 74, 75, 84, 97, 99, 102, 103, 104, 105, 130, 141, 153, 156, 169, 180, 182, 200, 201, 202, 204, 228, 230; racial inferiority of, 49; as superior hunters, 202–4; and wolves, 47, 49. *See also* crossbreeding; designer dogs; eugenics
Morgan, John Pierpont, 52, 133, 137, 206
Morkies, 231
Mortimer, James, 135, 144
Mott, J. Varnum, 161
mutts. *See* mongrels

National Arts Club, 172
National Disaster Search Dog Foundation, 101
neurasthenia, 234
Newfoundlands: in disease research, 232; health problems in, 232
Nicholas II (czar), 141
Nightline (TV program), 7
Noel, Robert, 242
Norfolk terriers, 3, 159
Norwegian elkhounds, 52
Norwich terriers, 3, 159, 175

Olde English Bulldogges (Leavitt Bulldogs), 28
Old English sheepdogs, 119, 144
Olin, John Merrill, 207
On the Origin of Species (Darwin), 62
Orford, George Walpole, 3rd Earl of, 135
Orthopedic Foundation for Animals, 231
outcrossing: and purpose breeding, 91, 92; and traditional breeding, 90. *See also* American Kennel Club; genetic diversity; inbreeding

Pacific Urns, 224
Pape, W. R., 63

papillons, xi, 114, 121
Parson Russell terriers, 108
Paw Printz Pet Boutique, 223
Pedigree Dogs Exposed (BBC documentary), 5, 6, 225, 227, 231
Pedigree Health Report (RSPCA), 227
pedigrees, x, 6, 53, 60, 100, 102, 104, 136, 140, 201, 203, 223; *vs.* conformation, 88; and designer dogs, 231; in early New York shows, 141–42, 144; etymology of term, 115; fraudulence in, 46; and French bulldogs, 36; *vs.* health, 70; human, 57, 79, 81, 135, 139, 168, 213; and Labradors, 174, 179, 210–11; *vs.* purpose breeding, 92, 97, 99; and Talbots, 59. *See also* American Kennel Club
Pekingeses, 48, 65, 110, 114, 121, 141, 160, 171, 181, 251; in Communist China, 220; health problems in, 145, 171. *See also* founding father myths
Pembroke Welsh corgis, 34, 114, 115, 222; health problems in, 224, 229, 251. *See also* extreme anatomies; founding father myths
Perpetua Life Jewels, 224
Peters, Harry, 206
Petit Basset Griffon Vendéens, 3
Pharaoh hounds, 52, 217
pit bulls, 17, 105, 116, 160, 163, 230; Animal Farm Foundation, 98
pointers, 66, 73, 87, 114, 185, 186, 190, 193, 196–99, 205, 217; abnormal orienting response in, 197; and backing, 197–98; and early dog shows, 63, 199; and neoteny, 197; "Sensation," 119, 199. *See also* blood sport
Poland: dog extermination in, 221
police dogs, 92, 97, 100
Pomeranians, 141, 155
poodles, 102, 114, 119, 123, 128, 141, 145, 171, 178, 213; in disease research, 232; health problems in, 231, 232. *See also* blood sport
Portuguese water dogs, xi, 2, 3, 75, 123; in disease research, 260
Procrustes (myth), 44, 49, 129, 133, 227
Puggles, 231
pugs, 21, 113, 119, 121, 131, 162, 174, 207, 220, 222; in disease research, 232; health problems in, 4, 6–7, 41, 71, 171, 230, 232. *See also* extreme anatomies
Punch (magazine), 55
puppy mills, xi, 46, 83, 228, 232; and designer dogs, 231. *See also* American Kennel Club
Pyrenean shepherds, 171

Queen Elizabeth Pocket Beagles, 217

Raper, George, 38
Regal Point Vizslas (kennel), 170
Reigning Cats and Dogs (MacDonogh), 222
reproductive uniformity, 25, 36, 45, 86, 92, 154, 260; breediness, 36, 83, 154, 157; breeding true, 49, 93, 94, 111, 229; Caius's theory on, 46–47. *See also* breed standards; eugenics
retrievers, 190, 193; American fad for, 205; as assistance dogs,

98; breeds *vs.* nonbreeds, 201, 202–4; in cities, 175; early types of, 178; and field trials, 183; French fad for, 189; and neoteny, 197; in pigeon shooting, 195; in upper-class hunting, 86, 106, 178, 185, 196, 209, 217. *See also* blood sport; Chesapeake Bay retrievers; golden retrievers; Labrador retrievers
Rhodesian ridgebacks, 35, 113; health problems in, 171, 226
Richard III, 57, 67
Ritchie, Carson, 188, 219
Rockefeller Foundation, 81
rottweilers, 2
Royal Court (kennel), 170
Royal Society for the Prevention of Cruelty to Animals (RSPCA), 227, 229
Royal Veterinary College (University of London), 226
Royal Vista Miniature Pinschers (kennel), 170
Royal Windsor Kennel, 170
Rugoff, Milton, 138
Rural Sports (Daniel), 190

Saint Bernards, 3, 107, 147
Saint Hubert's hounds, 180
Saint John's water dogs, 34, 179–82, 204, 227
Salisbury, Robert Arthur Talbot Gascoyne-Cecil, 3rd Marquess of, 56
Sandringham, Royal Kennels at, 195, 211, 230
schnauzers: in disease research, 223; health problems in, 223
Scottish deer hounds, 59, 143; health problems in, 4, 59
Sealyham terriers, 45, 159
search-and-rescue dogs, 83, 109; mongrels as, 101–2; National Disaster Search Dog Foundation, 101; in 9/11 artwork, 50, 77, 109; pit bulls as, 98
Seranne, Ann, 225
setters, 72, 75, 102, 114, 186, 190, 192, 193, 196, 203; and class, 187; and early dog shows, 63, 199; and lion dogs, 122; and neoteny, 197. *See also* Gordon setters, Irish setters
Shar-peis, 71, 113, 114, 119; in disease research, 232; health problems in, 4, 232. *See also* extreme anatomies
Shetland sheepdogs, 121, 159
Shiba Inus, 15
shih tzus, 121
Shihtzapoos, 231
silky terriers: health problems in, 229. *See also* extreme anatomies
Social Register, 137
SOS Dog (Gallant), 26
Spratt's (dog food manufacturer), 146, 167
Stables, Gordon, 8, 9, 25, 49, 66, 78, 88, 145, 164, 201
Stafford, Kevin, 86, 94
Staffordshire terriers, 59, 111, 159, 170
Staverton, George, 21
Stephanopoulos, George, 76
Stifel, William, 199
Stockholm University, 93
Svartberg, Kenth, 93, 96, 97
Swedish Armed Forces, 91
Swedish Kennel Club, 91
Swedish University of Agricultural Studies, 91

tail docking, 117–18, 123
Talbot hounds, 59, 60. *See also* heraldry
Tegetmeier, William, 69, 71
terriers, 103, 104, 105, 111, 122, 143, 148, 167, 175, 202; in early dog shows, 72; as fighting dogs, 16, 159–60, 161, 163; and going to ground, 126; mythical origins of, 48, 110; tail docking of, 117; working *vs.* show, 85, 86
Thackeray, William Makepeace, 55, 216
therapy dogs, 83, 98–100; Karma Dogs, 99–100
Thomas, Elizabeth Marshall, 223
Tibetan mastiffs, 113, 121, 122
Tibetan spaniels, 121
Tibetan terriers, 122
Today Show, 70
Topsell, Edward, 110, 111, 112, 117, 123
Toy Dogs and Their Ancestors (Lytton), 135, 139, 145
Trafford, Henry de, 135
Transylvanian hounds: Romanian extermination of, 221
Tuxedo Park, 132
twisted stomach (gastric dilatation-volvulus): in Labrador retrievers, 229. *See also* extreme anatomies

Union Club, 137
United Kennel Club, 6
University Club, 137
University of Aberdeen, 97
University of California, Davis, 227–28

Veblen, Thorstein, 234
Victoria (queen), 68, 135, 143, 170, 251
Visconti, Bernabò, 219
vizslas, 120, 170

Walsingham, Thomas de Grey, 6th Baron, 194
war dogs, 49, 90, 92, 117, 122; alaunts as, 58, 194; ear cropping of, 116–17
Washington, George, 215, 251
Watson, James, 22, 23, 26, 41, 52, 159, 160
Wegman, William, 2
Weimaraners, 2, 120
Wellington, Arthur Valerian Wellesley, 8th Duke of, 206
Welsh springer spaniels, 75, 77, 88, 89, 97, 191; health problems in, 77; in mental illness research, 93–94; rage syndrome in, 94
West Highland terriers, 159
Westminster Kennel Club, 195, 205; logo for, 119, 199; and social clubs, 137. *See also* dog shows
Westminster Kennel Club Dog Show, xiii, 2, 3, 34, 52, 53, 62, 64, 65, 94, 133, 140, 168, 171, 174, 209, 216, 225, 228, 233; and blood sport, 66–68, 186, 199; and Crufts, 5, 87, 132; and eugenics, 77, 81, 87, 102; expansion of, 144, 146, 147; first, 63; and French bulldogs, 37, 38; and pedigrees, 141–42; and Scottish deer hounds, 59; sponsors of, 167. *See also* dog shows
Westminster Pit, 18. *See also* blood sport; dog shows

Wheaton terriers, 72, 103, 119
whippets, 60, 115
Whitney, Caspar, 198
Who's Who (social register), 137
Wilde, Oscar, 53
Willis, Malcolm, 94, 95
Wilsson, Erik, 91–92
Windham, William, 17
Windsor, Duke of, 120, 131, 174, 207
Wolters, Richard, 34, 204, 205, 206, 212
wolves, 6, 11, 106, 112, 113, 124, 130, 158, 185, 220; and dog ancestry, 47, 48, 51–52, 79, 110; behavior in dogs *vs.*, 16, 26, 48, 126, 130, 178, 197, 217; extinction of, 48; in heraldry, 58; and landraces, 50; and neoteny, 49; and tail docking, 117. *See also* blood purity; heraldry
Wyandanch Club (New York), 205

Yellow Labrador Club (UK), 178
Yorkshire terriers, 67, 147
The Young Sportsman's Manual (Craven), 202